Lillee

To Sue
Keep hitting 'em
for six

Lillee

Dennis Lillee

An Autobiography

HODDER

First published in 2003
by HEADLINE BOOK PUBLISHING

10 9 8 7 6 5 4 3 2 1

Cataloguing in Publication Data is
available from the British Library.

ISBN 0 7553 1231 7

Typeset in Garamond by
Letterpart Limited, Reigate, Surrey

Printed and bound in Australia by
Griffin Press

HEADLINE BOOK PUBLISHING
A division of Hodder Headline
338 Euston Road
LONDON NW1 3BH

www.headline.co.uk
www.hodderheadline.com

To dear Sid :
Happy 70th birthday.
To a great New South
Welshman about a
great West Australian.
Love. Bryan.

Contents

Acknowledgements

I would firstly like to thank Helen for the amazing time and effort put in to make this project possible.

Thanks also to the many people who have contributed their time, effort or memories, particularly Ian and Greg Chappell, Rod Marsh, Jim Woodward, Tracey Maitland of the WACA Museum and Rod Taylor.

Thank you to Jonathan Harris for bringing all parties together, Ian Marshall at Headline for his guidance and Bob Harris. For Bob and myself to still be talking after this monumental undertaking is nothing short of a miracle but we truly hope the result was worth it.

Thanks to Mum and Dad, for your love and a wonderful upbringing, as well as understanding my unusually busy lifestyle; to Helen for being a lovely person and great wife and mate; to our great sons, Adam and Dean, for lending their father to cricket. I love you all dearly.

A special thanks to Pop Len for his love, inspiration and guidance, and, most importantly, for preaching about the second wind.

Prologue

It is, for me, the ultimate challenge – the fast bowler preparing mentally and physically to face the oldest enemy, England. What makes the moment even more special is the game is at headquarters.

It all begins long before the toss or the first ball. It was there in my head when I went to sleep the night before and it is right there, in my face, when I woke up on this, the morning of the first day of a Test match – not just any Test match but against England for the Ashes at Lord's. It does not get any better than this.

I always start off with room service rather than breakfast in the dining room. I know even if I go down, few of my team-mates will be about because they feel much like I do. Why? We are comfortable in our own rooms, not having to talk about cricket and exchange pleasantries with other hotel guests. None of us wants to be with other people.

I arrange a late wake-up call at around 8.30 and have a quick skim through the papers over breakfast to see what the English cricket writers have to say. I leave it as late as I possibly can before finally going downstairs.

As usual I share a room with another fast bowler. They like to pair an experienced player with a newcomer. And this time, on the 1972 tour, I am rooming with Dave Colley. There is not a lot of conversation. I order grain-bread toast, orange juice, eggs and bacon, along with a lot of baked beans, and coffee. The modern dietician would probably squirm at that but we are not as knowledgeable and, in any case, there is not a lot of choice, even at the Waldorf just off the Strand. I decide to have cereal as well. We are talking about fuel for the body on the first day.

Breakfast over, it is time to get organised, pack the gear for the game and make a few telephone calls. It is a race to catch the team bus on time because the telephone keeps ringing with friends and relatives wishing me luck, and people wanting tickets. I wonder where some of them found the temerity to ring out of the blue like that on the first morning of a Lord's Test match.

Then it is down the ornate staircase to the lobby, running into team-mates, feeling the nervousness, the excitement. There is a lot of small talk – people are always on edge on the first day of an important Test match. On board the coach, some try to behave normally while others go a bit over the top because of the jangling nerves, talking in loud voices. Others, including me, just sit saying nothing much to anyone. As usual, Greg Chappell has verbal diarrhoea, just as he does while waiting to bat, manifesting itself in a few jokes. Rodney Marsh is fairly composed. Doug Walters is hiding behind a seat, trying to trick a nervous team manager into thinking he was late. The seating on the bus is never planned.

As we draw near the ground, everyone becomes quieter. We can see the queues, the bustle, the Grace Gates. People are yelling, waving and pointing at the team bus, which is lit up like a Christmas tree. I can feel the nervousness growing in my gut as we pass through those imposing gates. I focus on finding the best position in the dressing room. I like somewhere to spread out. I know where I want to put my gear but if that place is taken, I know the next best position. I keep my fingers crossed my bag will not be late off the bus so all the best places are gone, but my luck is out. The bag was slow in coming. I don't say anything even though I am thoroughly fed up about it and a bit angry. We all like to feel comfortable in what will be virtually our home for five or six days.

However, I grab a cup of tea and get over it in five minutes flat. It is 9.45. I unpack my bag, drink a second cup of tea and change to go to the nets. On the way down, I have a look at the pitch, going through the famous gate. To tell the truth, half the time I don't know what I am looking for but I am glad to see a bit of green on it. I bend down and feel it to see how hard it is. I decide I want to bowl first. There is something in the pitch, and the weather is a little overcast. That is my own preference but, of course, I am happy to go along with the team plan. I leave it to the captain to determine how the pitch is going to last over the five days. It is up to him and his generals to decide what to do.

After a run around and a stretch – not much, just enough for me personally – I spend 15 minutes in the nets at a fairly gentle pace, letting eight or so go to feel good at the end of the session. I wonder about a bat if there is time and maybe some fielding practice.

The opposition are in the nets next door but I take no notice. I don't want to speak to them. Even if one of my English mates spoke to me, I would just nod and not get involved in a conversation. But they know that; they feel the same. They ignore me just as I do them.

We wander back to the dressing room in twos or threes, a bit of a disjointed group as usual. Once there, I check that my boots are still all right, change out of my training gear and wait for the captains to make the toss. Generally, I prefer to be back in the dressing room by that time because otherwise I fret about not being as prepared as I should be. As the captain walks through the door, I want to know exactly what has been decided. I'm not waiting for him to tell me in his own time. I need to know.

I have my wish. We are in the field. Then it is a question of getting rid of the nervousness by going to the toilet and getting other mundane things out of the way. I don't want to be worrying about such matters just before going out on to the pitch.

I make a cursory check of the gear I had sorted out the night before: five or six shirts, three pairs of flannels, three or four jock straps, a couple of tracksuits, a few T-shirts, a pair of gloves, one bat – why would I need more than one bat? – and lots of pairs of socks, eight or so and as thick as I could get them because I wear two pairs at a time.

Ian and Greg Chappell's mum has knitted some socks for me for this tour. It all came about because I admired a pair that Ian was wearing and asked him where he had bought them because they were so good. The conversation ended there and then when he told me that they were home-made, but a short while later three pairs turned up as a gift from Mrs Chappell. I treasure them and look after them as well as I can.

I also have two pairs of boots, one for wearing and one wearing in. To anyone else, they look a mess. I like my boots to be firm fitting, which makes them ideal for running and walking but when I bowled and hit the hard ground, the boot stayed still and the foot moved, leaving me with a big toe that became bruised and painful. Once bruised, things can go from bad to worse, with infected toenails and all sorts of other ailments. So I have come up with the idea of slicing the big-toe area with a scalpel, which takes the pressure off totally. So the sock pokes through and looks odd – I don't care about sartorial elegance in that situation, just comfort. I don't know why other bowlers don't do the same thing.

I net in the spare pair, even playing a couple of minor games wearing them so they are ready to go. Also, I keep them with slightly longer spikes so I can wear them on soft or rubbley wickets. The regular boots have small spikes, mainly for the Australian type of wickets, and I will wear them until they fall apart.

Other items in the bag include the baggy green cap, which, to be honest, I never or rarely wear although I rather like the idea of every player wearing a cap for one session – good for team spirit.

The trouble is I sweat so much the perspiration runs into my eyes – a particular problem if I am using suncream. I once toyed with the idea of a wide-brimmed hat but, truth to tell, I never much cared for a hat at all. I tried wearing a sweatband around my forehead but, in the end, I stuff a soft hat in my pocket and will wear that if it gets really hot.

I make a last check. The sprig tighteners, spare sprigs, plasters, toe clippers, nail clippers, suncream, talcum powder, deodorant, scissors, shampoo, soap and all the rest are all there. I used to be big on the kit being right but I have to admit to being a bit slack in testing the sprigs in my boots. It was a blank spot. I just didn't think about it when they had been comfortable the previous time I had worn them. On this occasion, though, I check them. After all, it is Lord's.

Ten minutes before we are due to go out I am changed and ready. I move about, stretching, jogging on the spot, anything to get my body warm and loose, and to work up a light sweat. The captain has a brief word on the lines of, 'Let's get out there and have a good session,' and wishes us luck. There are no added barbs aimed England's way. We save those for individual batsmen.

I go out last. Occasionally, a few people have tried to usurp that position, hiding behind doors and things like that, but this time I watch carefully. I like going out last.

Downstairs no one says a lot. I feel like I am from outer space, making my way through those egg yolk and tomato ties. They just look and no one says a word. There is some polite applause. I don't take much of it in, anyway. All I see is a sea of white faces in front of me. Not even the steward holding the gate catches my eye. All I want at that stage is to get out on to the field and take hold of the new ball as quickly as possible. As usual, as soon as I step on to the field, everything changes. This is my job.

I indulge in a little shadow bowling as we walk to the pitch. I am thrown the ball and measure out my 24-pace run-up. I practise the run-in, stretch and wait impatiently to get under way. As usual, I acknowledge the umpire with a 'good morning', but nothing more than that. I certainly do not ask after his wife or kids.

Nervous energy courses through my body as I prepare to face the opening batsman. I don't know or care who he is. We know the team and what positions they are going to come in. There is no point confirming which one of them is going to take the first ball. When I see him, I'll know whether he is a left- or right-hander, but there will be no eye contact.

All that is going through my mind is to make sure the first ball is a good one. This time we have no plan of surprise. The first ball will be on a length, just going away from the right-hander, something he might be tempted to have a nibble at, or into a lefty, hoping to trap him in front. Provided I hit around that spot, I will be happy whether he hits it for a single or a four, or if it goes through to the keeper.

I plan to bowl as briskly as I can with the first delivery. I don't want to give the batsman any start, any opportunity; I want to be on top straightaway. The first ball will relieve the tension, particularly if I get it right. Then it is going to be down to hard work. I know what I am going to do.

My follow-through will take me quite near to the batsman. I don't do it for that reason. That has been my normal follow-through from the age of 16. If the batsman plays and misses, or if he plays a bad shot, I'll try to press home the advantage by looking him in the eye, complete with the hands on hips pose and a stare. Most batsmen will look down or away.

I know that the first over or two will be cat and mouse. I plan to make eye contact, looking for apprehension, to see if they are feeling the pressure of the game and the press build-up. I want the feedback that they do not want to give me. I am certainly not going to ask, 'How are you feeling, mate?' I will look for anything that will be to my benefit, anything that will fire me up. Batsmen tend to avoid eye contact early on because the eyes can betray nerves and edginess, the very things I am looking for.

Australia versus England at Lord's means so much more than any other game of cricket. I'm not decrying the other teams, but that game is in our culture, in our history. It's the old enemy, the old foe, 100 years of tradition and not wanting to let down the guys who went before you and the mates you're playing with. Sometimes, I feel that it means more to me than it does to some of the opposition. I don't mind because there can be small chinks in the armour of those who do not have the same full-on commitment. There is always a hard core of Englishmen who have the same intensity as us Aussies, but there isn't always full-term commitment from all of them. Over the years, we have come to know who they are.

'Play.' The umpire brings me back to the present. Geoff Boycott is at the other end and I want his wicket with the first ball because this is England, this is special, this is personal.

CHAPTER ONE

Childhood

There would have been long odds on a young Dennis Lillee becoming an international sportsman of any sort, let alone a fast bowler in Test cricket. I cut a sorry picture as a youngster. I had to wear special corrective boots because of weak ankles and I often fell over. Consequently, I developed a funny walk.

I was born in Subiaco, a suburb of Perth in Western Australia, on 18 July 1949 to long-distance truck-driver Keith, aged 22, and his 20-year-old wife Shirley. Dad was a fairly good amateur Australian Rules footballer and he tried out for South Fremantle and East Perth, then a First Division team, when he was only 17. But he was from the country and no one knew him. When he went down to try out for East Perth, he didn't see a lot of the ball. In the end, he was so sick of it that he left and carried on playing amateur football with his mates. When he told me about those early days, I thought out loud that it was quite a long way to drive, for training and a game of footy, some 20 to 25 miles, but he shook his head and told me, 'No – I cycled.' Maybe determination was genetic because it was something that I drew on a lot as I developed from that rather fragile youngster to become an Australian Test player.

I grew up with sport. I can remember the social times that went hand in hand with Australian Rules football. We would go down to the ground and the kids would play in the field while the grown-ups socialised and partied in the pavilion after the game. There were no problems; it was a great life, kicking a football around, playing on the swings, running around until our parents put us in the car to drive home when we promptly fell asleep.

It was so relaxed. Every Saturday night after football there was a party at our house or at one of the other players' houses, usually a barbecue with a big 18-gallon keg of beer to sustain the 50 or so people who were there. Often the men would go around to the party host's home the next day to clear up, or so they said. I quickly learned it was to finish off the keg of beer.

It was a very typical, very Australian upbringing. We lived in an old weatherboard and asbestos council house, mainly asbestos it has to be said. It was my job, with brother Trevor and sister Carmen, to have the fuel ready for the wood-chip stove and the wood-chip heater. The heater was a long, cylindrical effort made of tin with a chimney. The water heated up on top of it for the bath. Mum had a copper for boiling the linen, with a stick to push it down, which we copped across the back of the legs a few times when we were out of line. She did the washing by hand and had a mangle, or a hand-wringer. Mangles were lethal things and a couple of times she caught her fingers between the rollers. We heard her shout out but she was tough. She just flicked the safety switch to separate the rollers, released her trapped hand and got on with the job. She never moaned or cried.

Dad mostly drove up north on unsealed roads and dirt tracks, and when the rains came, he could be stuck for days. Sometimes he was away for weeks at a time, so Mum had to be the strong one, looking after three youngsters. It was pretty difficult for her. We were a spirited trio and pushed it to the edge as much as we could.

In those days, they had those huge trucks with two trailers and the drivers had to change the giant tyres themselves if they had a puncture.

There was no cabin to sleep in, just enough room for him and a passenger, if there was one. Whether it was raining or hot, he slept on an old gate, the criss-cross sort, welded on to the back of the truck's cabin. There were few shops in the outback, so the drivers lived on tinned food, and they kept warm on cold nights by sitting around a small fire. Dad loved it and would still be doing it if he could.

When Carmen was old enough, we made her take over most of the little household chores. Trevor and I carried on collecting wood from the surrounding country and Dad would chop it when he was at home. It came naturally to him because he was from a timber-working family. On the odd weekend when the wood was low, Dad would down trees with an old handsaw. Our job was to cut it into fire-size pieces. Dad was a bushman and knew where to get the good wood. Nowadays, they would shoot you for taking the jarrah wood but, in those days, that's what you did. You took the best wood because it was there and available.

Dad's nickname was Cheyenne. He was a big, healthy man with a 44-inch chest and a 28-inch waist and huge arms. He had an amazing build but with truck driving, drinking cordials and eating canned foods, he gradually developed a truck driver's belly, although he kept pretty fit.

There was not a lot of money around and I suppose there were hard times. I know it now, of course, but it didn't make any difference then because we always had food in the fridge, would go for drives at the weekends, could have the occasional ice cream and played a lot of sport. We were fortunate to have a large fridge and a television. Mum had a job in a department store for most of her working life and got them at a discount. She still has an eye for a bargain, a talent she has passed on to me.

Mum would not get home from work until around six at night, so she would prepare the spuds and vegetables for our dinner the night before. It was our job to put them on to cook at a certain time so when she got home they would be ready and she would cook a steak or something. That was a problem because as soon as we got home from school, we would change and be off down the oval or out in the backyard. With no watches, we often lost track of the time and more than once we heard her bus arrive round the corner and quickly made up all the excuses under the sun. We would say we couldn't get the wood-chip stove going and all sorts of other things. But she knew.

Dad's parents had moved to Australia from Kent. They lived in the country, 25 miles out from Perth, which was very much country in those days. My granddad had the night-cart contract, or the ice-cream-cart as it was called – in other words the toilet run, collecting the big outdoor toilet pans on a horse and cart, emptying them out and replacing them with clean ones. Their house had a dirt floor and was incredibly basic. They had nothing except ten healthy kids to feed! Every Friday, after doing his last run, Granddad would go to the pub and drink until closing time. Then he would slump on the back of the cart, slap the horse and it would take him home. If he was late, my grandmother, who I believe was descended from an American Jewish family, would send my dad and his brothers to get him out of the pub and they would put him on the cart and take him home. It must have been desperate and depressing to clear everyone's crap.

My mother's father, Len Halifax, was a big influence on me. I don't remember much about my maternal grandmother because she died in her 50s when I was still very young. Pop Len's background and passion was boxing. A true Cockney born and bred, he was a coach but he wouldn't let us anywhere near the sport, calling it a mug's game. He coached some very good State amateur boxers. He had a belief in what he called a second wind whereby you trained so hard that you went through the pain barrier and then discovered your second wind and came back strong.

Whenever we went to his place, the cricket ball and bat came out very quickly. He bowled to us and batted. He was a clever bowler even though he did not play at any great level. He had served in the Second World War and would make us laugh when he ran up to bowl with a funny action, saying just before he let go, 'Coming up with the pin out,' pretending he was bowling a hand grenade.

He lived on his own and, later, we would often stay at his house before a game on a Friday night. We might have a practice and then, because I got nervous before a game, we would go for a walk and talk, or I would go for a jog before going to bed. Then he would take us down to the game the next day. He was almost like a father to us. He had retired so he had more time to give us than Dad had. Dad wasn't around a lot. Some people say it's bad for children not having their father around but I never thought about it. I just thought that was what everyone's dad did. I didn't think it strange and I'm sure it had no adverse affect on my upbringing. When he was at home we made the most of it. He would come out and play cricket or footy with my friends and me in the backyard, even if it was late and he'd been driving since six in the morning.

We made our own fun and had mates round to play, or we would jump on our bikes and go down to the school nets or play in the middle. When we were short of fielders, we were ever so grateful to our mate Chris McLeod's dog, who fetched the boundary hits!

Sport was seasonal with football in the winter and cricket in the summer. I had a go at athletics but I wasn't great. I tried high jump, long jump, 100 metres – shorter stuff rather than long, funnily enough, given how much long-distance training I was to do in later years. I wasn't great but I was competitive, just as I was a competitive swimmer for Belmay Primary School, near my home in Belmont. I have to admit that I was a bit of a thrasher in the water and I have never really improved. Primary school was an exciting place for me. I was keen to learn and I loved my teachers.

If you can have an idyllic childhood, I had one; at least, I thought of it as such. One of the great benefits was having such young parents. It was an amazing bonus; there's no doubt about that. I suppose it was like having an extra older brother and sister, except there was a clear line drawn between us and they were strict in some things, insisting that we showed good manners, went to bed at the right time with lights off and all the rest of it. But when we had people round on a Saturday night, they would let us stay up until eight or nine. Later on, Dad would sneak out Trevor – 18 months my junior – and the men would huddle round to listen to his risqué stories. They thought it was a hoot coming from an eight or nine year old. Dad was very proud of him.

Carmen, four years younger than me, was fabulous. We allowed her to play cricket with us, but only to field. We rarely let her have a bat – only if we got very tired. Most of the time she spent chasing the ball but she didn't seem to complain. She had to put up with plenty of rough and tumble, and became a bit of a tomboy.

Carmen was a very good all-round sportswoman. She played netball well but didn't continue with it once she started to meet boys. We were all supportive of each other; we would watch her play, and she would occasionally come to the cricket with Mum and Dad. She eventually got married and had children of her own. Her husband, Ray, is a great bloke. He used to play a bit of cricket with us. They lived in Melbourne for a while but are back in Perth now.

Of course, we fought like all kids do but generally we all got on. In fact, we were very close.

Fire was a fascination for me and a couple of experiments got out of control in the backyard, but generally I was pretty well behaved and too scared of the law to get into real trouble like a few of my mates. I guess we were brought up to respect authority. For example, I remember the time Carmen told us she knew there was no Father Christmas. Mum and Dad would have killed us if we'd let on to her, but she knew anyway, and just before the big day, when our parents were out, she disappeared out of the room and came back with all the presents. We didn't want to look; we were petrified because we knew Mum and Dad would realise that they had been moved. It took Trevor and me hours to put them back in the same position in Father Christmas's hiding place.

It was a blessing that I enjoyed school even though I was of only average intelligence. I guess I went to school to play sport rather than to work. I couldn't wait for Friday afternoons because weekends were devoted to sport. I used to get so excited about it I couldn't sleep at the end of the week, and would even get nosebleeds with the adrenaline and nervousness flowing through me. I was a very nervy youngster.

The teachers were generally fantastic. There was one, Ken Watters, who was always immaculately turned out for football and cricket, and he expected you to be the same. We had to have our boots polished, shirts tucked in and everything had to be done up properly. We had to be groomed to look the part. But more than that, he was very skilful in the way he taught us and we won a few tournaments during his time. Quite rightly, the school was proud of its football.

He had a big influence on me, developing my will to win and teaching me never to give up. He gave inspiring talks before the game and at half-time. He was just a really good bloke who knew how to wield authority and at the same time, while not a mate, get close enough to young people. He was a role model.

Perth was developing rapidly as I grew up, and Belmont High was one of the biggest schools in the entire area, fed by the new housing commission developments. I guess there were around 1,200 to 1,400 pupils, if I recall correctly, a very big school for that part of the world.

When I started, it was newly built on the outer fringes of the city and our playground was still bush country. The bush was pristine and stretched for four, maybe five, acres at the most. It's hard to judge now because perceptions are awry as a youngster. I used to think my back garden was huge, that we had a full-size cricket pitch in there, but when I went back ten years or so ago, I was amazed at how small it really was.

There was an airport close by the school and the planes scared off the kangaroos, but bobtail lizards, snakes and magpies were around. When the magpies were nesting, they would swoop down on the schoolchildren. One of them attacked me, buzzing around my ears and petrifying me so much that I admit I am still wary of magpies to this day.

I was not a model pupil by any means. Lessons were genuinely hard work for me but I was interested and wanted to learn. I admit my attention span was not great because I would be thinking of the next game of footy or cricket. We played cricket every day at lunchtime. Before the oval was ready, we would play right near the school in an area of mainly black sand next to the driveway and the portable school cabins. We got so black we would have to get under the tap before we were allowed back into the classroom.

Looking back, the constant exercise almost certainly helped my general fitness later in life. Running on sand gives you good balance and helps the stamina. I also used to walk the kilometre or so to school – along the tops of the neighbours' fences where I could. That helped balance and coordination, especially jumping over the gates! Small things, but they all helped me to learn control, determination and stuff like that without really knowing or thinking about it.

Even though I was shy, I had some good close friends. I was the only one of the group to come through and make it at cricket although some of those I played against made their names in football. One young Italian boy looked as though he would really make the grade. He was muscular, quick and inspirational to the rest of us, but suddenly he stopped growing and never made it all the way. It just went to show how big a part luck could play in your sporting future.

One of the subjects I really loved was geography. I enjoyed learning Western Australia was big enough to swallow up the United Kingdom, Japan and Germany and still leave plenty of space over. I was well aware of how under-populated and remote we were, even though in those days not many Western Australians travelled – just to Perth and that was it. The south west was logging country and apart from that no one seemed to move out of Perth much at all, other than to the coast. When we went on holidays when we were young, we would drive to a place I thought was miles away down gravel and limestone roads, but now with highways that same beach is just 30 minutes out of Perth. It seemed to take us half a day to get there when I was a schoolboy . . . and probably did.

History was another subject which fascinated me as a youngster. I found it exciting, especially the Elizabethan era, the explorers, the Cortezes and the other guys who were tough, hard people ready to take on the unknown. I also imagined the early pioneers in my country going into the bush in 40 degrees heat with the kangaroos, the flies, the snakes and the wild dogs, let alone there being no track, and exploring that wild countryside. They were either mad or superhuman. Even nowadays it would be tough doing what they did then. I found it romantic but realised, of course, what a hard slog it would have been. As a youngster, I was enchanted by the vision, just as youngsters are these days by sport – without knowing the hard work it takes to get to the top in that as well.

I got by all right with maths, English wasn't a great subject but I enjoyed French and hands-on things such as technical drawing and art, but I certainly didn't have the same feelings for senior school as I had for my junior school. It was too much like hard work. I didn't like the homework, much preferring to go outdoors to play football or cricket when I returned home in the afternoons, and I would cram everything in the last couple of weeks before exams.

I was nervous in exams and would go totally blank, not just because I hadn't done the work. I was frightened and had a nervous block even with the things I knew well. They just disappeared. Yet I could work on a project and receive top marks.

Even now, I find it hard giving interviews, making ads for television or standing up to speak at dinners. That's just me. I have always been self-conscious which brings on the nerves, thinking you are not good enough for whatever it is you are doing. I have got through it mainly but I have had to work very hard at it. Some things that I know well I'm confident about, but in other things I'm still not.

One of the reasons I didn't much like high school was that there was so little organised sport. There was no school cricket team, so I never had the chance to try out for the State junior teams, the target for all sports-minded youngsters of my age. There were guys getting games who I knew were no better than me. The only cricket we played was a couple of lessons during the week. We had inter-school athletics matches but I didn't make the team because we had some superb athletes. I don't recall us having a football team; maybe it was because we were such a new school.

However, we did have a big field and cricket nets and a teacher called Dr Frank Pyke, who became a great friend and influence later in life. He played A Grade cricket and first-division football and was one of our cricket coaches.

I wasn't a bad kid. I remember getting six of the best from the headmaster, Clive Elliott, who was an old schoolmate of my mother's – not that it helped me when it came to the punishment meted out because I refused to dance. I was very shy as a kid and far too embarrassed to dance in front of all the others. I didn't like dancing then and I still don't like it now. I felt strongly about it and no one was going to make me dance in the schoolyard.

I remember going back at the school's invitation following the 1972 tour to England and Mr Elliott stood up and told the school assembly that I was a model student, an example to follow etc, etc. I gave him a sideways glance and wondered whether he was talking about Bob Massie or me! It was all I could do not to laugh and I had to control myself as I remembered being punished for not dancing.

In my teens I had a few fights – it was only a few because I was basically scared of getting hurt. I remember coming home from a drive-in theatre with a mate with a big bandage around my finger. Mum wanted to know what had happened and I told her I had slammed it in a car door. I thought I had got away with it until she had a chat with one of her colleagues in the department store. Her friend also worked part-time at the drive-in and she told my mother about the young lad she had to treat with a deep gash across his knuckles where he had been in a fight. Mum asked her what the boy looked like and the game was up. I was in big trouble but more for telling fibs than for fighting.

By the time I was 14, I was more interested in club cricket than anything the school provided. I played Under-16 cricket for South Belmont and Metropolitan Seniors and in the combined sides with my brother. In the afternoons, I occasionally played men's B Grade cricket.

Pop Len came to every game he could. He used to walk the boundary and when Trevor or I was out, we would go and sit with him and talk about cricket and life, or we would walk the boundaries, too. He was very big on me doing lots of running, both sprint and distance, and sit-ups and push-ups.

My parents also came to every game they could, particularly club and later Shield cricket. The nice thing was that they never interfered. They never tried to tell me what I should do, never criticised; they were just there supporting and watching. Dad tells the story that if they didn't manage to get to the game they would ask me the next day how it went. Dad says it was so hard to prise the information out of me that they would go and look in the newspaper. Apparently, I would say, 'Oh, I took a couple,' and they would look in the local newspaper and see I had taken five. I wasn't into bragging – my family just weren't like that.

I batted fairly high in the order in junior cricket, often going in at number four, but I always opened the bowling. I always had the new ball and Trevor was an opening batsman. Perhaps that is significant after our early contests in the nets and the backyard, with me bowling and him batting.

I just ran in and bowled as fast as I could and occasionally tried to bowl an outswinger. A yorker wasn't in my thoughts at that stage. I did bowl short of a length a great deal because I did not have great control, but from what I was told I was pretty quick for my age. The problem was, untutored, I fell away as I bowled so a lot of balls slanted in. I read Don Bradman's *The Art of Cricket* and any other cricket instructional books I could lay my hands on. I used to take them out into the backyard, prop them up and try the various grips.

Of course, a lot of the instruction contained in those books is dated by today's standards, and now we know that much of the advice was bad and led to physical damage and injuries. Because I was twisting so much in my action, I was always aware of having a sore back. I was also asked to bowl a lot of overs as a youngster, and willingly did so. That was another problem, the overuse of young, willing, fast bowlers – you get tired, the action breaks down and the fault gets worse.

Now there is legislation in junior cricket limiting the number of overs a youngster may bowl in a competitive match. It works in two ways, protecting the player from over-bowling and also offering the chance for other youngsters to join in the game and bowl when previously they might not have been given the opportunity. You have to bring all the team into play and you never know what little gem you might find. My only complaint is that it does not teach youngsters about real cricket, four-day and Test cricket where you have to bowl longer spells and the better bowlers are going to bowl more. But that's only a small thing offset against the advantages of protecting the youngsters at a time when their bones are not anywhere near their strongest.

Trevor was a better sportsman than I was. He was a skinny kid but when he was young he was coordinated and balanced. As well as being an opening batsman, he bowled leg-spin or even medium pace with a lot of swing. He was short and frail and he scored painfully slowly because he basically didn't have the strength to force it. But they couldn't get him out. He had amazing defence, backward and forward, and he bored them to death as he hung in there. He played A Grade cricket at 16 and was a very good Australian Rules footballer, playing on the wing. Although he was skinny, he was as skilful in that position as anyone you could find. He used to get belted around and they really used to try to knock him off the game, but he would always get up and get on with it.

We were very competitive against each other in all our sports, with the usual fights about being out or not. I treated him as a younger brother but he was a tough young man and would take no rubbish from anyone, me included. We did a lot of things together.

Trevor eventually went away to do his National Service – his marble was pulled out of the bag and mine wasn't – and he met a girl while he was away in Melbourne and has stayed there ever since he was 20.

He also found religion. He played cricket until he was 18 and did not play again as he dedicated himself to the church. It was a shame. I was just getting into the Western Australia side then.

I suppose I was the opposite of him from then on. I have my own beliefs but keep them to myself. He was excited by his new-found commitment and, without realising it, tried to lay it on us a bit. I objected to that and for a while we went through the motions a bit. I didn't realise the religion had faded a little as he grew older because we did not talk about it. I'm sure he still has beliefs but he is no longer actively involved. I find it fascinating that he started off telling risqué stories and then found religion before going back to telling similar stories and jokes.

Someone once said to me, when Trevor was very young, he was going to be either a thug or a priest. That was his commitment and he was strong with whatever he did, so perhaps it was a good thing religion consumed his early days. I suppose I was just as strong with cricket and maybe at that age we both needed something to cling on to. We're close again now.

I played with some older guys in B Grade cricket and I will never forget our wicket-keeper, an aboriginal guy named Wally Bates, probably then in his mid 40s. We thought he was as old as the hills but he was terrific and took me under his wing. He had a kind face and was a lovely person. He was passionate about cricket, which was fast taking over as my be-all and end-all in sport.

I left school at 15 and went to work in a warehouse for a clothing firm for three months while I waited to see whether I would get the job in a bank which I had applied for. Cricket wasn't full-time in those days. I chose the bank because, naively, I thought that it would leave more time for cricket. After all, the bank didn't open until 10 a.m. and it closed at 3 p.m. It never occurred to me to find out what was actually involved. I thought I could lie in in the morning and be at the nets by 3.30 in the afternoon. When I got the job, I found out very quickly that it didn't work quite like that and sometimes it would be 6.30 or 7 in the evening before I balanced my till. Nevertheless, I wanted to make a career at the bank. I saw it as my future and I was very conscientious. In fact, I worked my guts out and developed the ambition to become a manager with the Commonwealth Bank.

I spent most of my time when I wasn't at work at South Belmont Cricket Club. Mick Basile, one of our Under-16s coaches, was a very good bowler and something of an independent spirit. He should have gone further but didn't because of his attitude and because of the politics within the team he played with as a youngster. He was a quick left-armer and one day he knocked over the top three in an A Grade game and then didn't get another bowl as the skipper brought on the old brigade to pick up a few cheap wickets. He was only 17 or 18 at the time but he blew his top and didn't have many more games for that team before he finally walked out, saying he would rather play with his mates at South Belmont.

Mick called me, and every other kid, Snowy. It was good he was there because he took a personal interest. He was brutally honest about what I had to do to be a top bowler and would not only tell me what I was doing wrong but actually show me. I would toss him the ball and, without warming up, he would whip one down in exactly the style he was trying to explain to me. He believed that a fast bowler was the most important player in the game. He said that, as a fast bowler, you are the game – you start the game, you can create opportunities, and you can control the game.

In those days, we played on artificial wickets made with a linoleum-type composite called Malthoid on a concrete base. They were very fast, very bouncy. For a fast bowler, it was some kind of heaven. Everywhere apart from non-government schools and the top-class game, cricket was played on this surface. Grass was totally different, which was why Mick Basile said to me after I finished with the Under-16s that I should not stay with the club any longer and if I did I would rot. He was convinced I could play better cricket and should test myself, and suggested I join Perth Cricket Club in the West Australian Pennant Cricket competition.

So I went down on my own, asked to register and was sent to the nets. Someone must have liked what I was doing because I was put straight into the Second Grade team for seven or eight games. Then I was promoted to play First Grade cricket. At the age of 16, that was quite unusual. At the time, I didn't think it strange to be playing cricket with players who were a lot older than me; it seemed natural and normal. I thought I fitted in, but if anyone had told my children at 16 that they were ready to play any sport at that level, I would have told them to hold on, even though they were better developed physically and mentally at that age than I was. When I think back, I wonder how I ever did it.

CHAPTER TWO

Heroes

I tried to imitate England's Freddie Trueman and Wes Hall of the West Indies. There was no Test cricket at the WACA in those days (the first Test held there was in December 1970) but the touring sides came to play Western Australia there. Trevor and I would hitchhike to the ground, pay to get into the general area and then sneak our way into the members' section. We couldn't afford to be members but we wanted to see the players close up.

We actually managed to meet some of our heroes and I will never forget Wes Hall. He had time for everyone, laughing, telling stories and having fun, even though we couldn't, and I still can't, understand him fully with his strong Bajan accent. Then we would watch him bowl. I had seen him on newsreels but this was different, seeing him in the flesh. He was a magnificent and awesome sight. I remember the shirt-tail flapping, arms and legs everywhere, and the big load-up, the follow-through and the big appeal. The follow-through was almost as long as his run-up and he would finish right near the batsman.

I followed Wes because of the exciting Caribbean side of 1961, especially as he was in tandem with the fearsome Charlie Griffith that day in Perth. I liked Griffith but for some reason I was not as influenced by him as I was by Wes. He was quiet, unmoving and didn't have the same charisma as Wes. In fact, he appeared gruff. He had been accused of chucking and probably wasn't a happy man at the time, but I have met him since, on a tour in 1973. I was shy and he was very insular but I got on well with him when we sat down and had a talk.

I couldn't get enough of Wes, either sitting and talking to him or, even better, watching him bowl. I used to think, 'What a bowler, what an athlete!' as every sinew and muscle stood out with every ball. I saw batsmen ducking and diving and others clean bowled. I especially admired his enthusiasm, not just for himself but when his team-mates took wickets as well. He was the absolute epitome for me as a young fast bowler.

I saw Fred Trueman towards the end of his career on some old newsreel film at the cinema. He was the guy who moved the ball around both ways. He was compact with a beautiful run-up, smooth and able to let one go now and again at real pace. To me, he seemed fast but smart, not as fast as Wes but a great bowler. I loved the aggressive way he rolled his sleeves back and had his hair plastered back against his head.

The others who took my fancy in those early formative days were the Aussie trio of Alan Davidson, Ray Lindwall and, of course, Keith Miller who could do anything with the ball. I saw them, too, on film because when they played at the WACA I was either playing myself or at school. It was only when the touring sides came that Trevor and I would make that real effort.

I liked Alan Davidson because he was like a left-handed Fred Trueman. He swung the ball around, used his head and had the most beautiful run-up and action. I loved Ray Lindwall because he was a great fast bowler. When I was just starting to play for Western Australia, I wrote to him for advice and he wrote back telling me to try this and try that. When I started to play some Test cricket, I asked him to watch me to see if I was doing anything wrong and he would make comments and suggest adjustments.

He was a lovely guy, unassuming and soft-spoken, who enjoyed himself with a few quiet beers. Unfortunately, I did not get really close at the time but later I did, and for the last 20 years I have also telephoned Keith Miller just to see how he is and to say hello. He is universally loved and he was my hero because I fancied myself as a bit of a batter when I was young – and he was the great all-rounder.

They were my major influences, together with Sir Garfield Sobers. Although our own Don Bradman was a great batter, Sobers was the player I always aspired to be. I saw him in a double-wicket competition at the WACA where he square drove a six, the first time I had seen it done; and that cat-like run-in when he bowled was awesome. I always thought his run-up and fielding was like a panther's with so much feline grace.

When I was coming through with Perth Cricket Club, my local hero was Graham McKenzie, who is now my near neighbour. Graham was a very quiet man; he played a lot in England in the off-season so I didn't see him around much. He used to have a couple of trial matches at the start of the season but was often tired when he arrived back after his efforts in England on the county circuit.

I don't think anyone realised at the time but he was suffering from stress fractures before they became medically recognised. He would get through a season, rest for a month when a bit of healing went on and then he would play again. So he wasn't around a lot at practice, but he was a genuine guy, one of nature's great people – and a great bowler.

I will never forget one trial match. He had just returned from England and I was keen to look at his action. Brian Hannah, a prolific run scorer in club cricket and a Shield player, came up in the stand with me to watch. Brian had played against Graham a few times and said he had never been troubled by him, and it seemed that day Graham was only turning his arm over.

A wicket fell and Brian was in. As he walked out to face Graham, I warned him to watch out but he just smiled. Graham bowled two or three balls, which Brian played really well, and you could see Graham give him a long, hard look. The next ball was a lot quicker, jagged back and bowled him between bat and pad. On the way back from the middle, Brian looked at me, said, 'You're right,' and carried on into the dressing room.

Graham knew when to turn it on and when to look after himself. He was a professional and as a fast bowler you cannot bowl fast all the time. That's the problem with English cricket and the number of games they are expected to play.

My mates and I used to try to imitate Graham's action. In training, we couldn't keep our eyes off him as we tried to learn from the expert. He had a very different action from mine but, playing around, I could copy it.

Graham is a retiring guy who didn't talk a lot, but nowadays if I see him over the road mowing his lawn when I come back from a jog, we talk more than we ever did.

When I progressed to State cricket, I warmed to the captain, Tony Lock, immediately. Sure he was hard and trod on a lot of people's toes but it was almost always for the good of the team or for the individual he was helping. He was undoubtedly the right person at the right time for me. If he liked you, he was great; if he didn't – you knew it.

A lasting memory is when the Western Australia side travelled to Brisbane. It was my first tour and my first Shield match. Tony paired the team and I was to share a room with Graham. When we got to our room, he asked me if I wanted the double or the single bed. I told him it was his choice but he insisted. Then he put the kettle on and made me a cup of tea. That was incredible; he made me so welcome and at home, treating me as an equal. It's just fabulous when one of your heroes turns out to be genuinely special like that.

CHAPTER THREE

The Young Cricketer

They treated me all right at Perth Cricket Club, I suppose because I was good at what I did. I never had any trouble and I was made welcome, particularly by the captain, the coach and the president of the club, Bert Rigg. He loved cricket and treated me as an adult. He was a very influential man at the WACA and was eventually on the Board of Control. He pushed my barrow with the State selectors, without me knowing it at the time. It would have made no difference to how I thought of him. I just loved him as a bloke, a great president, a great lover of cricket and a legend at our club. It was only ten years or so ago that I learned how influential he was in my progress.

Despite his support, my first couple of years of First Grade cricket were not exceptional. I bowled quickly but didn't take lots of wickets. If I look at both sides of the ledger, I played for a weak team on a dead, grassless wicket which was basically a football field and a pitch of rolled clay. It was hard work; there was no doubt about that. But I had the chance to play on other pitches around Perth which weren't like that and while I still did not set the world on fire, I did my bit. I was inconsistent and had a lot to learn about the art of bowling but I enjoyed it. I was enthusiastic and would keep bowling all day if they wanted me to. The endeavour was there – but not the skill.

It was a big step up. I was playing against boys one season and the next I was bowling to State and Test players such as Ken Meuleman who was a great performer for Western Australia, John Inverarity, Ross Edwards, Rod Marsh, Bruce Laird, Tony Mann and Keith Slater. In those days, there were only eight Sheffield Shield games a year and Western Australia would play their four away matches in a month. The other four were staged at home throughout the season, so everyone had to play club cricket, including the top players. There simply weren't the games available there are now, so you played against good players on good wickets most of the time. Often the shine would be quickly off the ball and it would be a batsman's dream.

Kevin Taylforth was my first A Grade captain. He had been a quickish bowler when he was young but by the time I started playing A Grade, he was down to medium-pace swing mixed with a good slower ball – he was one of the first I came across who did this – and quickish off-spin. He bowled a very good length and gave away few runs. He was a real student of the game, a hard man and a hard captain, especially where the opposition were concerned, because he was uncompromising. In one of the first games I played under his captaincy, I ran in, bowled a bouncer and hit the batsman. This was in the days before helmets. I rushed down the wicket to see how the batsman was, but Kevin came in from wherever he was fielding to intercept me. He took me away, telling me to go back to the end of my mark and wait while they got the batsman to his feet. He added, 'If he carries on, you run in and bowl to him as fast as you can.'

I have to admit I was not happy about it. Afterwards, we talked about it many times. He emphasised that if I was going to be a fast bowler, I was going to hit batsmen now and again because it's the nature of the game, and I was going to have to divorce myself from it. At times you have to pretend a little. It was not something which sat easily with me but I was eager to please my captain.

Kevin knew he had someone who was pretty quick and that word gets around the other clubs. His attitude was that if I knocked them down, he would pick them up. Apologising was a weakness until after the day's play. Then he liked us to have a few beers with the opposition. He played it tough and I hadn't had anything like a tough captain before him. The Second Grade captain for whom I played half a dozen games was a happy-go-lucky guy at the end of his career who loved a good time and playing cricket. This was my first experience of a hard nut. The second was Tony Lock, captain of Western Australia. Those two hardened me.

Kevin Taylforth played for the club for a long time. He was a respected mainstay and captain but known as a very hard guy around the traps. Now I think back, he was captain of a weak side, trying to get the players motivated and to win a few games because it's not great when you're losing all the time. I provided him with a bit of a potent weapon and he wanted to make sure that it worked. As I didn't drink, I wasn't mixing a lot after games so I don't know what the perception of the other teams were about my bowling. I did know by the look in their eyes during the game that I frightened a lot of the opposition more than a little – especially when they made the occasional step away towards the square-leg umpire. This was a powerful feeling and it gave me confidence. I realised I had them beaten and I liked the feeling.

There was plenty of sledging in both Second Grade and First Grade. In the old days, it was as subtle as a sledgehammer – hard-hitting but usually not of a personal nature. Often the remarks would be funny and make people laugh. Years later, it got a bit personal and out of order.

In my second or third First Grade game, I had a top bowler, Jim Hubble, coming in at me. I thought I handled a bat pretty well. This guy bowled a couple and I hit him through the covers. The next ball whistled by my ears, and the next, and I was out soon afterwards. At the end of the day's play, he spoke to me.

'Well bowled,' he said. 'Did you learn anything about batting out there today?' I told him I learned not to upset him but he shook his head. 'What you learned today is there are weak people and there are tough, strong people. Remember that because if I can give you one thing to think about, rather than talk about your bowling, it is your attitude out in the field. You have to be tough out there.'

Basically, he was saying I wasn't tough enough. He did it well by first praising my bowling and then pointing out a weakness. He told me that for my age I was doing well and I went away thoroughly encouraged.

He was showing me there were two games going on out there, a mind game as well as a physical game of cricket, and you must never let anyone dominate you. The tough survive and the weak do not. It was an interesting lesson to learn, especially at my young age with everything happening so quickly.

In the field, I was generally mid-on, mid-off, third man or fine leg, which is normal for a fast bowler. I wasn't a good slip catcher, not having the necessary quick reactions. It's tough to field in the slips as well as bowl fast because you have to stay alert for every ball and really you want to go somewhere where you can catch your breath and prepare for your next over. I was often away in Dixieland when I was fielding, thinking about what I had done in the previous overs and what I was going to do in the next one. I probably didn't concentrate as much as I should have done. The entire attitude to fielding has changed these days and quite rightly so.

It was tough going and I was not being talked of as a Shield player, never mind a future Test player. I was nowhere near. The nearest I got was a State bowling squad coached by Peter Loader, the former England Test player, and Charlie MacGill, grandfather of Aussie leg-spinner Stuart MacGill. They were two totally different people: Peter was a real swing bowler, quickish and a true pro while Charlie was one of those who just got out there and let it go. He gave them hell with little technique and a lot of motivation.

Then, when I was 17, I went away on a colts tour for the State, so I must have been showing some potential. The first game was against Victoria with Alan 'Froggy' Thompson and Max Walker opening the attack. We had a very good side and so I didn't get a game but I was named 12th man. Stan Wilson was the fast bowler and he was excellent, really quick, one of the quickest I ever played against in club cricket. Later, he played a few Shield games but, sadly, he got sick and by the time he bowled he had lost all his energy and performed poorly. He never quite made it but he was very good with the colts. Rod Marsh and Terry Gale, the golfer, were both in the side along with Bob Massie. There were a lot of good players and I simply couldn't get a look in.

The second game was in Adelaide and I was called in at the last minute because one of the batsmen had pulled out with a migraine. It was an odd choice, a quick bowler for an opening bat, but maybe they just wanted to have a look at me. I took wickets which must have helped my cause a bit.

By this time I'd got to know Helen. Her house backed on to ours, separated by a narrow lane. I'd met her down at the shops one day and we got talking. We liked each other straightaway, but she was only 14, and still at school, and I was 17. She used to come along to some of the games, but she wasn't into cricket and if the weather was nice she preferred the beach.

She had a steadying influence on me – going out with her meant I didn't go out with the boys. Anyway, they were into drinking and I wasn't; it did nothing for me, even shandy.

Her parents were very strict, and as a parent myself now, I can totally understand their attitude. We were allowed out only on a Saturday night and then not alone. If we went to the pictures, we had to be home within half an hour of the end of the movie. It was all above board in a very innocent era. It probably seems strange to youngsters today but I did not smoke, drink or go to bed with girls – and I was 17.

In 1969 I was picked for Western Australia and things were progressing nicely. Early in 1970, I was selected to go on a six- or seven-week trip to New Zealand for Australia A. I was working at the Mount Lawley branch of the bank at the time, and all the staff were delighted – except the manager. He fancied himself as a bit of a hockey player, going on about how good he was and showing his scars. He also claimed to love cricket.

When news came through of my first representative selection, the first phone call I received was from Pop Len. I was a teller and I asked a pal to take over for me while I spoke to him, but the accountant told me to 'get off the phone and look after the customers'. I apologised, explaining I had just been picked for a national team and was a bit excited about it and was talking to my grandfather. He gave me a dirty look and after another 30 or 40 seconds he stretched over and cut me off.

I was furious, upset as hell, and asked him what he thought he was doing. I told him never to do that again, but he was as feisty as I was and he told me to get back to work. I ignored him, picked up the phone, dialled my grandfather's number and talked to him for another two or three minutes while the accountant stood there with steam coming out of his ears, going purple in the face.

You could have cut the atmosphere with a knife and I suspect that was the beginning of the end of my banking career. The way the system worked was that you were the subject of regular progress reports, and once you had two or three in a row which were progressively better, you were given a Grade One, enabling you to be promoted, thus beginning the climb up the career ladder.

I was called into the manager's room with the accountant and he told me that while my last two reports were excellent he was marking my current one exactly the same as the previous one because cricket had dominated my thoughts and my time. He added that I had not been doing what they wanted me to do in the bank.

I looked him in the eye and told him I honestly believed what he said was wrong because I loved the bank but against that I was very excited at my breakthrough into international cricket as my heart had always been set on playing for my country. I told him he wasn't right at the moment but he probably would be in the future because cricket would eventually dominate for me. I walked out of the office. It was a bold thing to say because there was no career to be had in cricket and I had put 100 per cent into banking, the same as cricket.

But I could see the manager's point because people were talking to me a lot more than to the others in the bank. I was regarded differently. I was taking a lot more telephone calls than the others, and tried to get off work a little earlier to practise.

I worked for the bank for seven years but as time went on, I was away more and more, so they put me on what was called relieving staff duty, which meant you were expected to travel all over the State. I refused to go to the country because of my cricket practice and so I went all over the metropolitan area covering for people on holidays. It was interesting and I learned a lot more about the bank and banking than if I'd stayed at one branch.

I left the bank in 1973, after going on tour to the West Indies with the full Australia side. When I came back to Perth, instead of wearing the bank-style pastel or white shirt, I wore a newly purchased West Indian black shirt with yellow and white pinstripes and one of the older guys had a go at me for wearing 'pyjamas'. It struck me there was a bit of cattiness creeping in and, as I got older, I was no longer inclined to take it lying down.

We were switching to computers at the time, and all the records had to be transcribed from ledger to machine. I found myself setting down name, address, balance, account number for eight hours a day, all day, week after week. It was relentless and after three months or so, I had had enough. I went to see the boss, Roger Fitzharding, and told him I wasn't comfortable any more. There was envy within the staff, which I could understand because of the time off I was having. He asked if there was anything he could do to change my mind, but I'd decided to leave even without another job to go to and my cricket future in doubt because of the injuries I'd picked up. I'd come back from the West Indies with what turned out to be stress fractures in my back, not that anyone was aware what it was at the time. This was not the best of situations to be in but I'd been offered a partnership with a contract-cleaning firm so I took that.

It was hard to combine a career with sport at that level, but it was the same for all Australian cricketers in those days. In fact, it was the same for players in most other countries except England, where they had county cricket, and to a lesser degree India and Pakistan where they had full-time cricketers. In England's case, this strongly contributed to their domination of world cricket for so long.

But it was during that first tour, with Australia A, I bought an engagement ring. Things were done formally in those days and so I had to ask Helen's father for her hand in marriage. Shortly after I got back, I was invited to their house and when her father got up to leave the table after lunch, I followed him, thinking it would be a great opportunity to speak to him alone and ask for permission to marry his daughter. But instead of going outside as I'd thought he would, he turned left.

'Can I have a word with you?' I called after him.

'Sure,' he said. 'But I have to go to the toilet first.' He left me sweating for fully 20 minutes. 'Yes, Dennis. What is it?' he said when he finally came out.

'I want to know if Helen and I can get married,' I mumbled.

'Sure,' he replied with a smile. 'Not a problem,' and he walked straight back into the dining room. I'd been building up my courage for weeks and he completely stuffed me, knowing exactly what I was about to do.

Even though Helen was only just 17 there seemed to be no worries about her age. When I think back now, I'm quite surprised it was accepted so readily. Perhaps we were mature for our ages – even though I was naïve – but it was easy to see we were very much in love. We were married seven months later.

CHAPTER FOUR

Run, Dennis, run

Those sportsmen and women who have a good work ethic are the ones who last the longest. Jack Nicklaus is reputed to have responded to a young journalist who asked him if he was a lucky golfer, 'Sure I am. The harder I practise, the luckier I get.' That, to me, is a great answer.

I was great at practising. I couldn't wait to get out there and I would practise as long as possible. If the session was five hours, I'd be out there and involved for five hours. I used to get excited about anything to do with cricket, the practice, the game, and the dressing-room banter. I'd cram in a practice session and a run or some sit-ups and push-ups. I did that consistently. I was very big on practice and training. I rarely missed a session.

That was Pop Len's influence. He was a great believer in consistency and moderation. I didn't agree with him totally because I believe in consistency and intensity – not moderation. He would say don't go out and do a 12 kilometre run and then do nothing for five days. He claimed you were better off having five days of three kilometre runs. I think that's correct with the right measure of intensity.

The newspapers picked up on Pop Len's shout to me, 'Run, Dennis, run', and made it a catchphrase. He was encouraging me to work hard so I would still be going strong when others were fading – his second-wind theory. Because of his training tips and my work ethic, I bowled as quick at the end of the day as I did at the start. I'm sure this was a direct result of the sheer amount of aerobic fitness work I did.

I was fortunate, I suppose, that there was a shift towards the work ethic in sport in general in Australia at the time. With Western Australia, it was thanks to Darryl Foster, our fitness man at Perth, who eventually became State coach. Traditionally, a coach didn't do much other than organise practice and help out a guy or two with technique in the nets. By and large, they would bring in former bowlers to look after the bowlers and former batsmen to look after the batsmen. Darryl's expertise, however, lay in fitness.

Under Western Australian captain Tony Lock there was no fitness training. If we ran two laps it was as much as we did. Tony wouldn't, or couldn't, participate because his knees were stuffed. If we ran for fitness, it was done individually, and having done it from the age of 14 I kept it up. Some thought I was a bit mad because at the end of practice I would run hard until it was dark and then do a series of other exercises. Pre-season, I would be at it six days a week, running somewhere between four and six kilometres a day, and then, probably every second week, a 10- or 12-kilometre run.

Times and distances were religiously entered into my diary. When the season started, I would still run on Mondays, probably four kilometres on Tuesdays, and then on Wednesdays I'd do sprints or a long run, depending on what the coach wanted. This was tapered down for the Thursday practice session with a lighter run of 15 or 20 minutes plus a few sprints. I did a lot of aerobic work during the season. Maybe it was over-kill but I felt I needed it.

I always had a bat in the nets, the same as everyone else, 10 or 15 minutes or whatever I could get three times a week, but I would bowl for an hour or an hour and a half per practice session. At Perth, where I eventually became both captain and coach, we would bat against the best bowlers, but with the State, often by the time I batted, I faced the batsmen who couldn't bowl and it was a waste of time in terms of improving my own skills. It's a lot more professional now.

In 1969 a trial match for the Western Australian team was played at Perth Cricket Club to open our new ground. Usually, trial matches were held at the WACA, but probably because of Bert Riggs' influence, this one was played at our ground. There were a whole heap of fast bowlers around at the time: Jim Hubble, the experienced Stan Wilson, Lawrie Mayne, Sam Gannon and me. We were all probables for selection and all pretty good. Essentially, the match was Perth Cricket Club, bolstered by a few outsiders, against the State team.

My brother, a steady percentage player, opened the batting for Perth and took on the two really quick bowlers Gannon and Wilson, one a left-armer who swung it around and the other with a fast windmill action. Trevor scored 40 or 50 really quickly and tore them apart. When Perth took the field, I bowled and did pretty well. I was picked for Western Australia as a result of that and I've always thought I owe a debt of thanks to Trevor. He took on the two bowlers who were favourites to make the team, and gave them such a hiding as an 18-year-old that he made me look good when I bowled against the State batsmen.

We had to wait for the team to be announced a few days later. I was playing another game and my parents were at the ground, sitting in their car on the boundary. Dad said he would toot if he heard on the radio that I had been picked. The day went on and there was no toot. I was toiling away with hardly a wicket and becoming more and more despondent. Eventually, during the final session, I heard it and suddenly everyone sitting in their cars around the boundary edge picked it up off the radio and they all started tooting.

It was all very emotional – no tears but great relief. The longer the day had gone on, the more I felt I had missed out. Now I knew I was in the 12 with a pretty good chance of playing. It was a great feeling and nice that it happened at Fletcher Park, our club ground.

Tony Lock was a hard taskmaster, a tough uncompromising captain both on his team-mates and on the opposition. If you are talking sledging, he was a master. He had a great sense of humour. At the end of a day's play, first thing was the ritualistic unwrapping of his damaged knees. They would be swollen, knobbly and in all sorts of shapes, and he would sit there with a towel wrapped round him, with quite a big gut, and hold court. He was 20 years older than I was, and nearing the end of his career, eventually finishing in his early 40s. He had the respect of everyone, including the opposition, and was a lovely guy.

Locky left a lasting impression on me, not least because he was the one to nickname me Fot, short for 'fucking old tart'. It happened when I was dreaming in the outfield, thinking about my bowling. A ball was hit down to third man, I didn't go the right way and a single was turned into a two. Locky was livid and with hands on hips in typical pose, he yelled out in this near-empty ground, 'For fuck's sake, you fucking old tart.'

He got on with the game but John Inverarity, a cerebral giant, fielding in the slips, mulled it over, decided against using the full vulgar expression and, instead, used the acronym FOT – and it stuck. Before that I was 'Falcon' because of the nose or 'Swampy' because of the lilies found in swamps in Australia. But it was Fot that stuck, never to be lost. Even some of my mates' wives call me Fot. I'd think to myself, 'No, my name's Dennis,' but it was meant as an endearment and I guess I liked it, even though those ladies didn't realise what it stood for.

Locky had an amazing pair of hands. He took some of the greatest catches in the gully I have ever seen, even at 40 years of age. Every now and again he would put himself at silly mid-off, the ball would hit him, rebound and he would shout, 'Catch it!' That's how tough he was.

As far as I was concerned, he was very encouraging and seemed to have a bit of a soft spot for me, despite the fact that I was raw, naïve and didn't always bowl where he wanted me to bowl. Presumably he saw some potential, and I am totally indebted to him for the way he looked after me. I cannot speak highly enough of him. He taught me a great deal about the game at a time when I had just got into the State team.

My first State game was against Queensland in Brisbane. I took only one wicket but it was a top batsman, Sam Trimble. Sam was a run machine for his State and a hard player out in the field, but he laughed a lot and loved life. He and Locky got on well together and after the game they would hold court in tandem. They were a million laughs because they had the same attitude to the game – play hard and then forget any differences over a beer. If one had abused the other, it was forgotten, but then next day they would be at it tooth and nail again.

I can't remember how I got him out but I do remember Sam had scored 100. It was hardly an auspicious debut and no one was welcoming the new Ray Lindwall to State cricket; more likely they were saying where did they get this guy . . .and when is he going back!

I was very naïve in those days and became the butt of some of the older players' jokes. For instance, we had to travel by rail across the country to Victoria over three days. I roomed with one of the senior players, John Inverarity, and when we got to our cabin, John said that I had better get my sleeper bed ready. He said that as senior he was claiming the bottom bunk and that mine was the upper bunk. I looked up and there was this thing that looked like a hat rack. I thought to myself, 'Oh, shit!' but started to climb up anyway with my bedding. He fell about laughing. That's how naïve I was.

On another occasion, the rain had been pouring down in Brisbane. It was torrential and without great drainage the outfield quickly became flooded. When we arrived, there was a picture in the local paper showing in the foreground a tin can floating in what looked like deep water covering the playing field, and one of the boys said, 'There'll be no cricket today. Look at the result of all that rain.' They told me, and I believed them, that it was a 40-gallon drum. I really believed it. I was gullible because I wanted to believe everyone. I thought everyone told the truth in those days.

I must have improved and taken a few wickets to earn my place on the trip to New Zealand with Australia A. The selectors were searching for new blood at the end of an era – Graham McKenzie was coming to the end of his career, Lawrie Mayne hadn't set the world alight on the recent Test tour of South Africa, Dave Renneberg was at the end of his career and hadn't even made the Test side. Eric Freeman was around with his medium swing and Froggy Thomson was there – he made his Test debut in the 1970–71 series against England – but there weren't many others around.

During the trip to New Zealand, the bastards stuffed me at every turn. They took advantage of me being so young, naïve and gullible. It rained for two of the six weeks but the way they spun me along during that rain-induced rest made it feel more like two months than two weeks.

Greg Chappell was the ringleader. He took full advantage when he saw me watching him sniff his wine before swilling it around his mouth. I leant over and observed, 'You'd be a bit of a toff, wouldn't you?' Greg looked offended and responded that he worked for McWilliams wines. Of course, I apologised. Just to be sure, I checked him out and discovered he didn't work for the wine company at all but for a soft drink company, Coca-Cola. I challenged him but, as usual, Greg had an answer. He had worked for a wine company and was now a Coke taster, he said, but he never swallowed a mouthful, always spitting it out.

He quickly changed the subject and asked me what I did for a living. I told him I worked in a bank and he responded, 'So did I – until I got caught with my hands in the till!'

Unfortunately, Greg did not keep this incident to himself and told Graeme Watson and Renneberg that he had found a ripe one, someone they could tell anything to. They decided to make a real job of it and for the entire trip I became the target of a constant stream of stories, each one bigger than the one before. The whole team caught on and even manager Frank Bryant became a party to it. They said some travellers' cheques and other valuables had been taken from Graeme Watson's room. They set up Froggy Thomson to check Greg's room, and he came back with money, passports and all sorts of other stuff, saying he had found it all in Greg's room.

The manager stood up, shook his head and said what a grave situation it was and that Greg would have to be sent home. This was a guy I looked up to and I jumped up and yelled out, 'No, he wouldn't have done that. You're lying.' I was almost in tears that they should accuse Greg of something like that.

It was too much. Everyone collapsed in laughter and I was transfixed for a few seconds, frozen in time until I caught on and yelled at Greg, 'You bastards! You've done me!' I was embarrassed and felt humiliated. I decided there and then it would never happen again.

Greg quoted the cameo in his autobiography:

Dennis was one of the most naïve blokes to come into cricket but we never, ever put another thing over him. From that day onwards he became the most cynical. He wouldn't believe anything you told him unless it was in black and white.

On that tour, I hid the fact that I had a hernia. I knew something was wrong because it was hurting and I had a big lump. It got worse as the tour progressed, affecting my bowling, and in our last game I asked to see a doctor because of the persistent ache. He told me how stupid I was, failing to report it earlier, and told me if I had left it any longer it could have killed me. But the last thing I wanted was for them to send me home during the tour. However, once the last game had finished, I was whisked back home and straight into hospital.

I didn't have a great tour and there can't have been many people who thought I was going to make it. I recall bowling in the last two unofficial 'Tests' when it was cold and windy, and I found myself bowling into a gale in Wellington. This was my first trip abroad and I was all starry eyed with so many good players around me. A number of the squad went on to play many times for Australia, but one player who later became a Test regular who didn't make the trip was wicket-keeper Rod Marsh. John Maclean of Queensland was preferred – not that it affected Rod because he went on to play for Australia before the year was out, while I had to wait a little longer.

When I first met Rod I was 17 and he was 19. He was a scruffy, overweight, beer-swilling intellectual, a pianist and a good singer. He was also a hooker, cutter and slogger. Well, I called him a slogger because he was such an aggressive batsman. I don't remember much about his keeping, but I do remember him hitting me out of the ground a few times. He was not my sort of person and I wasn't his choice of friend because I was too straight and didn't drink.

We did not hit it off and it appeared we were never going to, even though we both came from the country – now the suburbs of Perth. It was a case of same background, different lifestyles. We were quite different people. He probably thought I was a bit of a nerd while he was a typical cricketer of that era, enjoying a drink and having a great time. At the same time, he was dedicated and would have died for his country. I admired him as a bloke, his ability, his cricket brain, his wit (he is an amazing storyteller) and enjoyed his comradeship within the team. He led the singsongs and contributed to everything we did. I guess I was a bit intimidated by all those assets, and the fact that he was a couple of years older and more experienced.

We didn't get close until probably halfway through my career, even though we played together so much, both for Western Australia and Australia. Gradually, I became a bit more outgoing and gained some respect along the way. People assume we were friends from the start, but it was a slow burner, developing slowly over some years and eventually growing very strong.

To his close circle of friends he is priceless. One of his epics was when he chased the record of Doug Walters who had set record 44 cans of beer in 1977 on the flight from Australia to England and Rod was determined to beat it. He was very excited about it. I got wind of it and I thought the best way to stop it was to take him on a big drinking binge the night before we left Melbourne. I wrongly assumed he wouldn't feel like drinking on the plane the next day and wouldn't be getting himself into bother with the team management.

I felt I was doing the right thing by my team-mates. We travelled across from Perth to Melbourne the day before and that night we went to a Qantas function. On the flight over I commented how he always reckoned rum drinkers were weak and now was the time to take me on. We had about eight rums each on the flight, and when we arrived in

Melbourne we went from the airport to the function and to join up with the rest of the team. To my delight Rod was straight onto the beer while I nursed a few quiet rums. I told him it was time we had a real drink and we went out with some others. I gave up around two in the morning and crawled off to my bed, leaving Rod still drinking with a few others of the hardier variety.

But I felt I had done my duty. Next morning I packed, and rang his room when I was ready to go. We were due to leave the country that afternoon and I asked him how he felt and he said he was fine and just about to go next door where a few of the local boys were arriving to have a lunch of a big steak and a few beers.

I arrived about half an hour after him and the restaurant table was littered with jugs of beer while the players cooked the steaks. In case he was still planning his assault on the record, I reminded him these beers did not count; they had to be on the plane. I thought my job had been done because of the big session the night before and now the lunchtime drinking before we boarded the plane

We went via Sydney and when we arrived he met up with his old mate Douggie Walters and, of course, had to have a couple of beers with him. We then met all the dignitaries in the airport and had a few drinks with them before boarding the plane. I was now sure my ruse had worked and he would be sleeping a lot more than drinking.

But, no. He was ready to start as soon as we got on the plane. It wasn't just a question of lining up the tinnies; he had pace-setters and scorers to make sure it was all official. He was taking this record very seriously. I was one of the pace-setters early on and I kept him company with a few rums until we reached Hawaii about eight hours later. I had enough and was ready to sleep.

We had the full backing of the aircraft crew, who knew he was trying to set the record, with one of the stewardesses telling him: 'You keep drinking them and I will keep bringing them.' I had a beautiful sleep for the next 12 hours, but when I woke up he was still going.

Eventually, as we were 20 minutes out of Heathrow, he was clearly struggling, but the betting was he was going to make it. I asked one of the stewardesses if she could make an announcement that Rod was about to break the record, as I thought this would be the spur a competitive man like him would need.

Sure enough the entire aircraft soon found out that Australian wicket-keeper Rod Marsh was bidding to break the record for the flight. Proud man that he was, he was clearly determined to finish it. I reckon the beer had reached the Plimsoll line and he was full up to the teeth by then.

After finally reaching the last can and drinking it down just as we came in to land at Heathrow, he collapsed. Now we had a problem. All the players had changed into their official gear from their tracksuits and were on their way off the plane. Graeme Wood and I wrestled Rod out of his tracksuit and into his blazer, trousers and tie.

We made our way through the passageways with the help of an arm around each other. By now we were half an hour behind the others and I thought what a good thing it was because, by the time we were through, I was sure all the press would have gone and we could sneak him out without anyone seeing or photographing him.

We eventually stopped an official on a buggy-type vehicle who told us to throw him on the back. We drove down the long corridor until we reached a fork where the driver had to go one way and he told us that a few yards the other way was the baggage reclaim area.

One either side of Rod we went around the corner and about 35 flashlights went off to take the three of us staggering into their sights. I'm sure they must have been tipped off that we were coming. The next day there were pictures and stories in all of the papers about Lillee, Wood and Marsh in this big drinking session. So the moral of the story is to never, ever help your mates in that sort of situation because it rebounds on you like a boomerang. He wasn't too good for several days but he blamed it on the jet lag.

Maybe it was stupid, but for me it showed the strength and character of the man and the fact that he loved a challenge, especially as it was his best mate Douggie who held the record. He did not hurt anyone, and the crew and the pilot joined in along with all the passengers, who clapped him when he broke the record before he collapsed, proving it was harmless. In those days it was a laugh, even in the papers, whereas nowadays we would have been disciplined, fined or locked up in the Tower of London.

CHAPTER FIVE

From Perth to Perth

After playing for Australia A in early 1970, my big hope was that I might make the step up to the full side in the next season. There was a big incentive to do so because our opposition was England, and the chance to play in the Ashes was one I'd always dreamed about.

But the season did not go well for me, and I began to fear I'd missed my chance. I did not have a good tour of the eastern states with Western Australia, taking only six wickets in the four games for lots of runs. It was not much better when we returned home, Barry Richards scoring 356 against us in November. I took 0–117.

I was selected as 12th man for the Western Australia game against the touring MCC side, but was reprieved when Graham McKenzie dropped out with injury and I was allowed to bowl with the wind for a change. I took Geoff Boycott's cap off with the first ball, but he had the last laugh and, once again, I was left without a wicket. I was beginning to think this might be the end of my international career, and so in the second innings I was a lot more relaxed. I just let myself go and took Colin

Cowdrey's wicket in my first spell and Boycott's in my second. That was just what my sagging confidence needed and, after the game, Jack Fingleton, a former Test opening batsmen and then one of the most respected journalists and commentators on the game, wrote that I should be tried in the Test team after what he had just seen in Perth.

Talk about a change of fortunes! It continued in the next game, against Queensland in Perth, when Bob Massie and I took 14 wickets between us. I took six of them and this was the turning point for me as I continued to pick up wickets.

Even so, I was staggered when I was selected for the sixth Test against England at the Adelaide Oval. I was almost the last one they could turn to, fifth cab off the rank, and few expected it, least of all me. But England were 1–0 up in the series and the selectors obviously felt they needed to try someone else.

I heard the news during the annual match between the State side and a Country XI at the WACA. I was sitting in the dressing room when the team was announced over the loudspeaker. People poured in to shake my hand, including my parents and my grandfather who were at the ground. Helen arrived during the tea interval to congratulate me, having heard the news on the radio. The Country team must have wondered what all the fuss was about because, after that, I could not concentrate enough to bowl well.

I travelled to Adelaide with Rod Marsh, the only other Western Australia player in the side. I remember the opening day clearly, even now. I always liked to go out last and I can remember seeing these 10 other guys in front of me, dressed in startling white, like something out of a soap powder advert, and in front of them a vivid green ground. Everything was vivid to me. I was nervous and my heart was pounding. It was all magnified in the bright Adelaide sunshine.

It was a bit of an anti-climax as I toiled against the wind. I had to wait a long time for my first wicket – John Edrich caught at slip by Keith Stackpole. It was a tired stroke, but then Edrich had scored 130! I finished the day on 1–41 off 14 eight-ball overs. It was the only wicket in the day to fall to a bowler as Boycott was run out. England finished on 276–2. The economy rate looked fine for my debut, but the truth is I probably did not make them play that many.

The next day everything changed. It was my turn to bowl with the wind and I soon accounted for the England nightwatchman Alan Knott, and clean bowled Ray Illingworth with a jaffa that moved away and then bit back off the pitch. I added tailenders John Snow and Bob Willis to finish my first Test match innings with 5–84 off 28.3 overs. I'd gained great confidence seeing the ball swinging away from the right-hander. My only regret was having persuaded my parents not to make the 1,500-mile drive from Perth to watch me.

With the wicket slowing down and becoming easier, I didn't add to my haul in the second innings but I was well pleased with my Test debut and even celebrated with a few drinks with Rod Marsh that night. Both he and Ian Chappell had been deeply suspicious of me before then, believing that all fast bowlers should drink.

It was a good start to my Test career and I kept my place for the seventh Test (the third Test had been abandoned and this one replaced it) in Sydney. Froggy Thomson gave way to the giant Tony Dell and I had the privilege of taking the first over. But I came back down to earth quickly as I tried to bowl too fast and lost my line and length. I was all over the place and bowled just one decent ball, yorking Ray Illingworth, finishing with three wickets in the match.

I was also set up by the skipper, Ian Chappell. I'd gone in to bat after Terry Jenner retired injured near the end of the second day. Ian came up the next morning, thanked me and told me the injured Jenner would resume batting. I was a bit perplexed but accepted the word of the captain and went to the nets to have a good bowl. The umpires were on the ground before Ian realised I had believed him and he hastily sent a runner out to the nets to tell me to get my pads on and get out to the middle. Not surprisingly, I was out almost straightaway.

It had hardly been a good time to come in the night before. John Snow, a very quick, truly great fast bowler, was not in the best of humour having been no-balled by umpire Lou Rowan. Snow became even quicker, and Terry Jenner ducked into a short-pitched ball. This was in the days before helmets and there was blood on the pitch as I came in to face up to John Snow, wondering whether I was in line for more of the same.

The Paddington Hill crowd were angry with Snow and began throwing cans at him. One of the crowd actually reached out and grabbed Snowy by the shirt. Seeing this, Ray Illingworth led the England team off the field, leaving Greg Chappell, the two umpires and myself on the ground. The mood Snow was in, I would have been happy to follow them off! Greg told me to stay where I was. We would be given the game if the England team did not come back, but they did once the field had been cleared of debris, and won the game and the Ashes 2–0.

During the series, I sounded out Geoff Boycott and John Snow about the possibility of playing in England. They were all for it and told me it could only help my cricket. Boycott even wrote a couple of letters for me but I couldn't get a county. So, taking extended unpaid leave from the bank, I went to play for Haslingden in the Lancashire League.

Playing in England was not only a steep learning curve cricket-wise; it was also great for Helen and me. We had not been married long and, aged 21 and 18, it was wonderful to go travelling. The furthest I had been was New Zealand the year before, and Helen had never flown at all.

As it turned out, I felt they got the better of me over the contract. I received £1,400 for the six months and I had to pay for our airfares, accommodation and a car, so we both had to work to make ends meet. I worked at a rubbish tip and Helen worked for a trucking company. At the end of the six months, we were left with about £30 in our pocket. I was young and didn't know better. You just hope people are going to do the right thing by you. I thought the club was going to pay for everything, but I was naïve and clearly a lousy negotiator.

Three other Western Australians were going over at the same time: Bruce Yardley and his wife Kath, Tony Mann and his wife Lyn, and Bob Massie. We learned later that not only was I paid a few hundred quid less than the others, but they didn't have to pay for their airfares, accommodation or cars. It was no one's fault but my own. I had done the negotiations and hadn't asked anyone for advice. However, the visit was to give me so much in cricket terms that it was worth it in the long run.

Tony had signed for Bacup in the same league as me, while Bruce and Bob were on their way to Perth and Kilmarnock in Scotland respectively. We took advantage of the trip by breaking the journey for a couple of days in Hong Kong and Zurich. They were exciting diversions and the group became very good friends. We got together from time to time during our stay in the UK although it was difficult for Bruce and Bob, playing in Scotland.

It was a huge shock when we arrived in May – freezing cold, wet and miserable. We didn't know anyone and were taken to an old, semi-detached house which was available for us to rent. An elderly lady had recently left it empty, having lived downstairs for many of her last years there. There was no heating and no fridge, which didn't matter because it was so cold we just put the milk and the butter in the pantry where it would keep for weeks.

The first night, we went upstairs and jumped into the double bed only for it to collapse. Imagine the embarrassment next day, having to ask the club if they knew of a carpenter to come and mend the bed. It was all very innocent but you can imagine how it went round first the club and then the town like wildfire.

The club was terrific, but I recall reading the president's report a year or so later, which said they had the young Australian Dennis Lillee as a professional and he was the worst professional they had ever had from the point of view of figures. I took 68 wickets at 13.85, scoring 207 runs, and they had obviously hoped for a lot more. What he did not say was that his side could not catch and almost every snick went for four. I was tempted to put all the slip catchers (or, in this case, droppers) on the boundary to save the runs because they weren't going to catch the ball too often.

It was usually wet and when I ran in from the boundary to bowl, I would slip and slide about. That taught me to slow down, bowl more accurately and hit the stumps far more often than I had done in

Australia. From that point of view, it was good value, and it was a great experience playing on grounds such as Bent Gate at Haslingden, Lanehead at Bacup and Alexandra Meadows at East Lancs in Blackburn – a constant test with the soapy, wet ball, the cold weather and the bad footholds. The only thing we escaped was the snow in the spring.

Another problem encountered was the fact that most of the grounds seemed to be on the side of the Pennines, most obviously at Colne, with its drop of 10 feet from one end to the other.

I didn't have too many collections but I got one at Colne. At one end of the ground there was a big chicken farm. The stench was terrible and on one fine day they opened the doors to air the barns. The smell was almost unbearable. I took eight wickets in the innings and I reckon it was because I wanted to get off the field as quickly as I could and, probably, so did the batsmen. I was awarded the collection along with the wicket-keeper who took seven catches. It came to £70, which meant £35 each – big money for me then.

The job at the tip, where I earned about a pound a day, meant I couldn't play as a guest in any of the other nearby leagues. Luckily, Helen was earning £15 a week, which brought our total income, on top of the cricket money, to the princely sum of £20 a week. All day, I sat on the weighbridge, eating sandwiches, drinking coffee and getting fat. I would have been better off training on my own but I thought all the professionals worked midweek and played on the weekends, much the same as we did at home.

What struck me most was the fanaticism people had for their clubs. The Lancastrians loved their cricket, turning out to support their teams whatever the weather. It was nothing like Perth where the players were fanatical but there weren't enough supporters to be that way inclined. In England, they expected their pro to perform and if you didn't, they looked down their noses at you. Fortunately, when the pitches dried out a bit, I scored a few runs and took more wickets. Anyway, friendly people took us under their wing and looked after us, and that was one of the best things about the whole experience. Joan and Jos Knowles, whose son Brian was just about to start playing Lancashire League cricket, befriended us and they were like second parents. We have remained friends to this day, as we have with others in the area.

If the supporters were fanatical, the players seemed less committed. What struck me was their attitude to training. I practised but few others bothered. Some would come down straight from work, take off their tie and jacket and have a hit before going into the bar for a few beers and then home for their evening meal. By the time I finished, I had a few of the youngsters coming down to the nets regularly with me, but I guess some of the older players thought I was a bit too keen although I got on with all of them. In my favour was the fact that I played with great intensity; I hadn't gone there for a holiday during the Australian off-season. They could see that for themselves when I trained, running the streets or running around the ground at practice, and I think I earned some respect for that.

John Ingham, who played for our side, was in his 40s then, still bowling his off-breaks and doubling up as groundsman. He said he would produce Australian-type wickets for me and he shaved off all the grass and rolled them and rolled them, which I didn't know was more likely to help him than me, as that style of preparation in England helps a spinner and not the quicks.

I realised when I went to other grounds in Lancashire all was not what it was supposed to be. At Neil Hawke's club, the wicket was green and the ball flew everywhere and did everything for the former Test star. After that, about five games in, I grabbed Ingham and told him I did not care what he did but I wanted some grass on the wicket and I wanted it green. The result wasn't very pretty with one end cut short for him and the other prepared for me. People began to make remarks about our track and it was certainly different.

We weren't the only club to prepare our wickets for certain individuals, as I discovered at Rawtenstall. The teams had met at our ground a week before. I had shaken them up with some quick bowling and I was planning to get stuck in again. The weather had been good and dry but when we arrived at their ground, the wicket was saturated around the bowlers' footholds. It was more like figure-skating than bowling and I simply couldn't keep my feet while their professional, South Australian Terry Jenner, had no problems running up to bowl his leg-spinners.

On one occasion at our home ground it had rained so hard that the pitch we had prepared was unplayable. So they just got out the mower, went up and down on the next track and, to my amazement, it played perfectly well. I couldn't imagine that happening in Perth.

The whole league was full of characters. John Ingham was one and he had us in stitches with great stories. My opening partner was a guy who used to come down to the ground wearing a huge cream cable-knit jumper. He would change into his whites and then put this jumper back on top of everything. After the game, he would change back, put his cable-knit back on and hit the bar. No one showered it seemed, except me, and one day I went to the sink, filled up a bucket of water and sprayed it all over them in a bid to get them to join the human race. I realised later that hardly another ground had showers, even if the players had wanted to tub.

One day I pitched a quick one right in front, hit the pads, turned round and screamed for an lbw. The umpire put his finger up but the batsman just stood there, not moving, until I asked him what the hell he was doing. With that, he said he wanted to go but he thought I had broken his leg. He had to be carried off.

Some great characters attended the matches as well, including a blind guy who would stand by the sightscreen with his pint, shouting abuse at the players, particularly aimed at the pros from both sides. He would tell them what they were doing wrong, even though he could not see what was happening.

Among the other pros in England at the time were the Indian Ramesh 'Bapoo' Nadkarni; Aussies Neil Hawke and Tony Mann; the South African Dik Abed who bowled big leg-cutters and led his side, Enfield, to the title, taking 101 wickets and scoring 662 runs; and Terry MacGill, a top mate, whose son went on to play for the same team, Todmorden, and then Australia.

Neil Hawke had a soft spot for visiting Australians. He married a girl from Leeds and had a long-term stay in the league. He would happily toss up a couple for a visiting Aussie pro – but only in return for a similar favour when he batted. I wasn't aware of this and when we batted first, he tossed me one up, a beautiful juicy half volley and I hit it for six to his absolute amazement. His look was nothing to the one which withered me when he came in to bat and I sent the first ball whistling past his ear as he played forward. It was only in the bar afterwards, when I was having my usual glass of lemonade, that he explained the facts of life to me. He told me that you always gave the opposition pro a single to get off the mark, especially if it was one of your countrymen, and they would do the same for you. I knew nothing about it because no one had told me. How embarrassing, particularly as he was another of my cricketing heroes.

Batting was difficult in these limited-over matches and my best score came in my last match when I made 48 before being run out – two short of a collection. But at least Dave McQuade, the room attendant and one of the nicest people I have ever met, presented me with the beautiful bat I had used, which he had carefully oiled all season waiting for me to produce a few more innings like that one.

Despite the problems, playing in the Lancashire League was a wonderful experience and I learned a great deal from the 20 or so games I played. Sometimes I wanted to pack it all in and go home but I'm glad I stuck it out. It wasn't always just about the opposition or even professional versus professional. On the whole, Helen and I had a fabulous time.

In between cricket and work, we were able to do some touring in our dilapidated old car and we visited the countryside of North Wales, Sherwood Forest in Nottingham and, of course, the Lake District. We found the countryside so varied and fascinating for such a small island.

When I was given a week off the tip job, Helen and I went to Scotland. We stayed with Bruce and Kath Yardley in Perth for a couple of days before we all set off for Bob Massie's wedding to local Scots lass Nancy Coulthard. When we arrived in Kilmarnock we went straight to the ground where we met up with the Manns, who had also travelled up, had a few drinks and set about barracking for Bob who was playing in a match that day.

At the wedding, the Australian contingent was swollen by the appearance of former fast bowler Lawrie Mayne and his wife Jackie, and we spent a memorable evening together which served to remind us all of home.

When we first arrived in England, we were just in time for the FA Cup final. I was not a soccer man at all and football meant something totally different to me. I had never been to a soccer match nor seen one on television. The chairman of Haslingden, Mr Entwhistle, invited us to go over to his home to watch the game between Arsenal and Liverpool. We arrived about an hour before the kick-off and Mrs Entwhistle made us cups of tea as we watched the build-up. At half-time, out came a big tray laden with hot pies and mushy peas. We hoed in and Mrs Entwhistle watched with ever-widening eyes as we wolfed it down. She replenished the stock as we enjoyed our 'dinner'. The debris was cleared away and we settled down to watch the second half of the game, and afterwards we sat around making small talk until Mrs Entwhistle came back into the room to announce that dinner was served.

The big tray was, evidently, TV snacks; dinner was the full roast complete with Yorkshire puddings. I guess we went green when we saw it, having stuffed ourselves during half-time. We hadn't understood that they served tea and then dinner. We didn't eat for days after.

When we went to Jos and Joan's for dinner, we sat down at five o'clock and had a big meal and then around nine Jos said, 'Come on, Blue, let's go and get some supper.' And off we went to the local chippie to buy huge greasy pieces of fish and bags full of chips, going back to eat a bigger supper than we had dinner. We went back home too full to sleep. I can only guess that it was fuel for the cold weather, who knows?

To us, that was England. Our only glimpse of London had been our arrival at the airport and Euston station. Towards the end of our stay, we returned in our old Anglia, bunny hopping our way towards the capital. The car had cost us £100 and wasn't in the greatest of shape. Every so often it was prone to skip dangerously towards the other side of the road. It had taken us to Scotland for Bob Massie's wedding, but that was the furthest we had driven until we ventured down to London for sightseeing and to watch *Love Story* with Ali MacGraw and Ryan O'Neal. As we left the cinema, the very first people we bumped into were Bruce and Kath Yardley. They had been to see the same movie. It was incredible because neither of us knew the other was even in London.

After that it was the grand sightseeing tour for the next three or four days, especially Baker Street where Sherlock Holmes had lived. I wanted him to be real. We did the entire bit, taking in Madame Tussauds, the Tower of London, the Houses of Parliament and so forth before heading north again.

It was, perhaps, a good thing we lived in the north and saw London, this great big monster city, late in our visit. Coming from Perth in Western Australia, which is only a small city, we were overwhelmed. We tended to live very quietly. There was no television in our house so we would go out for a meal when we could afford it, have a drink with friends or stay in together. It all sounds very tame by today's standards and it is hard to imagine following the same regime now, but at the time it was natural, and I was aware of being a professional cricketer for the first time in my life.

When I returned to England the following year, this time with Australia, I was approached by three counties, all offering mountains more money than I had earned in Lancashire, with Surrey topping the lot. I spoke to Ian Chappell about it, and a few other people, and they all thought it would ruin me because of the way I charged in and bowled, especially if I were to do it day-in and day-out on the busy county circuit.

However, after playing for Haslingden, I returned home to Perth and went straight into club cricket starting in the first week in October. My thoughts, of course, were centred on retaining my place in the Australian side to face the South Africans with the chilling prospect of bowling to such accomplished batsmen as Graeme Pollock and Barry Richards. However, I wasn't at all sure I would be picked and so my immediate thoughts were more on Shield cricket than bowling to those top stars.

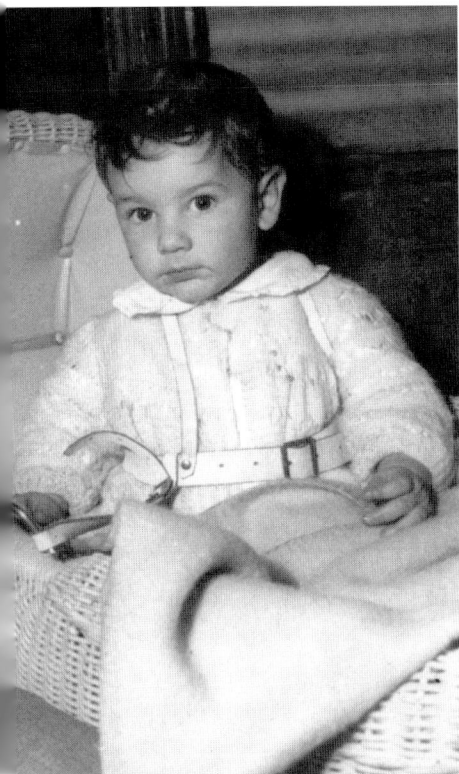

As a baby, obviously in the middle of winter!

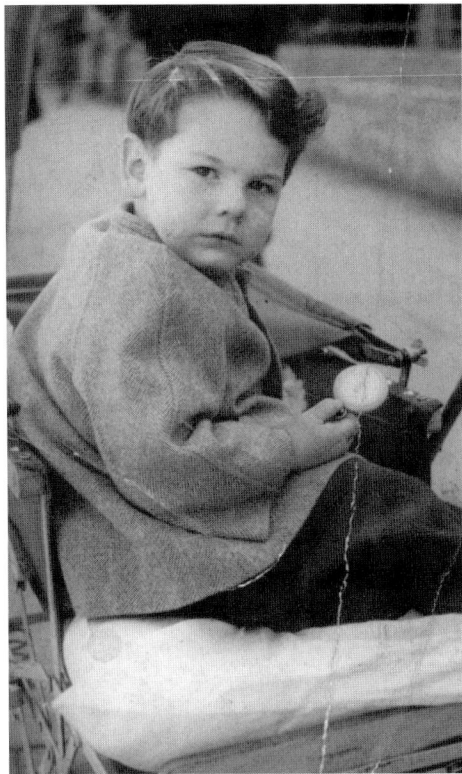

At 12 months – a big boy.

The Lillee clan – Mum (Shirley), me, Trevor, Dad (Keith) and the lovely baby of our family, Carmen.

Myself, Carmen and
Trevor. Butter wouldn't
melt in our mouths.

Mum and Dad and new
offspring on a beach
holiday near Perth.

Belmay Primary School. I am in the second row, second from left (where did that mop of hair go?).

Primary school time – buck teeth, big ears and thick hair (Brylcremed of course!).

High school years – sticking with the Brylcreme at 12 or 13 years old.

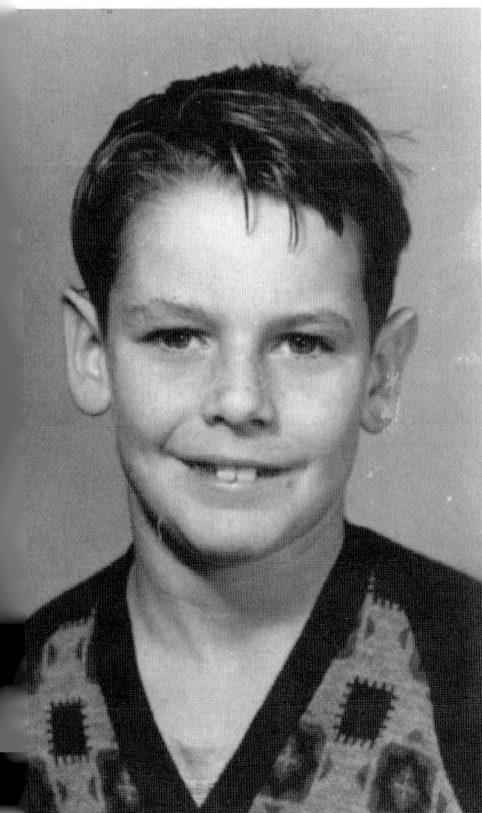

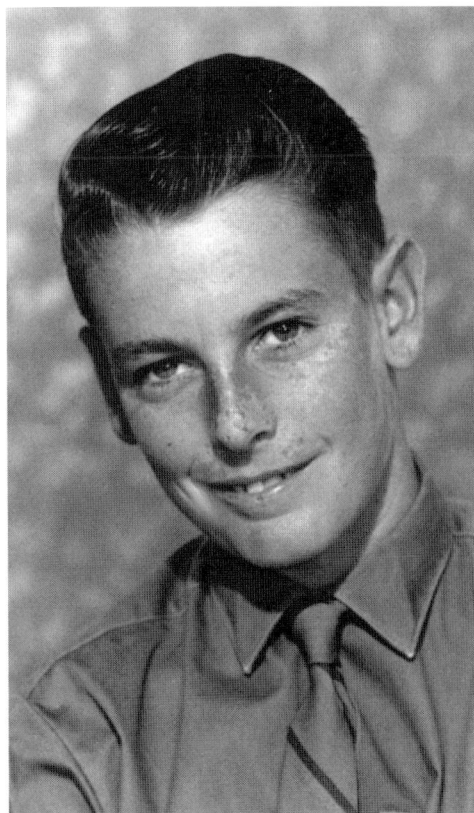

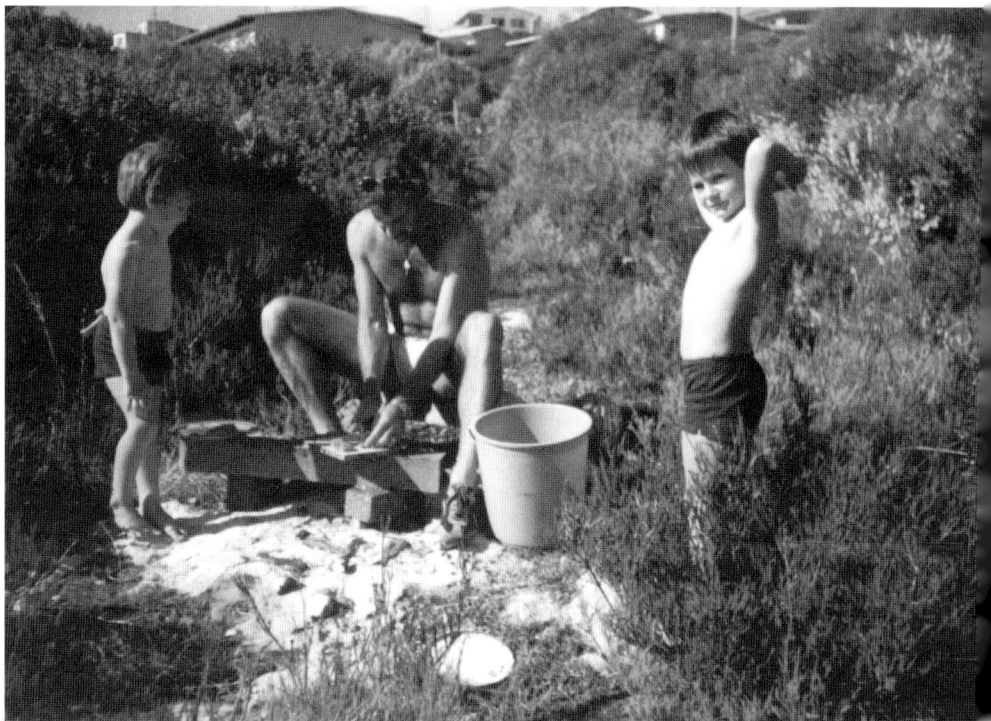

Dean, Adam and myself cleaning fish we had caught at Cowaramup Bay in the south-west of Western Australia.

On our trip around Australia in 1985. We are still smiling and not home yet.

Adam and Dean on Dean's first day of school.

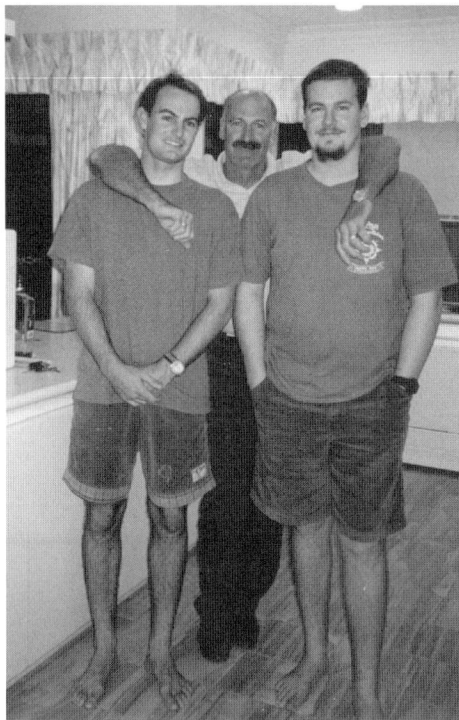

Adam, Dean and myself a few years ago. We are so lucky to have two great lads.

All dressed up and somewhere to go with my darling wife, Helen.

Jabiru Camp in the Northern Territory in 1985. Dean and me on borrowed vehicles. A sign of things to come with my hairstyle and Dean's mode of transport.

Dad checking out a horse's fetlocks and, although I am holding Dean, he is a little apprehensive about patting the horse. Helen says they eat money not hay!

Time out for my favourite
relaxation – London Lakes
in Tasmania.

Surfing – well, wave skiing –
washed among the rocks –
great fun, especially when
there are no sharks nearby.

Happy to be home with Helen, my lovely wife, after the long 1972 tour.

In the event, the tour was called off because of apartheid problems and we faced the bleak prospect of a summer without tourists as we built up to face the Poms in England in 1972. Fortunately, the Herald and Weekly Times group stepped into the breach and promoted an alternative touring side, the Rest of the World, led by the great Garry Sobers.

I had a quiet start to the season with 10 wickets from my first two games. There was a bit of a spat in the second game against Victoria when the quiet, well-mannered Aussie Rules footballer Peter Bedford ran into me while taking a run. I thought he had done it on purpose and had a few words with him. He didn't like what I said and advanced down the wicket at me until Graeme Watson threatened to run him out. The next ball was perhaps the fastest I ever bowled and, although Bedford got behind it, the ball knocked the bat out of the way and went on to hit the stumps. Peter told me afterwards he didn't even see the ball and had played out of instinct.

I was selected for the first international in Brisbane when a lot of rain fell, plenty of time was lost and the pitch was a batsman's paradise with five individual centuries scored in all. I also had a century, but not one to be proud of – I took 3–111. But I bowled fairly quickly and hit Sunil Gavaskar on the body several times while he was on the way to his hundred.

I must have done something to impress because I was picked for the second game, on my home ground. Australia batted first and, despite facing bowlers of the quality of Sobers, Tony Greig, Bob Cunis, Bishen Bedi, Intikhab Alam and Richard Hutton, mounted up a huge score.

I knew I needed a performance if I was to keep my place, but the problem was that I woke up on the morning of the day we were to bowl feeling groggy and didn't even want to get out of bed. I didn't tell anyone I felt bad and, fortunately, the first ball I bowled took off. The wicket had sweated under the covers and had speeded up considerably. With the second ball, I almost took the head off Sunil Gavaskar. The fourth caught his gloves and Rod Marsh was throwing up the ball for a catch behind the wicket. We rushed them out for 59 before lunch and I took 8–29 in 7.1 overs.

The remarkable thing was I still felt bad. In fact, after bowling four overs and having taken 2–29, I told Ian Chappell I did not feel too good and asked would he like to take me off. He told me to have another couple of overs and see how I felt. Nothing happened in the next over but the world turned upside down after that – I took the last six wickets, including Garry Sobers', in 15 balls.

That was probably the fastest wicket I ever bowled on and I bowled every ball flat out. It had been only 90 minutes but I was exhausted. I could have gone to sleep there and then, and had not even thought about the follow-on. Ian enforced it and I took my ninth wicket of the morning, Farokh Engineer. He had the embarrassment of being out twice before lunch in a first-class match – surely a record of sorts. I was shattered and added just three more wickets, making a total of 12 in the game.

It was a big match for me and, fortunately, the wicket was typical of Perth, with the additional help of some swing. It was a matter of running up and bowling straight and letting the conditions help me.

Sobers had dinner with his mate Ian Chappell before the next game, at Melbourne, and he told Ian that he would get hold of me and get some runs. He also bowled fast in the match – one of the four ways in which he bowled. After he had almost decapitated me with a bouncer, he said with a scowl followed by a huge grin, 'You are not the only one who can bowl bouncers!'

In their second innings, Sobers showed just how well he could bat. I remember a lot about it. For instance, I had man at square on the point boundary and he was hitting the ball behind and in front at will. I asked Ian Chappell for someone finer, just behind square, and he pierced that gap as well and continued to play in front of square until I asked Ian for another man in front of point – and still he hit it between those three fielders, several times.

When I took the second new ball, I attempted to bowl a big inswinging yorker. He leant into it with great power. I went down in my follow-through to try to stop it; by the time I was down, I was looking back and the ball had bounced back off the fence. I have never witnessed a shot of such power and grace. I thought to myself, 'We are in for some!' And how right I was.

It has to rate as one of the best innings I have ever seen – hard to judge when you are young because you have little to judge it by, but it was certainly the equal of anything I saw afterwards. Perhaps one to challenge it was Barry Richards' triple hundred at the WACA. The other was Kim Hughes against the West Indies at Melbourne in 1981–82 when the wicket was spiteful. Greg Chappell was injured in the same innings when the ball came off a length and hit him in the face. We were in deep trouble and Kim just danced down the track, drove, pulled and cut. Sobers' and Richards' innings were performed on great batting wickets; Hughes' was on a re-laid surface and the ball was doing all sorts of things. However, in context, this Sobers dig was truly amazing.

The great irony was that I had already captured the great man's wicket for a second time in the two matches when Graham McKenzie caught him at second slip for a duck in the first innings of this match. I fancied myself to get him again, especially when I almost had him caught by Kerry O'Keeffe in front of square-leg off one of my early balls. That was the last time any of us got anywhere near him as he compiled 254 majestic runs in just 376 minutes. It was wonderful controlled aggression and there was just nowhere I, or anyone else for that matter, could bowl to him.

I wasn't the only one who rated that innings. Sir Donald Bradman said afterwards, 'I believe Garry Sobers' innings was probably the best ever seen in Australia. The people who saw Sobers have enjoyed one of the historic events of cricket. They were privileged to have had such an experience.'

I certainly felt privileged, even though I had been right in the middle of the firing line. As much as I love to take a wicket, to get him out with that early ball would have been a heinous crime against world cricket.

Don't forget that at 36 he was, to me, an old man playing in the twilight of his career. I was only 22 and most top players retired before their mid thirties in those days. Despite that, before the series began, I was super nervous because of him. The other great names did not hold the same reverence. He was, and still is, the greatest all-rounder ever; I once wanted to emulate him. He showed me again why he was my childhood hero although I didn't think of him as a hero when I bowled to him. I might have been in awe of him but I wanted his wicket, not because he was a legend but because he was another batsman.

I did not try to intimidate him in Perth as some may think. What people don't remember is that bowling at around 100 miles per hour, you don't have that sort of control and this is why, quite often, express bowlers break down or eventually bowl within themselves. These days, Brett Lee or Shoaib Akhtar might be the comparisons. You have areas at which to bowl and you try to produce an outswinger or inswinger but I didn't try to think them out; I just tried to bowl at or around the off stump. That was how simple my game was. By the time I bowled to Sobers at Melbourne, I thought I was too quick for him and his reactions were beginning to fail. How stupid a judgement! Yet here was a guy who had to draw together a team of strangers and present cricket in the best possible light in view of the problems with South Africa that had brought this World XI tour about, as well as deal with all the other things in his life.

The series might not have counted in the Test averages but every match I played in, even a charity match, was important and I certainly treated them just as seriously as a Test match. That the authorities did not include the series in the averages after the promises they made is, to put it bluntly, very disappointing.

CHAPTER SIX

Back in trouble

My world collapsed in Sydney. The game was ambling towards a draw and I have to admit my mind was back with Helen in Perth. On a featherbed of a wicket, I was bowling at not much more than medium pace, so much so that Ian Chappell sidled over to me and said, 'If I'd wanted someone to bowl spinners, I'd have asked Terry Jenner to have a go.'

This snapped me out of my reverie and, next ball, I charged in and unleashed a really quick one that flew past a surprised Sunil Gavaskar. But I took no pleasure from it because all I felt was a stunning pain in my back. Ian asked me if I could finish the over, which I did with some trouble and then limped off in agony.

The Sydney physiotherapist Dave McErlane was anxious enough to call in the doctor, Brian Corrigan, who diagnosed muscular trouble. I assumed that because I had had no real break for over a year, it was the result of so much bowling. It finished my match there and then for there was no way I could carry on, any movement provoking sharp pain.

That night I could hardly sleep and getting dressed the next morning was a major effort. I was soon on a plane home to Perth and out of the one-day matches. When I arrived, I did an interview for a local television station and in return they sent Helen and me away to Yanchep about 50 miles north of Perth. My rest and recuperation were wrecked when I collapsed while rowing a dinghy and it needed a worried Helen to row back against the tide.

The tour to England was still a couple of months away, so I wasn't too bothered about that. The doctor in Perth gave me stretching exercises to do and I soon began to improve, with jogging, light exercises and eventually some work in the nets. I felt I was ready to play in a Shield match against New South Wales at the WACA and did not let a bout of influenza stop me. It should have been a warning because I got out of my sick bed and took no wickets for 119 runs off 19 overs.

I decided not to play again until I went to England, but after a couple of weeks I was ordered to take a fitness test at the WACA where John Inverarity, Rod Marsh, Ross Edwards, Graeme Watson and Bob Massie were preparing for the tour. I bowled a couple of overs at just over medium pace, went to the association doctor who put me through a few tests and was passed fit to travel to England.

I continued to work out with mates of mine, the late Greg Brehaut and Chubby Stiles, at the Perth Football Club, in addition to my usual training schedule, and I finally left for England feeling in terrific nick. But it wasn't long before I was having problems with my back again.

For me, this was a disaster. The meetings between England and Australia were the pinnacle as far as I was concerned, the ultimate test between cricket's most serious rivals. I desperately wanted to be at my best and to take the English batting apart but the back injury was casting real doubts over my participation, never mind running through the English batting. It was hardly the way to prepare for an Ashes series.

There was clearly a hint of a stress fracture. Stress fractures, we now know, do not heal without correct rehabilitation and, in fact, they become worse with overuse combined with a bad action.

I suppose it didn't help that it was bitterly cold when we arrived in England in April, and I was wearing two and three sweaters in the nets in the first couple of weeks. Although I felt good, I took no liberties and warmed up properly before every session, did a lot of floor exercises and ran three laps of Lord's before attempting anything. I built up my pace gradually and it wasn't until my fifth day in the nets that I let one go. Immediately I felt shooting pains in my back – just the same as I'd suffered when I bowled that ball in Australia.

I went straight to see Dave McErlane, who was on tour with us, and he gave me a rub down and a hot bath. The next morning he looked at me again and everything seemed to be back to normal. I did all my usual warm-up routine before going back to the nets and building up gradually to top pace. As soon as I tried to press the accelerator, the pain was back again. Ian Chappell could see I was having problems. He came across to me and we quietly moved away so as not to alert the media, who were after a story, any story. This one was right under their noses and they missed it.

I rested for a couple of weeks but as soon as I tried to bowl again, the pain came back. I was very depressed and broke down at Worcester after trying to bowl a session in the nets. Keith Stackpole, the vice captain, found me. He was terrific. The difficulty was that because no one could find out what the problem was, there were those in the squad who thought it must be in my mind. Whether he thought that or not, he consoled me and gave me a huge amount of support in a moment of great stress. At least I felt I had someone in my corner and this was a big help.

My mood hadn't been improved when we arrived at the hotel where we were due to stay for that game. There were two beds in each room with no more than a chair's width between them, a tiny wardrobe not big enough to hang our clothes in, and a minute amount of floor space, not enough for our cricket gear and our suitcases. We thought it pretty bad but before we knew it, Ian had spoken to the team's management and we were out of there. I had never heard of it happening before but it was exactly right that we moved. It was a two-star hotel at best and the rooms were far smaller than usual, although they were never very big anyway.

I went to see a specialist, Alun Thomas, in Harley Street. He was a tall, thin man with black curly hair, probably in his late 40s, and I took to him immediately. He was very relaxed and funny and, most important of all, he seemed to take a genuine interest in my problems. He was keen on sport and became a regular at the Australian matches in London. Everyone took a liking to the man. For me, he offered a ray of light and after a complete and thorough examination he assured me everything would be all right. I had some hope at last. That hope began to dissipate a little when the pains came back when I tried to bowl but Alun Thomas told Dave to keep me working.

Ian Chappell was also a big help, seeking me out every day to see how I was and arranging meetings with Keith Stackpole and the team manager, Ray Steele, to bring everyone up to date.

Eventually, I played against Lancashire at a very cold Old Trafford and bowled a very ordinary spell. The one bright spot was taking Clive Lloyd's wicket but even that was tempered by the fact that my short ball was so slow he mishooked me and was caught. It struck me then that my tour was over and I was dreadfully miserable, even though my team-mates tried to pick me up. In the end, it was journalist Jack Fingleton who gave me a lift with a late-night chat in my Manchester hotel room. He had been through a lot of back trouble and showed me a few exercises he thought might be useful and generally cheered me up.

Despite my pathetic performance at Old Trafford, I was selected for the next game, at Nottingham, and worked hard in the nets beforehand. But on the day of the match, I jumped out of bed, warmed up without problems and even let slip a couple of fast ones, only for it to go again. I was, once more, plunged to the depths of despair and I thought my career was over.

It was then Mr Thomas decided to try manipulating my back; with the first Test less than a month off, I was ready to try anything. I was put under, treated for half an hour and sent back to the hotel to rest with the instruction to bowl flat out the next day. When I did, the pain came back but the Doc had told me to ignore it and keep at it. The pain continued but I was bowling at pace again and, despite the agony, I was in ecstasy because it seemed the more I bowled, the more the pain subsided.

I bowled 16 overs against Hampshire at Southampton and began to smile again – I even had a drink on the way back to London and got a little tipsy with thoughts of the upcoming game against the MCC at Lord's. It was the first time on the tour I had bowled almost free of pain. Whether it was because I had slowed down a bit to compensate and maybe I had altered my action a little, taking the pressure off with less hyperextension, I don't know but suddenly there was little or no pain.

I was a little undercooked for the first Test but I got through; maybe someone was giving me a break. I was fine. I was stiff and sore in the back area and I was still tight but, thank goodness, there were no spasms and no searing pain. To my mind, it was a miracle, freakish that I was ready to play.

Before the start of the Test series, I was amazed at the remarkable amount of junketing. We had to attend all the formal gatherings such as the MCC dinner, Lord Whoever's dinner, the Sportsmen's Association dinner, the Lord's Taverners' dinner – there must have been 20 of them. I thought it was a load of bulldust. I wanted to practise and I wanted to play cricket. I now realise I heard some great speeches and some great speakers but I just didn't take them in or appreciate them at the time. It remains one of my great regrets that I didn't fully understand what was happening. I wasn't smart enough to realise and I missed so much of what went on. Fortunately, on the next tour I took in a lot more.

The 1972 series was great from our point of view. When we arrived, England held the Ashes and Australia had had little recent success, having been trounced on the previous tour to South Africa. A smattering of the old guard had been retained – Keith Stackpole, Ian Chappell, Doug Walters, John Inverarity, John Gleeson and Paul Sheahan – but the rest of the group were young and enthusiastic. The majority of us had been on the 1970 A tour to New Zealand but were a long way from being established players. Under the supervision of Ian Chappell, a great team spirit and camaraderie developed between the young and the mature players. We all got on well, which is not always the case for a touring side.

A lot of that was due to Ian Chappell, John Inverarity and Keith Stackpole. I suspect they were the tour selectors and, from the youth of the squad, Rodney Marsh emerged and joined the inner sanctum. It was the start of a great era.

We were real underdogs, inexperienced, given no chance and considered one of the worst teams to leave Australia. Then we lost the first Test at Old Trafford by 89 runs on the last day of a low-scoring match. I still believe had we played Bob Massie we would have won because the conditions suited him so much, as it did the English pace bowlers John Snow, Tony Greig and Geoff Arnold. I took eight wickets but the highlight for me was the 91 scored by Rod Marsh, including four sixes off the left-hand orthodox spin of Worcester's Norman Gifford.

Our confidence remained strong and we felt sure we could level the series at Lord's. This was my close friend Massie's match – at the age of 25 and largely unknown, he made history as he took 16 wickets for 137 runs on his debut. His bowling at Lord's was as near perfection as I had ever seen.

It was overcast and humid weather and Bob took full advantage with his swing, which bamboozled the English batsmen. In fact, the match was a triumph for Western Australia because I took the other four wickets.

It was the custom then for the Queen to be introduced to the teams at the Lord's Test on the Monday, the fourth day. As it became clear the game was heading for an early conclusion, there was a hasty reappraisal and it was decided we would, instead, go to the Palace at 5 p.m. that day. We won the match in three and a half days. It was all over by 2.30 and, as it was our first win in a dozen matches, the celebrations began instantly, despite warnings to go easy on the grog.

I was basically a teetotaller but, such was the excitement, I set to it and quietly downed a few beers. It was hard not to with Doug Walters and Rod Marsh around. I arrived at the Palace feeling very relaxed and took my place in the line next to John Gleeson. I am told Ian Chappell introduced the Queen to Gleeson who, as instructed, responded, 'How do you do, Ma'am?' Then Ian came to me and said, 'Your Majesty, this is Dennis Lillee,' to which I apparently responded, 'G'day.' It wasn't the politically correct greeting and Rod Marsh, next in the queue, apparently had problems keeping a straight face.

Later, Ian told Ray Steele, who had escorted the Duke of Edinburgh, 'You wouldn't want to know what Dennis Lillee said to the Queen.'

Ray replied, through gritted teeth, 'I suppose it was "G'day", exactly the same as he said to the Duke!'

I wasn't drunk; I was heady and relaxed. I didn't understand protocol and while we had been told what to say, with a few under the belt, I forgot and used my normal greeting. I didn't notice and clearly she didn't either.

However, this was nothing compared to the time I had the temerity to ask the Queen for her autograph. It happened during the Melbourne Centenary Test and her reply was to the effect that she couldn't do it in front of all the people at the ground and watching on television because she would be stopped and asked wherever she went. I asked because she was the ultimate hero to me, she was 'our' Queen. I had thought about it and took something out for her to sign.

I understood her explanation and forgot all about it until a week or so later when an aide-de-camp from the Palace got in touch and asked me for my address as the Queen wanted to send me a signed photograph. You could have picked me up off the floor and the picture takes pride of place in my house, the only memorabilia displayed apart from a few things in my office. It's a picture of me being introduced to the Queen at the very moment I was asking for her autograph, and it's signed 'Elizabeth R,1977'.

You can imagine how chuffed I was. I had probably embarrassed her and all the cricket officials but, at the time, I could not see the reason not to ask. People asked me for my autograph and I signed; at least, that was my logic. Maybe I was getting to know why the hierarchy didn't like me so much.

I met Her Majesty again at the Test match in England in 1981 but this time I refrained from any special requests! From that occasion, there is a jolly picture of us having a laugh but I can reveal it was not over the autograph incident.

The celebrations after the Lord's Test victory in 1972 hardly stopped. The next evening we were off to the National Sportsmen's Club where we had a memorable night in the company of many British sportsmen. At midnight, off we went to a recording studio to tape some songs including 'Here Come the Aussies' and 'Bowl a Ball, Swing a Bat'. It was riotous. Some of the non-singers were manoeuvred into position behind dead microphones – I was one of those in front of a dummy mike.

I was beginning to find my feet in international cricket and decided it was time to have a little fun. In a county game at Leicester's Grace Road, I surprised the crowd and my old Western Australia team-mate Graham McKenzie when I fired a tennis ball at him when he was bathing. At Hove, celebrating Sussex's centenary, I bowled a shiny red apple to the amazement of the umpire, former Aussie campaigner Bill Alley, who responded to my lbw appeal with a cry of 'No ball' – a very quick play on words.

We drew the Test at Trent Bridge on a featherbed and then went on to Leeds where the Headingley pitch had been a seamer's paradise all season, but they pulled a fast one on us. Derek Underwood and Ray Illingworth had our best batsmen groping through the two innings on a grassless wicket, ideally suited to spin for once. How amazing that this fusarium (a fungus associated with warmer climes) seemed to occur only on a stretch of turf 22 yards long by about eight feet wide. I was quite indignant about it. The wicket made me feel like a medium pacer. Even so, we might have had the last laugh if we had turned the screw when they were 128–7 in reply to our first innings of 146, but Illingworth and Snow put on 100.

We felt deflated and cheated but it was an indication of our spirit that we came back fighting. We had lost the Ashes but we could at least share the series if we won the last one at The Oval on a real old-fashioned Oval wicket – a fast bowler's graveyard.

It was a six-day Test and we managed to get out of jail and win it. The lasting memory is of Paul Sheehan and Rod Marsh running off the ground after they had put on 71 to square the series, with Rod whirling the bat around his head wearing a smile which couldn't be wiped from his face. Displays of unbridled excitement like that hadn't been seen before at Test level, certainly not in England, and that expression of our team spirit was a symbol of what was to come.

During that game, I found an affinity with the Caribbean contingent in the crowd. One particular guy was clearly a fan of mine because whenever I was having a rest, he would call out in a foghorn voice, 'Chappell, let de tiger loose, let de tiger loose', getting louder the longer I was not bowling.

When I was struggling to take a wicket, the same guy screamed across at me, 'Lillee, if you take a wicket you can have my wife.' We all looked across to where he was sitting and there was this huge woman waving to me. Rod Marsh took one look and said, 'For God's sake, Dennis, don't take a wicket.'

Six months later, we were in the field in the West Indies when, to my great surprise, up came this cry, 'Chappell, let de tiger loose.' He was there again.

In truth, it is a great feeling when someone out there is shouting for you and willing you on. It was the same when the crowd started chanting my name on my run up. It was a little embarrassing in one way but in another it was those people expressing their desire for us to do well for Australia.

At the end of the game, the Caribbean fans gathered around the pavilion gate to tell us how hard it was going to be to beat the West Indies on our next tour there in 1973. We had enjoyed their raucous support and, as we celebrated, we sent down a bottle of champagne for them because they had barracked for us. It was lovely that these guys supported us and we looked forward to seeing their smiling faces when we played against England. It was nice to have people supporting you and in those days not many Aussies made the journey – not that the English crowds were ever hostile.

Although we had failed to regain the Ashes, a new side had emerged.

We had proved we were able to get out of trouble and fight back against a great England team to level the series. That, I am sure, was the making of our side; I know we gained so much confidence from the result.

In the last Test match, I took 10 wickets and I rate it as one of my best performances ever in Test cricket because it was a hard slog from start to finish to get those wickets. It was not an easy track to bowl on and it was a question of powering away – a reward for all the training and those long, hard runs because this was about stamina and belief.

During our second innings, I was not watching events out in the middle. Instead, I took a hot bath at the back of the pavilion and must have been there for an hour when Ian Chappell came in.

'I want to thank you for everything you have done on this tour,' he said. 'You and I are going to have some time off in London. We'll eat out, have a great time and forget about cricket. That's my thanks to you.'

He looked me in the eyes as he said it and I was stunned, knocked over. I wasn't an established player in the side. I had taken 31 wickets and set a record, but that had not registered at the time. Anyway, the praise from the captain was worth far more than records.

He was as good as his word and we lazed around during the Munich Olympics in a flat in central London belonging to John and Dumpy Morley, great friends of Australian cricketers and particularly of the Benauds.

But before the relaxation we played a one-day series, the first-ever limited-overs international series. In the first game I bowled off a short run and took some stick from Geoff Boycott, prompting the English press to declare that he had won the war against me.

That was just what I needed. I have to confess that we were not taking these games quite as seriously as we would a five-day Test match, but in the next one I went back to my full-length run-up and knocked Geoff's middle stump out in my second over. That was very satisfying as was the fact that, after that awful start to the tour when I believed my career might be over, I bowled 456.5 overs in first-class games, 249.5 of them in the Tests, and 33 more in that one-day series. In fact, I bowled more overs than our leading spinner Ashley Mallett, bearing in mind they were eight-ball overs.

Certainly England was one of the best tours socially, with people wanting you around and putting on parties at the end of games. These were true cricket people who made you feel welcome; there was a genuine love of the sport in England compared with the fanaticism of India and the extensive knowledge of the game in the West Indies. The people in England were also very knowledgeable and strangely unbiased.

I reckon I was more appreciated by the cricket followers in England at certain times than in Australia. Perhaps that's putting it too strongly but the letters they wrote and the things they said to me made me feel that way. In Australia, supporters and other people were generally more blasé. In England, they wanted a piece of you, they wanted to talk and they wanted to know about the game. That made you feel appreciated, more so than an Aussie saying, 'Great . . . have a beer . . . see you later.'

The friends we made in England were often people who had long associations with Australian teams – the Morleys, Charles Benson, Robert Sangster and so many others who invited us around to their houses for a drink or a party. I believe they appreciated that we were amateurs without much money and they did it in that way rather than embarrass us. There was no obligation; it was terrific. Charles Benson, the sportswriter, who has now sadly passed away, was fabulous, taking us to the races, organising golf tournaments and many other things, including a trip to the Wimbledon tennis championships. From that point of view, I found the English very warm to us and warm about their cricket. Maybe they liked the way we were. We were uncomplicated, grateful, and perhaps the English players took them for granted or didn't appreciate people's generosity.

On that tour the English players tended to be cricketers during cricket hours and afterwards kept to themselves. I understand that more now than I used to because I eventually realised they played professionally day in day out and they wanted to get home. I couldn't understand it at the time and, in fact, I despised them for it because I felt they were basically shunning us, although not all of them shot off at the close of play. A few wanted to have a drink and chat with us. From memory, Edrich would stay around for a couple, as did one of the great captains, Ray Illingworth. Peter Lever, known as 'the Plank', was fantastic, and Derek Underwood usually did his bit. There might have been others but, in truth, there weren't many.

A few years later, this was all to change, but during that first tour to England, there was little mixing. Each day when it was our turn to pop in their dressing room for a chat, in we would go, but when it was their turn only a few would show and not for long. Eventually, they stopped altogether, and so did we. We felt they didn't want us around or didn't want us to do it.

It was a shame because I always liked that aspect of the game. Anything that happened out in the field could be forgotten once the boundary rope was crossed and you knew you were going to share a beer. If you had been the catalyst in a controversial incident, having a drink together eased the tension. To me, it was important, even if it was only for 10 minutes.

After such a long tour, I returned to Australia very tired. Helen and I had just a week's holiday before I was back in action again, training for the new season with Western Australia, preparing for the series against Pakistan and then a trip to the West Indies the following February.

Our domestic season was ridiculous, with five tough interstate games and one against the tourists in as many weeks, followed by three Tests in successive weeks. This meant a total of nine games in nine weeks beginning with a game in Perth against New South Wales at the start of November.

I was entitled to be concerned about the workload. Against New South Wales in Perth, I bowled a total of 34.7 eight-ball overs and took eight wickets. Eleven days later, in the game against the tourists, I bowled 23.7 overs and took another eight wickets. Between then and the Test series, I bowled 26 overs against Queensland in Brisbane; 41.4 overs against New South Wales in Sydney; 41 overs in Melbourne against Victoria and 40 overs against South Australia in Adelaide. My preparations for the series totalled 207.2 eight-ball overs and 44 wickets.

This was more deliveries at that stage of the summer than any other bowler, including the spinners.

At the end of that exhausting tour of duty, I had just four days before the first Test in Adelaide against Pakistan and I elected to go home with the Western Australia team so I could see Helen for a couple of days before flying back.

I forgot how tired I was when the Adelaide wicket proved to be surprisingly quick on the first day of the Test. I helped myself to four wickets but it became flatter and flatter and I finished with just one more wicket from a match total of 35.3 overs.

When I arrived at the ground on the first day, an hour and a half before the start of play, a few hundred people were already there. I climbed out of the cab and started walking towards the dressing rooms, and a young Pakistani lad came up to me, offering to carry my bag. I declined but he persisted and I let him carry it to the dressing-room door.

'You are my ultimate hero and I hope you get five wickets in every match,' he said, as I relieved him of the bag. I thanked him politely for carrying the bag and for his good wishes.

Pakistan were to bat first and I went through my usual routine to be ready to bowl the first over. The first ball went down the off side and as I began my walk back to my mark, I looked at the batsman at the non-striker's end and there, with a huge smile on his face, was the young boy who had carried my bag. I was stunned. Sadly, a few overs later, I fractured his thumb. As he headed off, he gave me that huge grin again. I almost felt guilty. I couldn't even remember his name, but a little research reveals it was Talat Ali who had an unhappy debut Test match.

There was only a day before the second Test in Melbourne, so I was happy when we batted first and I could put my feet up. When we did bowl, I tired quickly and began to have the feeling something was wrong, but I dismissed it as tiredness. However, I found myself dragging my feet after bowling another 27.6 overs for my three hard-earned wickets.

Even though I was not always bowling off full throttle, my pace unsettled the Pakistanis in Melbourne, but when we got to Sydney, I felt a nasty twinge in my back in the nets before the first day. I ignored it and worked up quite a bit of pace in my first spell. I returned for a second spell full of confidence, but just when I was building up some speed my back went. I was struggling with a shooting pain and immediately left the field to be examined by Dr Brian Corrigan, who told me I had been playing too much cricket and needed a rest. With plenty of rest and physiotherapy, he was sure I would be all right for the trip to the West Indies. The selectors, including Sir Donald Bradman, popped in and told me to 'do what the doctors said'.

Pakistan's first innings had ended in a 26-run lead and we were in trouble at 94–7 ahead of the rest day. I had time to recover and began to feel a lot better. With Bob Massie and John Watkins then putting on 83 for the ninth wicket, we were left with an outside chance of victory as Pakistan needed 159 to win. I offered to do my bit, with the doctor reluctantly giving me the go-ahead, aided by some extra hot liniment and a couple of painkillers.

I bowled just above medium pace but fast enough to snap Nasim-ul-Ghani's stump in half. Max Walker cleaned them up with 6–15 off 16 overs while I trundled down 23 overs and took three wickets. I knew if I came off I wouldn't be able to bowl again and I had to bowl straight through as we bowled them out for 106.

Physically, it was almost certainly the wrong thing to do, but I just assumed it was the joint problem and once I got through the match I would be all right again. I suspected it had probably healed slightly since England and then gone again. It was a great victory, but I left for Perth feeling sore and tired, with the thought that we were due to leave for the West Indies in 10 days' time.

What I remember most about that series was bowling to the outstanding Majid Khan whom I rated as a fantastic player, one of the best I ever bowled to, a true stroke player who batted at number four. He had as much grace as anyone I had ever seen. Everything was done with style and elegance; he was like my image of a prince, and everything was just majestic.

We had some great tussles. He used to wear a big-rimmed, white canvas hat, which was unusual. We had gone from peaked caps to floppies and I had never seen one of these. He wore it out to bat. A couple of times, I went close to knocking it off his head with a few sharp deliveries. We got on very well and at the end of the tour he promised me that if ever I did knock it off, it was mine to keep.

I remembered and the next time we played them four years later, I actually did knock it off. I had followed through, as I was inclined to do, and he was so composed. He just bent down, picked it up, walked the couple of paces and gave it to me, saying, 'As promised.'

It was a great memento. Unfortunately, Helen did not know anything about our pact. He had worn this hat in every game he played and never had it washed. It was stained and dirty and when she found it she put it in the washing machine and it came out shrunk and shredded. I kept it anyway. It is a relic I treasure because of what happened and the fact that he remembered what had been said years before.

There is no doubt that, because of my back problems, I should have called it a day after the Pakistan series, but I was 23 years old and thought I was invincible. The prospect of touring those Caribbean islands filled me with excitement and by the end of January I was in Jamaica.

I had to prove my fitness but what happens with stress fractures is with rest the pain will ease off and there is a bit of healing. I did a lot of trunk-strengthening work and bowled in the nets. Sure, I was a bit sore, and not knowing what the injury really was, I thought I would get through it again.

However, as soon as I got to the West Indies I knew I was in trouble. There were a few aches and pains, the usual thing when you have gone a while without bowling, but there was something more. I missed the opening game against the University of West Indies but played against Jamaica, operating off my long run, and built up some decent pace with just a few more aches. I missed the next game against the President's XI and visited the set for the film *Papillon*, starring Steve McQueen. What a thrill that was! I kept myself fit with plenty of running, preparing for the first Test in Kingston. On a fairly unresponsive wicket, I bowled 32 overs but I knew I was in trouble. I felt the soreness and the spasms in the first spell and I wasn't very quick because I couldn't put any pressure on my back.

On the social side, we were full of silly pranks. When we first arrived in Jamaica, there was an amazing scene with a large crowd, steel bands and the local press waiting to meet us, along with plenty of potent rum punches. A few of us were asked to do interviews and we stayed on while the others made their way to the hotel. Those of us who were delayed were looked after by a lady liaison officer, Celia, who offered to give us a lift to our hotel. On the way, we were talking about Alan McGilvray, the Aussie commentator, whom she much admired. We said what a lovely guy he was, how very proper, very English with his manners and his approach to life. We were due at a reception later and we couldn't resist a set-up, so we told her that an Australian greeting of warmth and feeling was, 'Get rooted!' A couple of us coached her to say, when she met the great man, 'Pleased to meet you, Mr McGilvray, get rooted.'

She delivered the line perfectly and he snapped back, 'I have never been so insulted in my life,' and stormed off. Celia didn't know what was wrong and was hugely embarrassed. Greg Chappell and I had set it up and we finished up having to apologise profusely to both of them. It took McGilvers a while to get over it and talk to us again.

In Trinidad, we attended a big cocktail party at the Governor's residence. When it was time to go, four of us jumped in a cab waiting outside the front door. There was no outside lighting and the grounds were enveloped in thick shrubs and trees until you reached the street. The cab driver was clearly nervous about collecting Australian cricketers from the Residence. I was in the back seat on the left and thought what a good opportunity it was for another little jape. The windows were wound down and as we arrived at the gate, I gave the outside of the cab a hard whack with the flat of my hand and made a screaming noise like a wounded animal.

The driver slammed on the brakes and asked what had happened. I said it sounded like a dog. I jumped out and made some more squealing noises and pretended to carry the injured animal into the shrubs by the side of the road.

I ran back to the cab, jumped in and told him to get out of there as quickly as he could. He sped off out of the gates and took us to the hotel. He was shaking with fear and wanted to know what to do. I told him not to go back there for a while and that I was sure he was safe because no one could have taken his number. He never realised it was a set-up, probably still doesn't.

Clearly this had worked so well it was worth another try. Coming back from the ground in Barbados there was an old guy on a push-bike. I guess he was about 70 and a bit wobbly riding along the edge of the road just to the side of a small drainage ditch. I hit the side of the bus as we went past and he was so scared he toppled off into the ditch, waving his fist at us in annoyance.

I didn't feel too good about that one in case he had hurt himself but the ruse worked. I did it on another occasion as we passed a car and they stopped, thinking there had been a coming together of the two vehicles. They looked everywhere for the dent or the scratch but, obviously, could find nothing.

The pranks were just to release a little pressure, have a laugh; otherwise I would have gone crazy with the worry about my fitness. My back had been causing problems for a year now and I collapsed in the game against the Leeward Islands in Antigua. The pain was so intense I told Ian Chappell I thought my back was broken. What I did not know was that my spine was indeed fractured – in three places. The most heartbreaking factor was I finally broke down in the last over of the day, coming back for a one-over spell. It was the last over I bowled on that tour.

For me, the rest of the tour was a continual trail to a succession of specialists who offered an array of diagnoses. The ironic thing about stress fractures is they settle down after a few days, so I was able to run and swim. I know some of the guys and the manager, Bill Jacobs, thought I was putting it on. I was getting short shrift from him and I was positive he had written me off and wanted to send me home. To give him credit, he tried everything but nothing helped. In the end, I missed three Tests and the tour turned into a personal nightmare. It seemed the only reason I was not replaced was because of the financial agreement between the West Indies Board and ours.

It was a very emotional time for me. The one hope was former Warwickshire cricketer Rudi Webster whom I had met in Perth when he played some cricket in Australia. He was a radiologist and had suffered back problems himself, so he suggested I might be suffering from the same problem he encountered in England – stress fractures of the spine. He felt he couldn't help because someone else was treating me but eventually I persuaded Bill Jacobs to let Rudi have a look at me.

Rudi took me to a hospital in Bridgetown, Barbados, where he took a series of X-rays. They showed three fractures on two of my lumbar vertebrae. Rudi suggested a programme of exercises to strengthen back and stomach muscles in order to take the strain off the damaged area as part of a long-term rehabilitation.

All the manipulations had not helped; in fact nothing had helped. On one occasion I had been jabbed with a huge hypodermic needle full of cortisone and told to rest for a day or two and then have a bowl. I bowled for about 10 minutes and the pain was excruciating. I knew I was in serious trouble. It was all so frustrating until Rudi found the real problem – of course, then the enormity of the situation sank in. It was very depressing.

I also discovered something about how the inter-island jealousies worked when we travelled on to Trinidad for the third Test. A doctor there would not believe my problem had been exposed on X-rays and insisted that it was muscular trouble. He refused to have Rudi's pictures sent from Bridgetown. In his defence, spinal stress fractures were relatively unknown at the time.

On the first morning of the match, they sent me to a specialist to have a manipulation under anaesthetic. What really annoyed me and got me offside was that I was left at the doctor's on my own because David McErlane, our physio, was wanted at the ground. I was out to the world and when I came round I did not have a clue where I was or what I was doing. I signed myself out of the clinic and somehow made my way back to the ground where I discovered they had picked that morning to have a team photograph, that morning of all mornings. It was as if I was *persona non-grata*.

Bill was one of the most loved managers of all time. Maybe I built the situation up in my own mind to be more than it was but I did not see it that way at the time and it began to sour me against authority.

They did consider sending me back to London to see Alun Thomas but when he was told about the stress fractures he told the English press there was little he could do.

I told Ian Chappell my back was no good and there was no chance of me bowling. He was incredibly supportive and said he wanted me to stay, join in what I could and be part of the group.

When we arrived in Montserrat he told me I had bugged him enough about my batting over the years and he was going to play me as a specialist batsman, opening the batting. I have never had such a torrid time in my life. The West Indian bowlers thought it was Christmas as they bounced and yorked me, knowing they wouldn't have to face any retaliation from me, until I was eventually out trying to hook. Never again did I pester Ian over my supposed batting prowess.

On reflection, the unfortunate thing about my injury was that no one understood much about stress fractures at the time, especially that it allowed you to do everything else except bowl. I can understand some of the players thinking it was in my head. I am forever indebted to Ian Chappell for his attitude and for believing what I was telling him, despite the flak he must have been getting from other areas. He knew. Why would I not want to play cricket? It was what I lived for at the time.

CHAPTER SEVEN

The incredible Doug Walters

Doug Walters was an enigma who would drink from five minutes past six, at the end of a day's play, until the early hours of the morning. None of us knew until exactly when because by then we had all gone to bed. He drank only beer and in all the years I knew him I can never, ever remember him being drunk. It was amazing. Obviously, he knew how to hold it and probably how to pace it, but he never missed a round and always had a beer in his hand.

Kerry Packer was insistent that when we went into the World Series we were fit. He was not pointing the bone at anyone in particular but he just wanted us in shape. Everyone had to do it without exception, otherwise they were to be fined and fined heavily.

When we went on the World Series tour to New Zealand there was some form of fitness routine scheduled for every day as we prepared for the games. Now Douggie had never been a great one for physical exercise. Well, I for one had never seen him do anything, and as he'd been part of the Australian team for over a decade, I guess he knew what he needed to do.

When we came down from our rooms for our first jog around the streets of Christchurch from our base at the Avon Motel, there was Douggie decked out in a new T-shirt, or rather a jogging singlet, with the words 'Jogging Kills' splashed across the front. We took off with Douggie in the middle of the pack. No one was taking much notice of him so he slipped into a convenient doorway and was not seen again until the end of the run.

Our captain, Greg Chappell, woke up to this ploy after a couple of days and decided we would run around a great big oval in the park so he could keep an eye on Douggie. As usual, Douggie took off with the bunch, keeping out of Greg's eyeline. Eventually, he disappeared behind the bushes not to be seen again until we came to the end of the run when he suddenly reappeared from behind a tree for the sprint home, complete with his 'Jogging Kills' T-shirt. Everyone fell about, except Greg.

Douggie stood with his hands on his hips saying what hard work it had been, adding, 'I'm too fit for you guys – I don't think I'll be doing it again,' hinting he was too fit to bother running with us. Of course, we knew that he had run around the block, hidden behind a tree, waited for us and jogged in ahead of us.

Soon afterwards, Douggie went up to Greg and said to him, 'I've decided – I'm not going.'

'Where?'

'The Montreal Olympics,' answered Douggie, deadpan.

At that, Greg gave up. Douggie was just a one-off and you had to accept him as he was. He wasn't going to change for anyone.

But Doug wasn't the only one who seemed a reluctant trainer. I remember one occasion at the end of the 1975 tour when Ian Chappell and I were staying at John Morley's flat in central London. After a couple of days, I felt a little lethargic and suggested a run around the streets. When Ian said he would like a jog as well, I nearly fell over because I had never seen him do more than a lap and a few sprints, and I had assumed he was one of these fortunate naturally fit people.

I did not expect him to be anywhere near my level – I ran pretty well most days – and so thought I would more than give the skipper a run for his money. He says he didn't beat me but I swear that if he didn't win, he was hot on my heels as we completed the five or six kilometres.

I quizzed him about his fitness and he admitted that he did what he needed to do but in his own time. He didn't need other people to train with and could do it against the clock. I took my hat off to him. I had previously put him in the same category as Douggie, but clearly he was totally different – unless Douggie was a really secret trainer. Somehow, I think not.

But for a true indication of Doug's methods, it's hard to beat the first Test in Christchurch in February 1977. Doug had come to our rescue, with Gary Gilmour, and scored 129 not out overnight against New Zealand after we'd been 208–6. At close of play he had a few beers at the ground as usual, then trundled back to the Avon Motel, taking up his usual spot at the bar. Everyone congratulated him and bought him a drink. Some ate early, some ate later, but everyone made the bar their focal point.

Everyone eventually drifted off to bed leaving him there, with his drink still in front of him. At around 2.30 in the morning, the manager of the motel telephoned Roger Wotton, the team manager and a lovely guy. Roger was startled and wondered what had happened, and the motel manager admitted he had a problem with Doug Walters. Doug was still in the bar and the manager had staff on duty who were now being paid double time. It was costing him a lot of money to cater for one drinker.

Roger, relieved it was nothing more serious, put on his dressing gown and went to find Douggie in the bar. He looked at his watch and looked at Douggie and asked him if he didn't think it was time to go to bed.

'I'm just having a celebratory drink for today's century,' Douggie responded. 'Have one with me and I'll go to bed.'

Roger declined but Douggie persisted and eventually they had another beer and off Douggie went to bed.

The next day, he took his score to a staggering 250 and, sure enough, exactly the same thing happened. Douggie was last in the bar and Roger was summoned again by the motel manager. This time Roger said straight out, 'I'll have a beer with you to celebrate your two hundred and fifty,' knowing that Douggie would be true to his word and go to bed afterwards, as he dutifully did.

Clearly the late nights were doing Douggie no harm for the next night he was back in the bar. This time Roger didn't even wait for the call. He set his alarm clock for 2.30, went and had a beer, and then Douggie went off to his bed and never bothered Roger again.

Doug was the most amazing bloke. There will never ever be another like him. I never saw him upset, never saw him throw a bat, never heard him talk badly of anyone. He was so cool. He also smoked cigarettes one after another. How he survived on the field all day without a smoke I don't know.

The captains quickly came to realise they could get away with very little where Douggie was concerned. Ian Chappell, on his first tour as captain, made a costly error when he said to everyone that his door would be open until three every morning if anyone had any problems. It was, of course, a figure of speech, but Douggie took it literally and at 2.55 in the morning he would pop in to Ian's bedroom just to annoy him. In the end, Ian decided the only way to keep him happy and get some peace himself was to have one beer with him, say goodnight and they would both go off to bed.

One of my favourite stories about Douggie took place in the West Indies in 1973 when our sponsors, unfortunately, were Red Stripe beer. I say unfortunately because, being sponsors, they kept us constantly supplied with their product. The two who enjoyed a drink more than most were Terry Jenner and Doug. We were staying at the Courtly Manor Hotel, which consisted of a series of rooms around a pool, sounding rather better than it actually was. The sponsors put a keg of chilled beer with a template in the outside section of Terry and Doug's room, number nine, which quickly became known as Club Nine.

During the first Test, there was one morning when Terry and Douggie didn't receive their wake-up call. That can happen in the West Indies where the catchline is 'come soon'. You often have to put in an early request at the hotels if you want to get anything. Terry eventually made the bus, albeit late. He had shaken Doug awake when someone hammered on the door of Club Nine. Terry flew out but Doug must have rolled over and gone back to sleep. Everyone was asking where Doug was and even Terry believed he must have nipped out and be hiding at the back of the bus somewhere. Realisation dawned when we arrived at the ground and there was still no sign of him.

Doug and Ian Chappell were great mates but there was a distinctly frosty atmosphere when it came to 15 minutes before the start and there was still no sign. Ian turned to Terry and said coldly, 'You'd better ring your mate and if he's not here before the start of play, there'll be trouble.' I have never seen him so cross.

Terry rushed off and made the call while we took the field with the 12th man. Doug arrived around 10 minutes late, changed and rushed down to the front of the pavilion. He waved and waved but Ian totally ignored him until the drinks interval. When Doug came on to the field and went to take his place in the slips, Ian said nothing but just waved him down to third man and made him field there – running him from one end of Sabina Park to the other at the end of each over.

Ian was hurrying the overs through and Doug was sweating profusely, rushing from end to end in the hot Jamaican sun, until he finally conned one of the spectators into lending him his bike and used that to change ends. Fortunately for him, Ian broke up and called him back to the slips. As we went off for lunch, Ian hung back to have a word with Douggie.

'You won't do this again, will you?' he said.

Douggie looked at him dumbfounded and said, quite seriously, 'Ian, I can't promise you that.' If nothing else, Douggie was honest.

Douggie's other love was cards and while he was quite happy playing solitaire, if there was a card game going he would join in, or he would be showing card tricks. In other words, he loved absolutely anything to do with cards.

He would play while he was padded up ready to go. He would have his bat, gloves and cap at his side and when a wicket fell, he would pass

We settled for the second option and he encased me in a plaster cast from my backside to just above my stomach so I had to do everything with a perfectly straight back. I looked like a goon. I couldn't wash the car or do any gardening; in fact, I was limited to nothing more than walking or sitting. It was a nightmare. The only time I was comfortable was when I was standing up straight. Lying down, dressing and washing were close to impossible and I was almost totally reliant on Helen to help me for six weeks. She acted as my valet for that period without a word of complaint because she was fully aware of the discomfort I was in. I was also reduced to wearing the one pair of trousers which fitted over the plaster, and a sweater, which did not please the bank with their formal dress code.

My mind was in turmoil. I didn't know if I would play first-class cricket again or even if it was worth the pain if I did. The frustrations were enormous but I knew I had to put up with it and see where I was at the end of the six weeks.

The relief when the doctor hacked off the plaster cast was immense. To my horror, he wanted to put on another one but I persuaded him I would be careful and we settled for a much simpler brace. That was even more uncomfortable than the cast but at least I could take it off while I enjoyed a soak in the bath. After dispensing with the brace, I had to be careful for a further three weeks while I regained some strength and movement. Then, at last, I was allowed some light exercise.

John Inverarity called to see how I was and when I would be ready to play and I had to admit I would not be bowling that coming summer. Who knew what lay in the future?

Dr Frank Pyke and I sat down to map out a recovery programme. He felt he could help me in two areas. One was to open up my action a little, something which had never been heard of before. I believed in him and agreed, but he spoilt it a bit by adding that even getting to work on my action was a long time away, and, honestly, it might never happen.

However, the first thing to do when I was able to resume exercising, he said, was to work on the core group of muscles until they were so strong they would take a lot of the pressure from the spine. As a fast bowler, it was important to contract through the trunk quickly and, therefore, to be strong and flexible in that area. He explained it wasn't just a six-pack that was necessary; it was important to be strong all round the trunk area. I did a series of exercises every second day from then on, during pre-season and throughout the season.

I left the bank while all this was going on to take up a partnership in a contract-cleaning business, plus we were building a new house. I put a lot of time into both, and Helen was pregnant, so there was enough happening to keep me occupied.

Cricket still took up a lot of my time and, while I was not bowling, I felt I learned a lot about the finer points of the game. I was made captain of Perth Cricket Club, which I found a little embarrassing at first, being preferred to players of far greater experience at such a young age. But I was determined to learn from my inevitable mistakes, and enjoyed that side of the game. I maintained my competitive edge by working hard on my batting and fielding. With a lot of help and advice, I began to function reasonably well, playing as a batsman about nine months after coming back from the Caribbean. I finished up scoring plenty of runs at an average of over 40 and with a top score just two short of a century.

When the doctor gave me permission to bowl sooner than expected, towards the end of 1973, I nervously brought myself on against Melville Cricket Club as the game threatened to slip away. To everyone's surprise, I came in off six paces and instantly hit a line. I wasn't going to get carried away, though, and the actual bowling was pretty ordinary stuff, gentle medium pace, but there was no backache, which was interesting. Of course, I had stiffness but I bowled a few overs in that game and then a few more in the next and after Christmas, I actually began to work up a little pace. I finished the season with 48 wickets and was well satisfied.

So in the following off season I was able to get down to some really hard work in the university gym, working on the trunk exercises for two to three hours in the evening every other day. On the off days, I went running. Ian King helped enormously. A lot of the exercises were isometric and you needed someone there to hold on to you to exert pressure. Ian was a team-mate, a fast bowler who opened the bowling with me. He was also a physical-fitness fanatic and he did the entire workout with me, including the running.

The strength work was going so well and I was pushing myself hard. Then one day, in the middle of an exercise, my back collapsed. I was distraught because I thought it had gone again, despite all the hard work. We walked up to Dr Pyke's office and I told him what had happened. He sent me back to Dr Gilmour who examined me and explained that all I had done was sprained a joint because of the hard work. He assured me it would settle down within a week. Imagine my relief. I did nothing for a couple of weeks and then eased in again. It had been a timely warning, showing me there was a limit to what I could do, and I stopped pushing myself like a man possessed.

By this time, the new season had begun and I played a few matches before being called up for a Shield game against South Australia in Adelaide. John Inverarity, the captain, and Ian Brayshaw, the vice captain, warned me the world's press would be looking on, especially as the Poms had arrived. They were having a week of nets before playing South Australia in a warm-up game. The captain wanted to get all the fuss over with, so he called a press conference. I wasn't happy about it at first but it worked.

Dr Pyke, John and I decided that, although it might take a while, I had to start off by bowling within myself and work up gradually. I noticed a number of the English players wandered over from the nets when I opened the bowling; I also saw they walked away fairly swiftly, after watching a few balls. They clearly thought this new-look Dennis Lillee was going to be no threat to them at all. As with the previous Ashes series, I was more pre-occupied with my fitness than with taking on England.

I didn't realise the relevance of their attitude until the first Test against England at the Gabba in Brisbane. I hadn't played Test cricket since Sabina Park in February 1973 when I took no wickets for plenty. It was now the end of November 1974 and I don't suppose I set the world on fire, but I was happy with my performance. In fact, I was happy to get through it – at the start, I didn't know whether I was going to last or what was going to happen to my reconstructed back and me. Australia batted first and my many innings for the club had clearly done me no harm as I scored 15 batting at number nine.

We bowled England out in the first innings for 265, and they scored that many only thanks to a century from Tony Greig, who was one of my two wickets in the innings. I took another couple in the second but it was my opening partner Jeff Thomson who took 6–46 to win the match for us.

The funny thing was that before the game, the press had written us both off. They didn't rate me because they had seen me bowling gentle medium pace in the lead-up matches after a long time out. They didn't rate Thommo because in his one previous Test, against Pakistan, he had taken none for plenty. They had underestimated us both and we finished with 13 wickets between us.

I have to admit during those 18 months or so between Sabina Park and Brisbane, I often thought I would never make it back to the top. I guess I thought all the hard work could have been for nothing, but I had tasted top-class cricket and I couldn't let it go without giving it at least one more shot. I don't think it was until the third or fourth Test back that I felt I was actually winning the battle. Even then, I was not sure if I would break down again; there was just no history of this type of injury, no comparisons were available. Dr Pyke had told me to bowl within myself and only let the odd one rip, but after the first Test I began to build up my pace without really realising it.

I suppose the amazing thing was the Board had enough faith to select me – and then I could have blown it. A week before the team for the first Test was to be announced, I rang up the secretary of the Board and told him if they were considering picking me to think again because they hadn't paid my medical bills as promised. He said they had all been paid but I had checked beforehand and they hadn't. What was more, if I was selected and the money had not arrived, I would go straight to the press and tell them exactly why I wasn't going to play.

It was a strong reaction but I was so annoyed because the bills had been sent to them right through my rehabilitation and they were dragging their feet. It was not a lot of money to the Board but it was a lot for me, and I could hardly afford it. Dr Gilmour was fantastic and refused to ask me to pay the account personally. He continued to send his bills to the Board.

The Board knew me by then and realised I wasn't bluffing. They settled the account in full. As far as I was concerned, it was money well spent for it was the start of a great partnership between Thommo and me. We went on to take 58 wickets between us in the series against England with Thommo having a field day, blitzing them from the very first day. When I look back, it was amazing we got together – Thommo failed in his first Test and was then dropped for the entire time I was out with my injured back. It was a gamble for me to play at all and it was a surprise they picked him.

Thommo and I hardly knew each other. We had played against each other a couple of times and exchanged cursory nods, but we got on straightaway once we were in the same team. You could never fail to get on with Thommo because he was just the easiest going guy of all time. I don't remember there being any competition between us over who took the most wickets. He just wanted to get out there in the middle and bowl as fast as he could. Thommo's mates jibed that he was not as quick as me and he had told them he was quicker, so initially he wanted to prove to them he was right. I have no doubt he was quicker than me, quicker even than when I was bowling at my fastest which was about 97 miles per hour. He was once recorded at 99.98 and he wasn't even sure that was the fastest he had ever bowled. We weren't recorded very often in those days.

He was the quickest I ever saw and certainly the quickest I ever faced. It was at the end of his career when I felt the full brunt of his speed. We bounced each other for the first time when we were the captains of Western Australia and Queensland, and I'm so glad I didn't start it 10 years earlier. Before that, we had an unspoken agreement not to do it.

One of the early things I remember about Thommo was when we had our team dinner the night before the first day of the first Test in Brisbane. I was walking out after the dinner to catch a cab and I saw

Thommo at the bar, sitting down with a tumbler full of ice and liquid three-quarters of the way up the glass. I said what a good idea it was to have a drink of water before going home, adding that I would join him and have one as well.

'Water?' he said incredulously. 'That's straight scotch. I don't want water.'

'Scotch?' I couldn't believe what I was hearing.

'Yes,' he responded casually. 'And I'm going to have a few of them.'

Open-mouthed I asked, 'What if you have to bowl tomorrow?'

He shrugged. 'That's just what I hope happens because when I go out to bowl I want a hangover from hell. I bowl real well when I have a headache. It makes me just want to get in there and get them.'

Me, I needed sleep and a good, solid meal. He could keep his headache; that was no sort of motivation to me. It showed what an unusual character the man was.

Thommo was an uncomplicated guy, but streetwise and smart. He could turn his hand to most sports. He played a good game of tennis and could hit a golf ball as far as anyone I have ever seen; on a good day, he could murder the longest course. He loved fishing, knew all about boats and I believe he has a skipper's ticket and even now runs a river boat in Queensland. He was always confident in his ability, not boastful but stating what he believed was true. For me, he was a regular guy. I enjoyed spending time with him and still do.

In England in 1975, he didn't look after himself. He wasn't bowling well and, to compound it, he put his name to a fractious piece in an English newspaper to which the Board objected. The Board decided to send him home. He admitted he had been, in his own words, a real dickhead, and accepted the rather harsh punishment. As he left the manager Fred Bennett's suite, he passed Ian Chappell and Rod Marsh who were sitting outside waiting to go in. He had his head down and Ian asked him what was the matter. Thommo told him what had happened and said it was his own fault he was being sent home.

'Be buggered you're going home,' Ian responded. 'Follow me – and you, Rod,' and with that all three went into the manager's room.

'Fred,' said Ian, 'if you're organising a ticket home for Thommo, make out seventeen for me and the rest of the team.'

Ian promptly turned round and walked off, followed by Marsh and Thommo, leaving Fred Bennett spluttering in his wake. They went down to the bar and waited. Sure enough, Fred came down and reversed his decision. Thommo said it was like a thunderbolt had hit him.

'I realised I had been such a bloody idiot. I hadn't been putting in for the team, but what hit me most was the captain knew that but still backed me. You could have hit me with a bat. It was then I realised what I was there for.'

From then on he bowled beautifully and really went for it. He hadn't realised before what a hole he was digging for himself, but was sensitive enough to realise it then. It was an amazing thing Ian did not only for Thommo but also for the team.

When people hear these stories about Ian, they may understand why we held the man in such high esteem. The public are more likely to remember him dropping his trousers, putting two fingers up and his well-publicised rows in the West Indies where he was taken to court for alleged assault. We saw the other side and how he protected his men, a real leader.

Thommo played a bit of soccer in the off-season but reckoned his pre-season consisted of water-skiing, pig-shooting and drinking and the captain had to understand he was different from everyone else and had to be nurtured in an alternative way. This was a man who used to chase down wild boars. If they turned on you, those creatures would rip you to pieces. These guys didn't just shoot them, they used to grab them by the horns and wrestle them to the ground. Then they would kill them and eat them while they were camping out. Admittedly, that was a lot of running around and good exercise, but it was more than compensated for by the amount of drinking they did afterwards.

What he gambled on was the first few Shield games giving him enough bowling to get ready for the Tests. He was fortunate in that he was a naturally fit person, but one particular season he showed up for practice a week or so before the first game and Greg Chappell watched him bowl a succession of no balls. Greg chatted to him and they worked on his run-up. They eventually sorted it out, but in their first Shield game, sure enough, the first ball was a no ball. In the first two overs Thommo must have bowled nine of them and was struggling to finish the overs.

After the ninth no ball, Greg ran from first slip, about 50 metres away from Thommo as he trudged back to the end of his run-up, and asked him what was going on.

Thommo looked round and said, 'I dunno. Whatever I do, I just keep bowling no balls.'

'That's stating the obvious,' snapped Greg. 'We worked on this a few days ago. What's gone wrong?' Thommo thought about it.

'In the nets, was I taking off on my right foot or my left foot?'

The exasperated Chappell snorted, 'Whichever foot you have been bowling off, try the other one,' and promptly marched back to his position. Problem solved!

On another occasion, Thommo was bowling at Brisbane with Greg setting a big offside field – only for every ball to swing away down leg side. Once again, Greg stormed up from his place in the slips to ask what the hell was going on. Thommo replied that the ball would not go where he wanted it to go.

'I don't care what you do,' Greg said, 'just hold the ball across the seam and let it go, and bowl it where we want them to play at it.'

Thommo nodded his assent and then said, 'By the way, Greg. What side do you hold the shine for the outswinger?' He was serious. Greg told him and Thommo replied, 'No wonder I couldn't get it to go where I wanted it to.'

That was Thommo, a natural. The guy did it easy so he didn't think a lot about the technicalities or the mechanics of bowling.

During the Test in Adelaide against England that 1974-75 series, he damaged his shoulder, but not playing cricket – playing tennis on a rest day at Yalumba Winery in the Barossa Valley. The injury was to put him out for the rest of the series. Thommo being Thommo had to do everything flat out whether it was driving, drinking, bowling or golf and it was the same with his tennis. He possessed a million miles an hour serve and he was out there without a warm-up, crashing down these gigantic serves. It had been a tradition for 40-odd years that on the rest day both teams would go up to the property in the Barossa Valley where the owner, Windy Hill-Smith, would put on food, wine and beers. There was a great pool as well as the tennis courts, and you could have a terrific time mixing with your own team, the opposition and assorted friends of the owner.

On his Test debut, Ian asked Thommo how he was going, and Thommo answered not too good because he had broken a bone in his foot before the game but hadn't said anything because he wanted to play. It wasn't obvious to us because Thommo never showed too much pain and somehow he still got through the match.

There is no doubt that, even with all his idiosyncrasies, Jeff Thomson was an excellent fast bowler, and Ian Chappell was one of the first to spot his massive potential. Ian Redpath, the great Australian opener, said to Ian during that Test against Pakistan, 'We have a great find here.' Ian agreed that, indeed, they had.

'So you agree Max Walker is a great find?' Redpath said.

'You can find his sort of medium pacer on any park but you cannot find a Thommo every day with his pace,' Ian replied.

This was no detriment to Max, who was a terrific bowler for Australia and made his debut in the same Test, but simply a recognition that Thommo had that something extra. Such were Ian's qualities he could spot talent even in a bowler with a broken bone in his foot who had figures of 0–110.

However, that first series back for me was not about my new opening partner, it was at first a question of getting through without further injury problems. It was always in my mind that my back could go at any time. Then there was the new action. I did not know whether it was going to work, whether it was going to be successful. I had the guidelines from playing in a couple of Shield games where it was comfortable – but this was a big step up from that.

I was taking very heavy-duty painkillers because the pain was still there, although not the stabbing, excruciating agony of before. Talk to anyone who has had stress fractures and they will tell you there is lasting pain, almost like toothache. As I played on, there was more stiffness and soreness but the surgeon just gave me tablets. It was also a mental problem; I was waiting for the breakdown to happen, particularly in the early days. Taking the painkillers meant I covered up the nagging ache but I did feel sore the next day. It was a continuing situation but the important thing was I got through.

I believed I was still fast enough to bowl bouncers and frighten batsmen, and I was quoted as saying, 'I bowl bouncers for one reason and that is to hit the batsman and thus intimidate him . . . I try to hit the batsman in the rib cage when I bowl a purposeful bouncer and I want it to hurt, so the batsman doesn't want to face me any more.' It was a statement I had made in a book some time before and it had been picked up and regurgitated. What I was trying to say was if you bowl a bouncer, you are usually aiming at the bloke's body, but what it came across as was that I bowled to intimidate. What I did not want was to hit someone on the head. I didn't like guys being badly hurt and it was a relief when helmets came in because it lessened the risk of permanent damage. I didn't mind making them duck and dive because it gave me an edge by keeping them thinking. A bouncer is like a yorker – a genuine fast bowler's weapon. I always felt a couple of broken ribs were the batsman's fault – not mine.

I also said bouncers should be bowled only to those batsmen who appear capable of handling them, but I have to confess I did not always follow those noble words. Sometimes my judgement would let me down.

Thommo, however, was far more bloodthirsty and he made my comments look gentle when it was reported he liked to hit batsmen better than getting them out, adding that it did not worry him to see a batsman 'rolling around screaming, with blood on the pitch'. I certainly did not agree with that kind of doctrine. The quote appeared in a magazine and Thommo claims the writer overdid it.

I suppose to some degree we lived up to those words in that series because my first ball to the prolific batsman Dennis Amiss hit him in the Adam's apple before a quick one from Thommo broke his thumb. I also broke Edrich's hand in the first Test and fractured two of his ribs with the first ball of the second innings, softening him up for Thommo to bowl him for six.

In England in 1972 I had bowled quicker but here, bowling a touch slower, I was operating on harder wickets and I was considerably more accurate than I had been on tour. Also in England, John Snow never minded handing it out to our blokes. Fast bowlers remember those sorts of things just as I remembered Shuttleworth not holding back with the bouncers on that tour. It's like the song 'We Didn't Start the Fire'.

We batted first in the first Test in Brisbane, and I know for a fact Tony Greig told Peter Lever to bounce me. Lever made a pathetic attempt at it so Greig took the ball himself, bounced me twice and had me caught behind on the second attempt. As I walked past, I said to him, 'Just you remember who started this.' People often remember who did the damage and not who started the fire. I bowled him a bouncer first ball, then walked down the pitch and made a mark on my forehead to tell him I was after him. It was pre-planned.

Tony Greig and Ian Chappell were of the same ilk. I have never seen two players at each other as much as them – apart from, perhaps, Javed and myself. It went back to a tour to South Africa. Let's just say Ian and Greigy clashed and they weren't the best of mates. In one game when Greig was bowling and clearing the rubble off the wicket, Chappell would brush it straight back. I thought Greig was super-competitive. He wasn't a mate but I enjoyed his company and his competitive streak.

The second Test in Perth turned into a full-frontal assault on the Poms. On my fast home track, Thommo hit Brian Luckhurst's top hand and smashed David Lloyd's pink plastic protector. Amazingly, they sent for the 42-year-old Colin Cowdrey to fill the gaps the injuries to Amiss and Edrich had caused.

We were surprised when Cowdrey flew out. We all respected what he had done in an illustrious career but we were a bit bemused to find him returning to the arena at his age. I take my hat off to him because he played well despite not having played Test cricket for more than three years prior to his belated call-up.

He told the story of how he took the telephone call in the middle of winter, watching the series on television in front of a blazing fire with his pipe and a glass of port, thinking how much better it was to be here than there. The call was from one of the officials who asked him if he wanted to go to Australia. He thought a managerial or an advisory role was on offer and it sounded good – until the official told him they wanted him to go out and actually play.

Cowdrey said he was silent for some time, maybe minutes, before saying he'd have to ring back. He said he thought it was madness to give up the comfort of his home to face those two lunatics. But in the end he thought what the heck, and flew out to play in the Test without any practice other than a quick net.

He must have wondered what hit him, but even so, he played wonderfully well. He knew what to leave and his glides, using the pace of the ball, were perfection. We were astonished he did so well under the extreme circumstances of the WACA, where everything counted against him.

England were clearly troubled and unsettled by the hostile attack. Brian Luckhurst was quoted as saying, 'It was the most awe-inspiring spell of fast bowling I have ever faced. Lillee and Thomson bowled like men possessed, and Thomson was warned for sending three whistling past my chin in failing light. He did not take a blind bit of notice and made no attempt to pitch the ball up – if anything the next four flew even faster past my face.'

We won by nine wickets with only wicket-keeper Alan Knott and bowler Fred Titmus passing 50 in the two innings.

After a draw in the third Test in Melbourne, England's skipper Mike Denness dropped himself for the fourth Test in Sydney but it did little good. Their batting once again let them down with only John Edrich, Alan Knott and Tony Greig scoring half centuries while both Ian Redpath and Greg Chappell reached three figures in our second innings. The pattern was the same as I took four wickets and Thommo took six.

It was here that we regained the Ashes and began our celebrations at the Koala Motel and carried on at the Different Drummer in Kings Cross. Above the door read the words of the American author Henry Thoreau: 'If a man does not keep pace with his companions, perhaps it is because he hears a different drummer, let him step to the music he hears, however measured or far away.'

The music was far away for me that night as I wandered around the Different Drummer, signing all sorts of memorabilia from table napkins to the usual scraps of paper, soaking up the enormity of an Ashes win.

The English attitude was summed up when Keith Fletcher asked John Edrich how it was going and was told, 'One tour too many.'

Fletch had plenty to say and when I was rapped on the arm in our first innings, he pointed at me and told the bowler to 'let him have it'. This was worth picking up on and on national television that night I vowed a little revenge. When Fletcher came out to bat, I quietly said to him, 'Good luck, Fletch . . . you're going to need it!' Sure enough, Thommo bowled him an inswinging bouncer which hit his gloves, his hat and almost got him caught in the covers. He didn't last long.

By the time we reached Adelaide for the fifth Test it was all over and we clinched the six-match series 4–0 with a 163-run win.

Dennis Amiss had, quite rightly, come to Australia with a big reputation but by the time the fifth Test rolled around he was not fancying it at all and commented it was like leaving the condemned chair, coming out to face Thommo and me. He said, 'Several times I walked out to the middle beaten before I started. The bat in my hand was superfluous against those two . . . batting was a complete misery.'

He wasn't wrong. I got him for a duck in both innings, and again for a duck in England's only innings in the sixth Test in Melbourne, where England exacted a little revenge by beating us by an innings. It had clearly got to the Warwickshire batsman for I took his wicket three times cheaply in his four knocks in England the following summer.

That tour didn't do the English morale a lot of good. We loved it and even frightened their tailenders with the odd short ball to Derek Underwood, Bob Willis and Geoff Arnold. In fact, I sent one whistling so close to Geoff's nose that it flew over Rod Marsh's head for four byes. Even I was relieved that one missed.

The one English player to come through it all unscathed was Tony Greig, who played as flamboyantly as ever, even going down on one knee to signal a boundary off my bowling and pretending to head my bouncers. Greig did well because he had us bowling to him where he wanted. We had a meeting in the dressing room about it and Rod Marsh came up with his 'sand-shoe crusher' theory – bowl the big inswinging yorker at Tony's toes.

Greig played aggressively. No one else was coping and he just took us on and hit some great cuts and great drives, as well as pulling a few. He had the same attitude as me and after play we'd enjoy a few beers and laugh about it in the dressing room. I liked Tony Greig.

But you could see in their eyes that some of the other English players were less than happy. Fletch was looking as though he wished he wasn't there, as did Amiss, Luckhurst and Edrich. I must admit, with Thommo bowling at 100 miles per hour on pitches that suited him, I would have been afraid.

Edrich, whom I liked and admired, Fletch and Amiss seemed bowed. When Amiss walked out, he looked almost apologetic, while Denness was clearly not comfortable. Add Brian Luckhurst, who never played for England again after that trip, and it was half the top order.

The atmosphere against England in that 1974–75 series was not the best. They were not happy with the aggressive way in which we approached the games and not many of them stayed around for a drink after play or came to our dressing room. They didn't want to mix. Perhaps this was partly due to the pressure, but it's part of the game and you have to be able to handle it.

We just thought of it as winning a series. Personally, I did not think there were too many bouncers. Two of us were bowling quite quickly but it was no different from Shield matches, and I don't remember bowling more short balls than I usually did.

I think England got to the stage where they were mentally defeated and played a lot of short balls they should have left. But we were bowling pretty well and Thommo was lethal, although not always accurate.

By now I was beginning to feel I had settled back into international cricket so in Sydney, in England's first innings, I drew on my own captaincy experience and insisted on a very fine, very short-leg slip to opener David Lloyd. I had Thommo standing nine metres from the bat while Rod Marsh was 20 metres back. Ian Chappell eventually agreed and Lloyd promptly tucked me off his hip straight into Thommo's waiting hands.

I was suggesting more and more, especially in terms of my field placings. Ian was terrific about it. If it had been Greg, he would have said we would talk about it later whereas Ian would simply say, 'Let's give it a go and if it doesn't work, we'll try something else.' I suppose, in Shield matches and Tests, I was suggesting things when perhaps I shouldn't have done. I only hoped the captain felt happy about my suggestions. At least it showed I was thinking what I wanted to do and where I wanted the field set.

I was certainly thinking about my bowling more than I had ever done before. I guess that was because I could no longer simply blast batsmen out; I had to have a better worked out plan than that. It was probably something to do with me maturing as a person, the catalyst being dealing with a career-threatening injury. Had I not had the problems, I would probably still have charged in. I had been through hardship and thought about survival and how to adapt. I did it on my own and I was able to experiment in club cricket and to a lesser extent in Shield cricket.

The penny started to drop at club level that if I started to drop down in pace, I would take more wickets than if I bowled quickly. I even learned to bowl off a very short run. I had the option of three different approaches. With the lesser players, you had to bowl them out or induce them in a different way from quality Test batsmen. Sometimes I found it easier to bowl against those Test batsmen than Shield batsmen, and Shield batsmen rather than club, because at the higher levels there is more intensity.

After an 18-month gap from Test cricket, I was satisfied. Maybe I bowled less quickly than before but I was a lot more accurate. With Amiss, I was getting his wicket from movement, caught behind or leg before wicket. I didn't get him out hooking, but nicking edges. We were also very well prepared and we had our plans for every batsman, which we tried to implement.

There was plenty of sledging from both sides with Greig and company never short of a word. The brooding Bob Willis didn't have a lot to say but the others made up for it. Who started it? Who knows? It certainly wasn't a one-way street. It may have seemed like it because they were down and we were cock-a-hoop. There was not a lot of personal abuse; some things were said in frustration and some simply in trying to get on top.

The strange thing was the animosity did not spill over to the English fans, or at least, not all of them. My postbag was far from being full of poison pen letters. Over the years, I have had thousands and thousands of fan letters and one of the many which made me laugh was from England a long time ago. An 18-year-old wrote and asked me for a fitness programme to become a very good fast bowler. I wrote back with my own programme because I was impressed with his enthusiasm. I warned him it would be tough and said I wouldn't blame him if he did not carry it through. I said he could modify it. I thought no more about it until 18 months later when I received a letter from the young man. It said:

Dear Mr Lillee,

Sorry for taking so long to answer your letter and thank you very much for your in-depth reply. I have followed your programme to the letter and I cannot bowl for shit anymore but I am now the County squash champion.

I thought it just goes to prove we are not all built the same but at least he must have been a very fit squash player.

CHAPTER NINE

Travelling the world

We broke our journey to England for the 1975 series with a visit to Canada and played cricket in the unlikely settings of Vancouver and Toronto. The whole trip was a great experience and I will long remember the day Bruce Laird and I went up into the mountains and I touched snow for the first time in my life. I had seen snow on the mountains in Europe, but this was the first time I had actually touched it. We threw snowballs at each other like little kids.

We were beaten by Canada in Canada without a Canadian in the team; they were all West Indians, Indians, English and Australians. It wasn't a great way to start the tour but it was understandable with the amount of alcohol consumed the night before the game. There had been a reception with unlimited drinks followed by a party at someone's house. It was a major plot and it worked because not only did they win, but we didn't mind losing before we got down to the serious business in England.

The first game in Canada was staged at one of the most beautiful cricket grounds I have ever seen, Stanley Park. Unfortunately, I did not play but as it was a very cold day it probably wasn't a bad thing. Bruce and Greg Chappell were not playing either, so we joined a small Caribbean section in the crowd for a few drinks. There was a crowd of about 500 and about 30 of them were from the Caribbean. We loved their company because they appreciated their cricket so much and were really on our side. They liked the way we played cricket.

Our team-mates did not know we were in the crowd and we fed our new friends a few relevant lines for them to shout and chant at our players out in the middle. They loved watching Thommo hurling them down West Indian style, even though, in the cold, he was a bit wild to say the least. Rod Marsh behind the stumps was struggling to keep down the byes when, helped by us, one of the guys shouted, 'Hey Rod, you stopping the ball like a full bus.' And then a bit later, 'Hey Rod, whatever happened to B.N. Jarman – he on sick leave?' When Ashley Mallett came on to bowl wearing dark sunglasses, they cried out, 'Ashley, you taking a dim view of de game?'

As the remarks degenerated, so the players began to twig that someone was in there, feeding them the lines while being fed with over-proofed rum. Rod Marsh was referred to as 'George the Gorilla', a name used by the team only, when he tried to slog. Soon we were spotted and the game was up.

The tour was simply a gesture by the Board and we were all billeted out to families. The people looking after Doug Walters came to the ground to the surprise of everyone, and when asked why, they replied, 'We thought we ought to come down and see what Doug Walters looked like!' They hadn't seen him from the time he arrived. He would arrive home after they were in bed and they had gone to work when he got up for the cricket. Naturally, it broke everyone up – another Doug Walters story for the annals.

I stayed with Denis Johnson, an ex-pat Australian, and his Canadian wife Cathy. They took the whole team out to Cathy's parents' shack for a barbecue. The place overlooked a magnificent lake surrounded by tall pines. None of us had seen anything like it in our lives and it was well worth the two- or three-hour trip on the bus. That was the perfect send-off before we left for England.

The trip showed the great side of playing amateur cricket. It is hard to imagine an Australian team doing a similar thing these days, staying with families, going on days out and playing in front of a handful of people before an Ashes series. I always counted myself lucky to have played half of my career as an amateur and the other half as a professional. It's good to have seen both sides of the game and the downside of the professional game now is that you do not have the opportunity to go on tours like the one to Canada and meet so many people socially.

When we arrived in England, we found we were to be loaned three Jaguar cars as part of the sponsorship of the tour. One of them was a V12 but as we were paid just £1,200 for the entire tour, Thommo was the only one who could afford the petrol to run it – he had secured a contract with radio station 4IP worth A$600,000 over 10 years. He had a car to himself for the entire tour.

Before the Ashes series, we took part in the first-ever World Cup. We loved the concept of this new one-day competition and were looking forward to some good competitive cricket.

We started off by beating Pakistan by 73 runs at Leeds, thanks to a brilliant not-out 80 by Ross Edwards. I robbed him of the man-of-the-match award with 5–34 off 12 overs. Next we faced Sri Lanka at The Oval when we rattled up a then record score of 328 off our 60 overs, with Alan Turner taking the batting honours. Sri Lanka might have been able to top our huge score had Thommo not produced the fieriest spell on what was a lovely batting wicket. He bowled Fernando and forced both Wettimuny and Mendis to retire hurt. At one stage, stretchers were almost passing on their way through to the pavilion. What's more, the injuries weren't all the result of bouncers; Thommo also used his sand-shoe crusher, hitting Wettimuny on the foot with a fast yorker, and Mendis on the head, others on the arms. It was an amazing spell and it transformed the game as they fell 52 runs short.

Next up were the West Indies – and they thrashed us. We were rushed out for 192 and they knocked off those runs for the loss of three wickets with 14 overs to spare. But it didn't matter as we were already safely through to the semi-final to meet England at Leeds and the home side's batting folded. They fell apart with only Denness (27) and Geoff Arnold (18) getting into double figures as Gary Gilmour stunned them with 6–14 off 12 overs. Old and Snow made sure we had to fight for our runs but we were into the final after 28.4 overs with six wickets down.

It meant we were to face the favourites, the West Indies, in the final at Lord's. We were off to a flying start when Roy Fredericks hooked me for a six. We watched the ball fly over the boundary but when we looked back, he had trodden on the stumps and was given out, hit wicket.

It turned out to be my only wicket as the West Indies rattled up 291 with Clive Lloyd hitting 102. We thought we were in with a chance when Gilmour bowled Viv Richards for five but all he had done was pull the tail of a sleeping tiger. Viv personally ran out Turner, Ian Chappell and Greg Chappell for a most unusual hat-trick while Alvin Kallicharran ran out Max Walker and Thommo at the end. Before that, we thought the runs were attainable on an easy wicket, but Viv came up with those three run-outs, which turned the match.

I came in last, joining Thommo, still needing 59 to win. It looked a hopeless task but we had got to within 17 runs of their total with eight balls left by the time Kallicharran ran out Thommo. The indelible memory for me was when I looked up at our balcony and saw there was no one there. Everyone had given up and they were away packing their gear, but as we began to put on the runs they began to reappear until the balcony was packed.

At one point, one of us hit a ball which went into the outfield and was caught. The crowd, largely West Indian, thought the game was over and started tumbling on to the field. I had heard the call of no ball and I just told Thommo to keep running for as many as we could. We ran three or four before umpire Dickie Bird stopped us. We felt aggrieved because we could have run seven, but obviously it would have been unfair.

Within another ball or two, Thommo was run out, leaving us just short but it was a magnificent match. On our way back to the pavilion, I looked up at the clock to discover it was a quarter to nine. But it was one of those beautiful English summer nights and I hadn't even noticed how late it was. I reckon we could have gone on for another hour, the light was so good.

The Test series was reduced to four matches because of the World Cup and, having made a mess of England in Australia, it was going to be interesting to note their reaction on their own soil. Clearly they still did not fancy taking us on and this was proved conclusively in the first Test at Edgbaston. It lasted barely four days as we won by an innings and 85 runs. The shell-shocked captain, Mike Denness, resigned. He had been caught by Greg Chappell off Max Walker for three in the first innings, and bowled for eight by Thommo in the second.

Dennis Amiss, another to suffer a crash of confidence in the previous series, was still suffering and even on his home wicket in Birmingham I had him caught by Thommo for four in the first innings while Thommo had him caught for five in the second.

Having scored 359 batting first, we whipped England out for 101 and 173. It would have been worse but for brave innings from Alan Knott and John Snow. I enjoyed myself with 5–15 off as many overs in the first innings and took a couple in the second while Max Walker also took seven in the match and Thommo grabbed five in the second innings.

I suspect I sealed Amiss's demise in the second Test at Lord's when I had him lbw for nought and then caught by Greg Chappell for 10. It was a shame because the guy had originally come to Australia having scored 1,000 Test runs in a calendar year and in the space of a few months he went from chocolates to boiled lollies. He was a fine player and a fine bloke but you have to forget about all those things when it comes to business.

For the Lord's Test, England shuffled their pack in a bid to stop the rot and the silver-haired David Steele, hardly in the first flush of youth, was one of their choices. At the time, we couldn't quite believe this bespectacled, compact guy with white hair, wearing his peaked hat on an upward tilt, was going to make any difference, but he made quite an entrance.

When he appeared, I asked, 'Who's the grey ghost?' The remark had nothing to do with his hair but the fact that he looked like one of our traffic wardens who dressed in grey.

When he first came in, someone made a comment out loud about his age and he turned to Rodney Marsh behind the wicket, patted his backside with his bat and said for all to hear, 'Take a good look because you're going to see a lot of that this summer.'

Steeley, with whom I keep in touch every time I come to England, takes great delight in telling that story – it's so good because he backed up his words with actions. They had lost four wickets for 49 – I had cleaned up Barry Wood, John Edrich, the hapless Amiss and Graham Gooch for next to nothing – when he and Tony Greig propped up the innings and put on almost 100 before Steele was bowled by Thommo for exactly 50.

England went on to make 315 and would have had us in serious trouble but for a fine 99 from Ross Edwards and a not-out 73 from yours truly, which carried us from a perilous 81–7 to a respectable 268 all out. I faced 103 balls and, according to the records, hit three sixes and eight fours. I always told them I could bat!

It was a different England in the second innings as they scored 436–7 before declaring with Edrich scoring 175 and David Steele another 45. The lowest scorer – and my only wicket – was Amiss.

I enjoyed that Test and did not tire of telling people it was another century nipped in the bud. It's nice to reflect that I made my top score on a ground which means so much, one of my favourite grounds in the world.

The wickets were all very different from in 1972 when there was lots of swing and they were helpful for seam. In 1975 it was a dry summer and the wickets were harder, a bit slower and with less assistance for the seamers. In the third Test at Leeds, Steele came out and played forward to everything we bowled at him whether it was a short-pitched delivery or a full length. I remember noticing his size 10 foot, toe pointing up, and his glasses as I delivered the ball. He just paddled the ball around and we bowled short balls to test him. Even though he hit them up in the air, he hit them squarish rather than down fine.

Interestingly, the next season when the West Indies were in England, they immediately put a fielder square and one fine and had great success. We weren't smart enough to dream up that ploy. Perhaps it was because we had enjoyed so much success against English players before that we thought if we were going to get him out it was going to be with a hook to fine leg. They did their homework. They realised that on the slow wickets of those two summers, hook and pull shots would not go as fine as on quick wickets.

But I take my hat off to Steeley, coming in against Australia with the attack we had at the time and being as successful as he was at 33, an age which usually heralded the end of a career. It was an amazing effort. At Leeds he scored 73 and 92. I had hoped the wicket would be a fast bowler's dream but I took one in the first innings and Thommo took two, with the reverse happening in the second innings. Fortunately, Gary Gilmour took nine in a low-scoring match which was brought to an unexpected conclusion when vandals, campaigning for the release of the convicted criminal George Davis, vandalised the pitch. The fifth day was ruled out with an even money bet on who would have won, though rain would have prevented a result anyway.

At last I got some measure of the Grey Ghost at The Oval, bowling him for 39 in the first innings as we ripped them out for 191. I had him again in the second innings, caught behind by Rod Marsh, but not until he had scored 66 as England fought back, following on 341 runs behind. They amassed 538 in their second innings and with so much time lost to rain there wasn't enough time for either side to force a result, even though the game ran into six days.

One truly memorable thing about the series was that my father, who had never been outside Western Australia, made a surprise visit. He turned up at Lord's on the day we were bowling. I didn't know he was watching as I took the first four wickets, three of them lbw. There were some rumblings over the fact that the umpire was Australian Bill Alley, silly as it sounds. He was one of the fairest umpires of all time. I guess it was because there were three out of four, but that was mainly because I bowled very straight.

It was great Dad was there to see me make my highest score. I saw him in the crowd when I reached my 50 and held the bat up to him. He was easy to pick out because he was wearing a purple safari suit and stood out like a beacon. It fitted him beautifully but by the end of the tour it seriously needed letting out. People were fabulous to him. He was rarely seen without a beer in his hand and was always being invited out to dinner.

We won the series 1–0 and retained the Ashes, which was a very good bonus after losing to the West Indies in the World Cup final. At the end of our trip, we were presented with Wombles, huge things. One of the team didn't want to cart his home, so I ended up with two, and I nursed them all the way home on the plane. I regret giving them away when the children grew up because they brought back such good memories of a fantastic tour, successful and with a good group of blokes.

We were given an instant chance to avenge that defeat as the West Indies were the visitors to Australia in 1975–76. They were just building up to their mighty peak in fast bowling, with Michael Holding and Andy Roberts plus Keith Boyce and Bernard Julien as back-up. We won the series 5–1, which shows just how good we were at the time, especially when you look at their top order: Roy Fredericks, Gordon Greenidge, Lawrence Rowe, Alvin Kallicharran, Viv Richards and Clive Lloyd – and that was without Rohan Kanhai. We had a good attack and our batting was absolutely superb but the West Indies were only just emerging as a really potent fast-bowling attack.

In Brisbane we beat them comfortably by eight wickets after bowling them out for 214 and 370. I took three wickets in both innings but it was the batting of the Chappell brothers that won the match. Ian scored 41 and 74 not out while Greg scored 123 in the first innings and 109 not out in the second, the two steering us to victory with an unbroken stand of over 150. Greg had taken over as captain after Ian announced his retirement during the last Ashes match.

The West Indies promptly bounced back in Perth, thrashing us by an innings and 87 runs even though Ian Chappell scored 156 in an Australian first innings total of 329. In response, West Indies ran up a massive 585 with big centuries from Roy Fredericks and Clive Lloyd. Thommo, Ashley Mallett, Gary Gilmour and I all had the dubious distinction of conceding over 100 runs apiece. Even though Michael Holding pulled a groin muscle in our second innings, Andy Roberts ripped through our top order to bowl us out for 169, taking 7–54.

At that point, it looked as though we were set up for a fantastic series. In Brisbane they had taken us on and scored their runs quickly but kept losing wickets. I remember looking up at the scoreboard and seeing them at 125 off 20-odd overs but with six wickets down. Then in Perth, on a beautiful track, they ripped us apart. Their bowlers just bowled a beautiful line and length while we tried to bounce them out. At one stage they were 130-1 after just 14 overs.

We had a team meeting after the second Test and decided it was back to basics. One advantage we had was that Viv Richards was not batting to his usual high standards, at least until Dr Rudi Webster, who had diagnosed my stress fracture, put him under hypnosis and helped him to recover his form. I wish he had just stuck to helping me.

In the third Test in Melbourne we put our game back together and regained the initiative with an eight-wicket victory as Thommo and I cleaned up with nine wickets between us in their first innings. The two of us then leant a hand with the bat, sharing a 56-run stand as I scored 25 before going to Holder caught by Richards, and Thommo went on to score 44. A century from Clive Lloyd was not enough to turn the game around for the West Indies and we were left needing just 52 for victory.

I missed the Sydney Test, suffering with pleurisy, at which we retained the Frank Worrell Trophy, but was well enough to return for the fifth in Adelaide, where we began to see the value of Rudi Webster's work with Viv as he opened. Thommo took his wicket in the first innings and I bowled him in the second – but not before he had scored a superb century. The wickets were shared around between Thommo, Gilmour,

Mallett and myself, as we ensured we won the series with another comfortable victory.

That Test was notable for another reason: I found myself bowling first change instead of opening in the first innings. The new ball was given to Gary Gilmour and Thommo and I was left fuming until I eventually got to bowl. I ran in and bowled a whole lot of rubbish, so much so that Greg came running up and demanded to know what I was doing; he had given me an off-side field and I was firing everything down leg.

I was annoyed and frustrated at being usurped and this was my protest but Rod Marsh, thankfully, came up when he saw what was going on. I told him I was upset, not so much at being used as first change, but at not having been told before we went out to field that, for the first time, I would not be opening the bowling for my country. Rod said he knew how I felt but added, 'Doing what you're doing is playing into Greg's hands – do you want him to have that satisfaction?'

That was all I needed. I bowled well after that and in the final Test took 5–63 in their first innings, including the wickets of Richards, admittedly after he had scored 50, and Lloyd, who was second top scorer with 37 in a total of 160. It still didn't stop Greg from changing things round in the second innings, but I took three more wickets and we came out very convincing winners in the match and the series.

The emergence of Viv Richards was one of the most significant factors of the series. He was clearly a batsman who could rip you apart in a very short time once he got going, as we began to see in the second half of the series.

I was satisfied with my total of 27 wickets, despite missing a Test, and with hauls of seven and eight in Melbourne. Years later, Melbourne was where I was expected to break the world record. My success rate at the MCG on good batting tracks was excellent. Melbourne, Adelaide and Sydney all demanded bloody hard work, and I worked differently and certainly a lot harder in those places than on the fast pitch in Perth. There you expected it to happen but it did not always. It had been a long, hard season during which I was asked to bowl an awful lot.

After the West Indies, I was asked to play with the International

Wanderers on a tour to South Africa under manager Richie Benaud. It was to be the first official multi-racial team to go to South Africa. A strong squad included Ian and Greg Chappell, Ashley Mallett, Alan Hurst, Martin Kent, Gary Gilmour, Mike Denness, Derek Underwood, Bob Taylor, Glenn Turner and John Morrison.

I was not included in the original squad but Ian Chappell called me when he had to return home on business and asked if I would replace him. I had not played for around a month I guess, and Helen was six months pregnant with Dean. I had not even thought about cricket and hadn't tried to keep in shape. In fact, I had deliberately let my body rest and my muscles heal by doing absolutely nothing. It was probably not the smart way to do it but it suited me to let my body completely recover after the season. It was never a problem to get back into my fitness programme at short notice.

To persuade me to go, Richie offered me an incentive per wicket which promised a nice little bonus with the baby on the way. We worked it out that Helen could safely fit in a trip.

On the way there, we were just taking off from Madagascar when there was a big bang and we came back down again, pulling up what seemed to me to be 40 or 50 metres from the edge of the cliff and the ocean. We taxied back and it was announced that a bird had flown into an engine, shutting it down. The pilot said he had had thirty seconds to make a decision whether to continue or to pull out. It affected me deeply and I didn't fancy taking off in the same plane again, but we did. I suppose I was a bit touchy with Helen being pregnant. She nearly had the baby on the spot.

It may have been a multi-racial trip but one thing that really stuck in my craw was when John Shepherd of Kent, who was of Caribbean descent, was made an honorary white to allow him to get into hotels and restaurants. It upset him, the entire team, and me, but what could we do? Obviously, there was a lot of baggage that would take more than a band of wandering cricketers to shift.

Naturally, I was uneasy about the possible problems before I went but I thought I could do more by being there than by staying away. It was an opportunity to go to South Africa and see for myself. I despised apartheid and felt I was playing my part in helping to break it down – but many things stuck in the throat, with the black citizens of South Africa being treated as second class.

In Johannesburg I went for a jog and had completed no more than half a lap when I thought my lungs were going to collapse. Later, in the nets, I wondered just how unfit I was before I realised it was the altitude affecting me rather than a lack of fitness. I backed off a bit after that and took it in small chunks, but I had just a few days before my first big game, having already played rather badly in a two-day, warm-up game.

During the long 1975–76 season just finished, my boots had worn out. There were virtually no sprigs left in them and I was slipping all over the place. So I rang Hope Sweeney, the guy who made my boots in Australia, and he had a pair almost ready. Fortunately, he knew a pilot on one of the airlines and they arrived in time for the second innings.

We came across some strange people on that trip. One night I took a call at some ungodly hour and a South African guy, very pleased with himself because Pollock had smashed us around the ground, gave me an earful, telling me how good the South Africans were and how poor we were, in particular me. I slammed the phone down, annoyed with this man for disturbing my sleep and with the hotel for putting the call through in the early hours of the morning.

The next day I was still seething about the unauthorised alarm call and I zipped through the South African batting. Having taken none for plenty in the first innings, I took eight for very few in the second, against a side which included Richards, Pollock, Barlow, Bacher and Irvine. I bowled very quickly – quicker than anyone they had faced since their exclusion. We had them nine down when we ran out of time. I wish to this day I had the caller's number because I would have loved to return the call and ask if he had changed his opinions.

We boarded a plane the same night and, having bowled my heart out, travelled across to Durban, arriving very late with an early start the next day. After two nights with not much sleep, I was not highly delighted when we lost the toss and were put in the field.

After the rigours of altitude in Johannesburg, it was humid in Durban, and bowling again after a maximum effort the previous day was a penance. It was my first experience of such a big change in playing conditions and being expected to perform on request.

The South Africans were playing to win, just as they always did. Greg Chappell had a run-in with an umpire in Durban. Three pretty dicey lbws were given against us right at the end of the session. After having been in a strong position, we were suddenly five wickets down and struggling. The next day we were quickly hustled out and, with the same umpire at the end I was bowling, I hit Barry Richards right in front of middle stump – not out. I did exactly the same in my second over but that was given not out, too. Greg went up to the umpire and asked him what was going on – three the day before were dicey and two plumb today. The umpire said he took a dim view of the comment and Greg answered him in kind and walked away. It was no more than an exchange.

Later, Greg came in and smashed a ball through the covers. Lee Irvine took the ball on the bounce and the umpire, with hardly an appeal, gave him out. Greg just stood there. He remembered in 1966, brother Ian, in the middle of a rough trot, nicked one just short of gully and the same thing happened to him. In that case, the other South African slips said it wasn't caught and the fielder said he caught it on first bounce. History was not to repeat itself. Irvine confirmed he'd caught it and, furious, Greg stormed off the ground. He went straight up to see Max Walker who had been videoing the innings. They replayed it and saw it was clearly not out.

In the bar afterwards, Greg went up to Irvine and said, 'I thought you nodded that you caught the ball?'

'Yes,' he said. 'I caught it. But you didn't ask me if I caught it on the bounce.'

It seemed that was how they played their cricket over there. Greg said the incident proved it didn't pay to argue with the umpires because they will always have the final say.

Generally, I found the South Africans were very like the Australians, playing very hard on the pitch and then throwing their arms around your shoulders afterwards, having a few drinks and a chat, and straight back into it the next day. They were fantastic hosts and I will never forget Eddie Barlow inviting us around to his house for a barbecue. It was just like the ones at home, totally different from England.

CHAPTER TEN

The Miracle Match and Viv Richards

The date was 12 December 1976 and, in the semi-final of the Gillette Cup, Western Australia were to play the holders, Queensland, with the winners meeting Victoria in the final. What could have been a disaster turned into what has become known as the Miracle Match.

There was little sign of it at the start. Queensland, with their superstars Australian captain Greg Chappell, the best batsman in the world Viv Richards and my old mate Jeff Thomson, put Western Australia in to bat on a beautiful, cloudless morning with the ground rapidly filling up.

With players such as skipper Rod Marsh, future Australian captain Kim Hughes and me, we fancied our chances on our own ground and were looking for a big score off our 40 eight-ball overs. But we were soon in trouble when Bruce Laird was brilliantly caught at slip by Ogilvie off a fired up Thommo, reducing us to 8–1.

It was a bad start but recoverable. Rick Charlesworth and Langer carried us to 50 before Langer was bowled by Geoff Dymock. Then the wickets went down with a clatter. Charlesworth was caught in front by Phil Carlson, Serjeant went the same way, lbw, Rod Marsh was caught by Viv Richards and Kim Hughes was bowled by a Carlson inswinger – suddenly we were 6–51 with Dymock having taken 3–20 off his eight overs.

Bruce Yardley and Ian Brayshaw pulled us back to 76 before Yardley was brilliantly caught behind the wicket by John Maclean off Greg Chappell. I went to the same bowler for a duck, Brayshaw was run out by Dymock and we were all out for a woeful 77.

It had been a difficult morning to say the least. With the 10 a.m. start, the ball was swinging and seaming all over the place. The day had warmed up nicely for Queensland and it was doubtful whether we would get anything like the assistance after lunch. It left us no sort of target and while I usually ate extremely healthily between innings in a one-day game, especially when I had to bowl, this time I ate a very large, compensatory meal of fish and chips instead of the usual fruit and carbs.

As we were getting dressed to go out, I said out loud, 'We *will* win this match.' Everyone looked at me like I was a dummy, and I have to admit my aim was to try to lift the atmosphere in the dressing room. Rod Marsh looked over the depressed faces and drooping shoulders and, just as he was about to lead us out on to the field, said there were three things he wanted to tell us. The first thing was that a lot of people had paid a lot of money to see us perform and we had disappointed them, and to keep this in mind when we went out. The second thing was he wanted us to bowl and field like we had never bowled and fielded before, to go out proudly and give 150 per cent. He turned on his heel, adding, 'Now come on,' and stormed out of the door with fire and brimstone coming out of his ears.

Rick Charlesworth, a doctor and a former Olympic hockey player, stopped him in his tracks.

'Excuse me, Rod.'

'Yeah?' said Rod, turning back.

'I just wanted to know what the third point was.'

Rod marched off, steaming more than ever, while for the rest of us the tension eased a little with stilted giggles.

When we went out, it appeared that not one spectator had left the ground, even after our miserable innings. What support and inspiration that was for each and every one of us.

Queensland were a pretty decent team and, even leaving aside Viv Richards and Greg Chappell, they had a competent batting side with a couple of decent all-rounders. I knew we had to get rid of Greg and Viv quickly and thought if we did that they might just panic. I thought if I bowled line and length they would get the runs but if I was aggressive and tried to blast them out by taking them on, we would either win it or be hammered off the face of the earth.

My plan was to try to get rid of Viv, even if I had to give away a few runs to get him playing his shots, which he loved to do. I was aiming to get him out on the hook with a bouncer, which was allowed in the one-day game in those days.

I charged in for the first over and bowled him four bouncers in a row with my first four balls, thinking I could probably get away with it in the circumstances. Initially, I did and it wasn't until after the third one that the umpire had a quiet word with me. As I walked back, Bruce Yardley, who was closest to me, ran up with the ball, worried the umpires would take me off after the warning. But I brushed him aside.

I bowled a fourth bouncer and this time the umpire left me and everyone else in no doubt that this was a serious warning. The next ball I bowled in Viv's block hole. He played it easily and as I walked back for the sixth, I made a signal to square-leg to drop back, to try to kid Viv that I was about to bowl yet another bouncer. I charged in but bowled a good length. Viv was already on the back foot, anticipating the bouncer, and the ball went between bat and pad and bowled him.

I then had Alan Jones dropped by Bruce Yardley but we quickly made amends with a spectacular catch in the slips by Mick Malone, diving forward to dismiss Ogilvie. Greg came in and my plan for him was to bowl six to nine inches outside the off stump and draw him in, but Rod walked down the leg side and put a hand up for me to bowl a high one, a foot outside leg stump. I charged in, everything went perfectly and

Greg gloved it. Rod had already moved across and took the catch.

Mick Malone trapped Phil Carlson leg before and had Alan Jones caught, and suddenly the title holders were 5–35 and in trouble.

Wayne Clark and Mick Malone picked up more wickets and the now packed WACA were going crazy, chanting 'Kill . . . kill . . . kill' as I came in for my second spell. The gritty Maclean was run out off my bowling by Dennis Schuller's bad call and I had the tailender caught in the gully. We had bowled them out and won by 11 runs in the most extraordinary game – I felt thrilled to have been part of such an occasion, especially as we won. The match has been replayed on television many times. We even had a 25th anniversary dinner for it and 600 people turned up.

The game was between two very strong sides and Queensland had already beaten us earlier in the season. Greg made them strong mentally and they always had a good import every season, this time the outstanding Viv Richards. Greg had given them a blueprint for success. He gave them confidence and helped bring on the youngsters. Thommo moved from Sydney and made his home there and much of the credit for that must go to Greg.

I had a great deal of respect for Viv and I suppose we were two of the fiercest competitors around at the time. He hated fast bowlers and I hated batsmen. We made no effort to socialise. Off the field, we were civil to each other, but only just. There were not many batsmen prepared to come down the wicket to fast bowlers and threaten them like he did, while I gave him no mercy and was prepared to die out there on the pitch. He was the first batsman I came across with the same combative attitude as me. He just wanted to smash fast bowlers, and it seemed particularly me, out of the park.

The strange thing is that since retiring from cricket, I have really enjoyed his company, in much the same way that I got to like Mike Brearley when we stopped playing cricket against each other. I never took the time to get to know him when we were playing, I suppose because he was the England captain. There was something about that I didn't want to know; we were opposition. Captains were prime targets for me. If the captain is struggling, it creates a rudderless ship. That was a bit of a theory anyway but, basically, the captain was in charge of a team who wanted to beat us.

At least Viv treated me with some respect. I would hear him say things like 'shit ball' to certain bowlers but he never did that to me, certainly not in my hearing. I never saw his lips move other than to chew gum.

With us it was more the stare than the words. He would make his point early on by playing a shot and then he would walk down the pitch as if to say, 'I am in control.' I remember him, chewing furiously, tapping down an imaginary bump and then making eye contact, which was pretty rare for a batsman in those days. It was just a look and then back to work. Viv reckoned in his autobiography that he learned the stare from me.

Some batsmen, when I gave them a stare or put hands on hips in front of them, would quickly look away. He did not. I tried never to be personal, just the occasional swear word and more often than not regretted it afterwards. It was the result of a fuse blowing and not premeditated.

I loved bowling to Viv. I had no fear of it. I enjoyed the challenge because I knew he was going to try to assert himself, and if he did it was bang, bang, bang and 25 were on the board. Then he would settle down and play properly like a normal genius, as though he was determined to make runs, and he usually did. We worried when he started like that but if he started like a normal human being we felt we were in with a chance.

We also felt we were in with a chance with an early blast, but if he survived it, we were in trouble. He was one of the most competitive batsmen I bowled to. When he was in the mood, you could bowl him your best ball and he would treat it with contempt. You would adjust your length and he would give it a flat bat through the covers or drive you to the boundary. Your margin for error when he was going like that was virtually nil. There was no real spot to bowl to him because he would create a shot from whatever you bowled.

The records show I got him a lot of times and he scored runs off me a lot of times. It was a nice even contest.

I remember a conversation I had with him some years later, when I was at Northampton. He asked me whether he should wear a helmet; he was reaching the age when he was not sure. I told him there was no shame in it at all. My advice was not to regard it as taking a backward step or belittling his manhood. I told him I thought it was a smart thing to do and if I saw him wearing a helmet next time I played against him, I would say, 'Good on you, mate' – not that he took a blind bit of notice of me. He carried on defiantly with that fearsome shaven head unprotected.

My feeling was that it's no use being macho six feet under, but you have to go with your own beliefs. I have seen too many players hit who could have been killed if they weren't wearing helmets. It has to be said, however, that very few cricketers died before the advent of helmets, and it does seem that batsmen who wear them are hit far more often than those who don't, or didn't. In the old, pre-helmet days, when you saw a short ball you made your decision to duck or put your bat up. Now you can keep your eye on the ball a lot longer before making the decision. With helmets, players back themselves against balls they would have evaded if they didn't have that protection.

As for the final, almost inevitably it faded into near oblivion when compared with the Miracle Match, but it deserved better because it was a magnificent game, too. It was played at the Melbourne Cricket Ground in front of a record crowd of 32,908 – perhaps the first inkling of the powerful attraction of the one-day game. We bowled Victoria out for just 164 but seemed to be heading for certain defeat when we slumped to 74–7. Then up stepped Mick Malone and, with the help of Craig Serjeant and Wayne Clark, he steered us to an unlikely victory with his man-of-the-match innings of 47 not out.

CHAPTER ELEVEN

Pakistan, New Zealand and the Centenary match

Pakistan were the tourists at the end of 1976, and we did not need telling they were getting a lot better at handling pace bowling. It helped from their perspective that Thommo was injured trying for a catch off his own bowling in the first Test in Adelaide. Alan Turner ran in from the leg side and they collided with Turner catching Thommo on the shoulder he had injured before, dislocating his collarbone. This time he had to have a pin inserted and his contribution to the three-match series was 8.5 overs and 2–34.

I also had an unhappy start with 1–104 but after that, things picked up for me. We drew the close-fought first Test and I had to do a lot of bowling in the second innings: 47.7 eight-ball overs, taking 5–163. To put that in context, it's the equivalent of 63.5 overs today, or more than four successive sessions. If ever proof was needed of the value of my extended training sessions, that was it.

In Melbourne we won by 348 runs although after two and a bit days the match seemed to be heading for a draw. We had scored over 500 in our first innings and they were sitting on 270 for two before they collapsed to 333 all out. I took 6–82 in the first innings and 4–53 in the second as Pakistan collapsed again, this time from 85–1 to 128–7 by the close of the fourth day. We bowled them out for 151 on the last morning.

It was during that match I had a run-in with umpire Tom Brooks who began wagging a finger at me over the number of bouncers I bowled. I wagged my finger back at him until Greg intervened to tell me we couldn't afford to upset the umpires. I was concerned at the way I was being treated but Greg tried to explain if I kept it up we would be the losers in the long run. Just then a balloon blew across the field and I caught it, ran in and attempted to bowl it towards the batsman. It was silly but it relieved all the pressure.

If we thought Pakistan were ready to roll over at that point, we were very much mistaken. This was the Pakistan of Imran Khan and Zaheer Abbas, emerging as feared competitors, and the irrepressible Javed Miandad and Asif Iqbal. Previously, Pakistan had fielded a team of players who didn't expect to have any success against us, despite the presence of Saeed Ahmed and the Mohammed brothers, Sadiq and Mushtaq. Now, they offered a much tougher attitude than we had seen from them before. It was a rapidly developing side, more aggressive in every area.

On the first day of the final Test in Sydney, they had us reeling at 198–9 and the fact that we raised 211 was due to the last-wicket stand, with Max Walker and me putting on over 50, the credit going to Max's 34.

Thanks largely to Asif Iqbal's 120, they piled on 360 and again I had a long bowl, taking 3–114. Imran Khan, who took six wickets in our first innings, ripped through us again with another six as we were bowled out for 180. It was so bad that I was third top scorer with my 27. I managed to snap up Sadiq Mohammed and Zaheer Abbas but it was a futile gesture as they levelled the short series with an eight-wicket win.

A month later, we were in New Zealand for a two-Test series and we fancied our chances of a comfortable time, especially when Doug

Walters scored 250 in the first innings and we totalled well over 500. But the Kiwis were obstinate and scored 357 in their first innings, saving the follow-on with the last pair at the wicket.

They then scored 293–8 as they chased a target of 350 to win, holding on at the end with Dayle Hadlee surviving the last hour to earn the draw as I bowled to a field of nine slips and a wicket-keeper. I did my share of bowling with nearly 50 overs in the match for a return of just four wickets.

The second Test went much more to plan and we won by 10 wickets. I took 5–51 in the first innings as we bowled them out for 229, and then went one better with 6–72 in the second innings as we bowled them out again, this time for 175. We knocked off the few runs required with two days to spare. Apparently, my 11–123 was the best Test return in Auckland.

Richard Hadlee was a young tearaway fast bowler. I knew his brother Dayle much better, having played against him in 1970 when I toured with the Australia A team. Dayle injured his back in that series and never bowled fast again. Richard did not have the pace of Dayle, but he came in off a long run and gave it a real go. I remember having a talk with Richard in our dressing room at the end of the game when he asked me about training and diet. He went on record later saying he took what I'd said on board and became quite dedicated to it all. He said watching me on video helped his career. It was a nice compliment from someone who was to go on to be such a success.

It was great to go back to New Zealand, a country I love. They made us very welcome and it was always a great place to tour. That short trip was a good warm-up for the Centenary Test in Melbourne a couple of weeks later, in March 1977, when we took on the Poms. The match was to celebrate a hundred years of Test cricket between England and Australia and the whole thing was just fabulous, the feel of it all, the huge build-up and the history of it. It was a great event, so much so that it almost felt mystical. It meant so much to me and I just could not believe it was happening and that I was involved.

There were a lot of receptions, dinners and functions with former and current Test cricketers – a week of events leading up to the game, plus practice. It was absolutely terrific; some of it was a bit stiff, formal and hard to take, but it was wonderful meeting the greats of yesteryear.

I will never forget one reception just before the match when every single living cricketer who had played for England and Australia was in the one room. I was like a kid in a lolly shop. All my heroes were there from the two countries, and the hairs on the back of my neck were standing up. I half expected W.G. Grace to strut through the door. I didn't think you could have 100 years of cricket without the Doctor being there. The odd thing was I didn't think about an Australian cricketer from the past, but of the famed W.G. Grace.

The game took amazing turns, and the spooky thing was Australia won by the same margin, 45 runs, as they had 100 years earlier. The whole thing was surreal.

John Lever, Bob Willis, Chris Old and Derek Underwood threatened to spoil the party when they bowled us out for a miserable 138 in 43.6 overs. Bob Willis broke Rick McCosker's jaw, forcing him to fall onto his stumps. Before stumps I was able to hit back with the wicket of Bob Woolmer. The next day we came back and finished off the job, bowling them out for 95 with no one scoring 20 as I took 6–26 and Max Walker 4–54.

The second innings was like starting the game all over again but it went well this time. Incredibly, Rick came back to bat at number 10 with a bandage wrapped around his face, insisting on carrying on with no helmet. He couldn't move his jaw. I winced when the first ball he faced was another bouncer from Willis, who said afterwards, 'I had to bowl him a bouncer.' The crowd and our players were incensed but when I reflected on it later, Bob was right. I would have done the same thing in his position.

It was a good job Rick did come back and help add 54 more runs with Rod Marsh because the match was very tight and although we scored 419 in the second innings, with Marsh 110 not out, it was only just enough. At 346–4 England were favourites. Derek Randall, the eventual man-of-the-match, was enjoying the innings of his life, going on to score 174. England came desperately close to beating us and spoiling the party.

I finished with 5–139 off 34.4 overs but the highlight was undoubtedly Randall's innings. It was a knock I will never forget from a nice guy. There is no doubt he had his share of luck and could have been out at any stage but that was the way he batted. He was cheeky, took us on, attacked and played every shot in the book, which was impressive. He was like a circus act, and we had never seen anything like it before. At one stage, he nicked a ball, Rod Marsh dived for it and Derek walked, but Rodney believed it was scooped and called him back. That was fantastic and shows no matter how hard we played, we played fair.

So did Randall, doffing his cap and smiling at us and making remarks such as, 'That was a good one, Mr Lillee.' When I knocked him over he would just pick himself up, dust himself down and then grin down the wicket at me. He also moved around the crease just before actually playing the ball. It got so much that in the end I snarled at him, 'Stand still! It's so much harder to hit a moving target.' It was true and he never kept still. But I did hit him once, a sickening blow on the head, but again he just grinned and said later, 'I was lucky. If it had hit me anywhere else it would have probably killed me but as it hit me on the side of the head it wasn't too bad.' I laughed out loud at that comment.

The Queen came on to the field to meet the players at the afternoon tea break. Just after that Kerry O'Keeffe bowled to Randall and Gary Cosier took a fantastic diving catch at forward short-leg, going backwards. That turned the tide because Randall was the one man who was going to win it. I'm sure it was the Queen who helped us get the crucial wicket. Maybe it was just us courteous colonials making sure the Queen had left the ground before beating England.

I finished it off, taking the wickets of Alan Knott, Chris Old and Derek Underwood and we won a fantastic game, which could have gone either way. With nearly 250,000 watching the Test, it was a truly wonderful occasion.

CHAPTER TWELVE

Packer

While the celebrations were going on at the Centenary Test, World Series Cricket was in an advanced stage of planning. Not many knew about it but I did. I was deeply involved; in fact, I was an integral part of it.

The whole thing began the year before with a suggestion I made to John Cornell. John and Austin Robertson were my managers at the time. John likes to think it was his idea but Austin knows the full story and I am happy to share the credit, as my original suggestion was different from how it ended up.

It came about because of the amount of cricket being played and the fact that it was becoming harder for Test players to hold down regular jobs. Understandably, our employers were saying they could not keep paying us because we were never around and cricket was paying near on nothing. We had reached a Catch-22 situation. The employers weren't going to change their stance, so cricket had to produce the money. The ACB were not prepared to listen or discuss the matter and we were fast heading for an impasse.

My idea was to organise a couple of five-day games, and some one-days, to be played against a World XI at the beginning and end of the season. We were the best side in the world at the time and the Aussie supporters, I reckoned, would love to see the Aussies versus the best of the rest. The matches, which would be additional to the usual Test and one-day cricket, would attract big crowds and command substantial television fees. With the players getting a good percentage of the gate and television money, it would have taken the pressure off the board, who did not want to pay us, and the players, who were feeling the pinch. I was certainly not thinking of splitting the game or provoking a fight with the ACB. I was simply being practical. The Board was making more and more demands on our time and, without a job, we would not be able to support our families.

I knew I could get the players to agree because they had had enough. There was discontent and unrest in the dressing room. I could name seven or eight players straightaway who I was sure would be ready to sign up.

I told John Cornell, his wife Delvene, the actor Paul Hogan and Austin Robertson about my idea in Perth one day, when Hogan was working there. When I had finished, John asked if I had ever heard of Kerry Packer. I hadn't but he explained Packer was a television man, desperate to get cricket on his channel and having no joy with the ACB, who already had a deal with the Australian Broadcasting Commission. John believed Packer would buy in to the idea and fund it.

That was the original seed. From there, we started talking to Packer. Austin and John handled the nuts and bolts of the deal on a day-to-day basis while the rest of us dipped in and out.

John, Austin and Paul went to New Zealand during our tour there to sign up a few players. John, who played 'Strop' in the 'Paul Hogan Show', had a sense of humour. He asked me to arrange a meeting with Doug Walters where no one would see them together, so I asked the curator for a room where I could rest, somewhere on my own where I wouldn't be disturbed. The curator gave me the key to a small dressing room, which I passed on to John, and I sent Doug down at lunchtime.

Doug had no idea what was going on; I'm sure this was the first time they had ever met. John asked if he could borrow a few dollars and Douggie took it seriously until we started laughing. Then he shut the door and told Doug what was happening.

During the Auckland Test, John told me he wanted to test out whether incentives would work, and said he would give me A$200 a wicket. As I was getting A$400 a Test match, it was a lot of money. When I came off, it transpired John had had to return to Sydney on business. Austin found me and said, 'Here's the dough Corney left for you. He said sorry he had to leave so early but he'd promised you he would pay up till he left for the airport, and you were going so well he had to leave early before he ran out of money.' He did eventually pay me in full when I saw him the next time.

I had to withdraw from the 1977 Ashes tour to England, having developed a hot spot in my back again, so I covered it for Channel Nine from their television studios in Sydney. This also meant I was able to talk to Packer without being secretive. Packer was just so keen on sport, and especially cricket. He could not get enough. He would even wait on the end of the telephone while I went to do my piece during the lunch interval and then carry on our discussion when I picked up the receiver again. He would talk for hours.

The initial plan was to run three Super Tests – he wanted more than the two I had originally suggested – plus some one-day games, which he was going to slot in between the official Tests, so they did not interfere. But when the ACB were approached with the plan, they simply said, 'No way,' to which Packer responded, 'Stuff them – it's them versus us now.'

When Tony Greig let it all slip out about his involvement at a party during the tour, all hell broke loose. The story broke in the English newspapers and the ACB immediately issued a statement saying the Australian players were under the threat of suspension if they played for Packer. Greig himself was relieved of the England captaincy, replaced by Mike Brearley.

A newspaper in South Africa revealed that four leading players had signed contracts and a month later, on 11 April, the full story broke in

Packer's newspaper the *Bulletin,* announcing that 35 of the world's leading players had signed up for three years to play World Series Cricket.

Packer rescheduled the games to compete directly with the official matches. It was a massive operation, trying to stage a cricket series outside the official game. He led from the front and while he surrounded himself with experts, he was never afraid of voicing his own opinions and ideas. A good example was when we were unable to find good enough grounds, and there was no time to get other pitches up to standard. It reached the stage where Packer suggested we should build our own so we could put them into any ground we wanted. It made sense, especially as time was running short. He came up with the idea of growing wickets in tubs with heating rods running through them, so the grass grew quicker and gave a better coverage more rapidly. By this means, Packer ensured that at least the wickets were good, something everyone thought was impossible.

The first game was played later that year at Waverley Park, way out of Melbourne. Packer and the Victorian Football League struck a deal, and Packer erected the first floodlights for a cricket ground. There could not have been more than 200 people there. It was an empty concrete jungle, but we played good competitive cricket. We played it like a Test match, Australia against the World XI. One problem was that the cranes they used to position the tubs desecrated the area around the pitch, particularly the run-up. No one had told the drivers to come in from the sides of the pitch area instead of going top and bottom. The run-up was completely disturbed and then top-dressed with a bit of sand. It was uneven and slippery for anyone who ran in fast.

I had injury problems for the first game, and I wished I was still injured for the second one when they scored 625 all out and the first wicket fell at 369! This was at Gloucester Park in Perth and this wicket also had dodgy run-ups. In fact, as most of the grounds in the first season were not normal grassed surfaces, in most cases running in to bowl was like running through sand, uneven and maybe even moving a little. It was dangerous and unsettling for fast bowlers. No one had considered this and it is often the small things which can destroy such a project.

At Gloucester Park, you didn't know where to put the ball, especially against Barry Richards and Gordon Greenidge; they must have thought it was their birthday. In the end, I thought I did pretty well to have figures of 4–149. It was a case of bowling and hoping, especially the way they batted. It was an amazing opening partnership. It helped that I took 5–82 in the second innings as the wicket broke down just a little to give me a reasonable analysis.

However, John Maley, our curator, was the ace up our sleeves. John was a former player – an attacking batsman – whom we always thought should have been a West Indian with his cavalier style of cricket. He even had a craving for rum and raisin chocolate bars. He proved to be not only a hard worker but also very innovative. He took it all on board and worked day and night to make sure the pitches were right.

Gloucester Park was a trotting ground opposite the WACA with no pitch at all. The middle had been neglected and it wasn't even flat. They rolled it, put in turf and when I went to check the progress, there were ladies in hats planting grass tuft by tuft to get good coverage. It helped that money was no object, but John made sure that we had a very good wicket, flat and true. Not enough credit was given to him. The pitches were slow but safe, well prepared and made to last. The credibility of WSC could have gone down the drain had the pitches been bad. John played a back-room part but it was probably one of the most important roles.

There was an awful lot of animosity between the State sides and the players who were involved in the World Series. It was so bad in Victoria that the players were told not to mix socially with the Packer players. We were basically *persona non grata* in cricket.

One day I was in a grocery store when I saw a guy I had played cricket with for years. When he spotted me he ducked his head and made to go in another direction. I walked up and said, 'Hi mate, how's it going?' He was too embarrassed to talk to me. I asked him, 'How are you?' and, 'What's happening?' all without any response. It was a short, one-way conversation and in the end I bade him a sad, 'Goodbye.' It was all very emotional for me.

We did not realise it was going to be as bad as it turned out and it made us bind together to fight against this huge negative force arrayed against us. In Perth, the written press basically ignored us. I took that very hard in my own State. It was almost as if we did not exist, or WSC was unimportant. If they did mention it, it was in a totally derogatory way. They didn't even try to understand the position of the players, just referring to us as mercenaries. It hurt me to the core. In the other States where the Packer group was involved, the newspapers were split into three, those for, those against and those who were still making up their minds. It was much more balanced. I would have thought the smart people would have waited, especially as tennis had already gone through this same business and the sport had emerged stronger than ever. I found it hard to get their feel for it, maybe because I was so involved, but I could not understand why we were pilloried.

When I was introduced to Kerry Packer, he treated me like a mate, a good friend, and I felt the same towards him. There was a passionate side to him and he had a big heart, but I also discovered there was another side which was tough. He was ferociously uncompromising about everything he believed in and stood for. Seeing him in action first-hand, I quickly realised what power he wielded.

When he went into cricket, he had so many good ideas about televising it. He brought in the best people and sent them to America to check on all the new technology and ideas for television coverage of sport. In the old days, the Australian Broadcasting Commission had one camera at one end of the ground and one side-on to the pitch, but Packer decided he was going to have eight camera points. Everyone thought that was odd until they saw it working. He was a perfectionist and expected perfection from other people. There is no doubt he moved the one-day game on internationally and brought about important changes, not least in terms of rewards for the players involved, and more importantly for the next generation of players.

He did a lot for players in terms of simply looking after them and their families; flying in wives for Christmas, inviting everybody around to his house. One Christmas there was an airline strike and a mate of

Packer's, who was in mining, chartered a plane to fly back to Perth. Packer asked him if he would take Rod Marsh, Bruce Laird and me with him.

Christmas was always difficult for the players from Perth because of the traditional fixture in Melbourne, starting on Boxing Day. We did everything we could to spend at least part of Christmas day at home with the family. Our routine was to get up at about 5 a.m., to give out Christmas presents, have a quick breakfast and then head for the 11 a.m. flight. Usually you had to be at a Test venue two days before a game to recover from the travelling, but for this match we suffered with jetlag because of the three-hour time difference and the fact that we had got up so early. We never thought about it. We did that every year for 14 years because of the Boxing Day tradition; we accepted it as part of our Christmas.

Nowadays, the players probably have their families join them three days beforehand but we weren't professionals and we couldn't afford it. When Packer came on the scene, we earned good money and yet he was big-hearted enough to help us out. It was much appreciated.

Packer loved every minute of the cricket to the extent that he would even put on pads and have a hit against Ashley Mallett and the others. He wasn't a good player but he just wanted to see what it was like. But he was also strict and the West Indies were almost thrown out because they started to complain about minor issues. He was a strong man, a tough man, who didn't mess around, but in all my dealings with him he was totally fair and everything he promised he delivered.

I had one interesting peek into the inner sanctum. Someone came into his office to present some idea to him and dropped down in a chair without being invited. He was out on his ear. It didn't matter if he had the best package available. I will never forget the look on the bloke's face; he couldn't believe it.

Considering the lack of preparation time, the entire thing ran like clockwork. I believe it had a lot to do with the fact that Packer, who was the equivalent of the Board of Control, listened to the players whereas in the past, the players and the Board were always on a collision course.

This was so refreshing. Packer always wanted to know how playing conditions could be improved and he consulted the players, even about such matters as accommodation. This engendered a good feeling, with the players being away from home for months at a time. We stayed in four and five-star hotels in comparison to the hotels booked by the board, which were usually three star, sometimes two and even less on the subcontinent.

Packer led the whole shooting match, but it was Packer the company and not just him alone. His people related everything to the players and involved us in discussions – so much so that it was almost like a Players' Association. In fact, Packer encouraged us to form an association and continue with it after the amalgamation with the ACB. There was, of course, resistance because the Board thought we wanted to run the game ourselves. It took a while, but a Players' Association was started 15 years after WSC.

In the first year, the format was six five-day Super Tests, three versus the West Indies and three versus the World XI; plus the Country Cup, which consisted of 14 two and three-day matches to keep the players who were not playing fit; and the International Cup, which was a series of six one-day matches. I thought it worked very well.

The only real problem was when players suddenly found themselves out of form; there wasn't much we could do to put it right. We played against top-tier players only, even in country games, and if you were an out-of-touch batsman, it didn't help to find yourself facing Imran Khan and Sarfraz Nawaz. There was simply no chance of playing yourself back into form against lesser players.

But those country games certainly worked for the spectators. They loved them. We went to country towns, played good cricket, did some coaching and signed autographs. The papers were saying the players were rebels, pirates, and should be outcast, but the country people said, 'Bulldust. They are coaching our kids, playing great cricket and they are our heroes.' It shows what a good move it was to go to the country. We took the game to people who usually watched it on television and made the long trips to the big games. Apart from that, those games played a vital role in keeping everyone match fit.

The night games always attracted reasonable crowds, but the Super Tests were a bit demoralising in that first year, playing in front of 200 or 300 people per day. Packer had invested, and lost, a lot of money, but he was happy with the fact that the cricket was going well. It continued to be competitive and taken seriously by those playing. In fact, the cricket was some of the best I ever played. It may have been on rolled clay in drop-in trays, which improved a bit in the second year, but I loved it. The players were worried about the lack of crowds, but forward-thinking people were already realising television was the future of the game. Anxious to get more people into the grounds, players started to do many more promotional visits, which was also the future of the game. It was the way the world of sport was going.

I had been watching Michael Holding, and his economy of move-ment during the run-up was impressive. He lost no pace and his arms were pretty still compared with the way mine flapped about, so I decided to make a concerted effort to change my action during the off-season. Austin Robertson's father, Austin senior, helped me learn how to run. He had been a professional sprinter, and held the 140-yards world record for 30 years.

I realised my run-up by comparison with Holding's was counter-productive, and I was wasting a lot of energy in the field, too, chasing balls and running around the boundary. I reckoned I could save up to 20 per cent of my energy in the outfield and bowling. I wasn't happy with the season's figures – 21 wickets at an average 36.42 in the five Tests – and felt I was at the crossroads as a fast bowler.

I always reassessed at the end of every season, looking critically at my action and training methods to see how I could improve, and seeking professional help if I felt I needed it. Of course, watching Holding day in and day out and being mesmerised by his fluency and grace, destroyed the old myth of the fast bowler running in as hard as he could to generate pace. Watching Michael and Andy Roberts certainly helped me later on when I went into coaching. They just glided in without any loss of pace.

More players were recruited for the second season, bringing in Clive Rice, Garth Le Roux, Javed Miandad and Sarfraz Nawaz among others. The concept of WSC was taken up a peg, too. In the first year, it was Australia versus a World XI and the West Indies, but in the second year, the World XI was to include the best West Indians. The West Indies side at that time would have held up in any era; to combine them with the best of the rest presented us with a monumental task and we had to fight hard to survive. Viv Richards who, in six Super Tests, had scored 862 runs at 86.2, summed up the quality of the opposition. Imagine those statistics being added to his record. The fact that the World Series statistics were never officially recognised was cruel because those runs and wickets were earned the hard way.

The format also changed. Not only did we have a Super Test in New Zealand but there was to be day–night cricket and a round robin to the final with winner takes all in terms of prize money. What Packer said was what he meant and the losers got zippo. There was no secret agreement to share the money after the game. It was played for real with the winners literally taking all. The losers just picked up their normal wages.

I worry about the future of sport with so much money coming in. I don't mind how much players earn, but I am all for a small base on the contract with the rest made up in incentives for doing well. That would include turning up for practice on time and all the pre-season training, with tests to prove your fitness. I am big on that. The system wouldn't bother the true professional because he does the right thing anyway, but it would sort out some of the others. I felt so strongly about it I happily backed the winner takes-all idea when it was put forward.

It was quite a concept for the players to play and take nothing, but we were on pretty good money anyway – especially compared with the miserly amount the Board had paid us – so this was more like a bonus if the team won. The lure of the big pot to be split up between the team drove us on. It was a substantial amount. For some guys, it was almost half of their salary.

The odd thing is that we didn't think about it once a game started. If you think about the money, you forget the work that's needed to win the money. Put everything in and the results will come; think about the rewards and it can confuse the process of getting to those rewards. That lesson stayed with me. I spoke about it when I was invited to talk to the Australian team many years later, after I had retired.

Before the new season started, there was the worry that we hadn't exactly pulled in the crowds, nor set television records apart from for the one-day matches; but establishment cricket was not doing well either. The first year had shown a lot of promise but it needed something extra to encourage the crowds to come. We knew we could win them over given the chance. Once they turned on their television sets, they would see our cricket was the best. In the off-season, John Cornell organised for an advertising agency, Mojo, to make a radio jingle and a television advert. When he played the jingle to me, I wasn't at all sure about it, although it was a very catchy number, 'C'mon, Aussie, C'mon', with lots of pertinent words added. He insisted it would grow on me and it did. Strange as it may sound, I believe using the jingle was one of the turning points for World Series Cricket.

The second season was much better than the first. With the help of politician Neville Wran, Packer was able to hire proper grounds, not through the ACB but through the trusts, including Sydney Cricket Ground Trust and Brisbane Trust. We played the first game of the season at the Sydney Cricket Ground. During a break in play, John Cornell said Packer wanted to see me. There were around 7,000 or 8,000 people in the ground, far from full, and I wondered if this was the end of the road for a brave and bold idea. When I arrived in his room upstairs, a number of other people were there, too. He called me over and took me to a window that looked out over the parkland at the back of the SCG. There were about 20,000 people trying to get in, with huge queues waiting at the gates. He put his arm around my shoulder and said, 'We've made it.'

The capacity of the ground was reduced to 40,000 because of renovation work and we must have turned away 15,000. From that moment, we knew we would win. Negotiations with the authorities began and I knew Packer would get what he wanted and we would get what we wanted.

I got off to a good start in the New Zealand Super Test, with 7–59 and 5–30 against a World XI at the Mount Smart Stadium in Auckland – but I take no credit. The pitch was so loaded in the favour of the bowler it was ridiculous. We bowled first and knocked them over. The pitch had seam and swing, as all New Zealand pitches do, but this one had pace as well. It was an athletics field and Maley had visited to sort it out for them.

There were a number of dressing rooms, round the back of the pavilion, and one of them had been allocated to the physios. As we walked past, I heard Collis King in the room having treatment because I had hit him on the thigh. When I popped my head around the corner, he grinned, and said, 'Come and see what you have done to me.' On his black skin was a red mark almost like the start of the bruise with a perfect imprint of the seam. They were about to apply ice but he still had the grace to laugh.

Ian Davis, known to everyone as the 'Wizard', was a very nervous player; he was extra nervous about going in to bat after seeing what had happened in their innings. He was quickly into the toilets before he went out, as is the practice of most batsmen at this level, as the nerves attacked. We had got hold of some big firecrackers about the size of a medium cigar and Mick Malone had strung six or seven of them together. When Ian went into the toilets, we all gathered around as they were thrown in.

You can imagine how loud the noise was in the confined space. The door flew open and there was Wiz with black smoke dust all over his flannels, standing there in total shock. He went out to face some of the fastest bowling in the world, face blank and without a word. He didn't last long. Richard Hadlee was allowed to play in that match, with the New Zealand cricket board's blessing. We were coming out of our isolation.

The atmosphere was a lot more settled in the second season than the first; we were getting the feel for it. Before that, we had never mixed with the opposition much, apart from a handful of people, but now we were travelling and staying together and there was much more of a comfort zone. I wasn't a fan of it but at the time we were being ostracised, not just by the cricket authorities, but also by people we thought were friends within cricket. So this drew us all together a lot more than it would have done otherwise. It was almost a siege mentality. We felt we were achieving something, playing well and proving we were the best.

It was hard work, harder for some than others, and we still had to contend with the fact that if you were out of form, there was nowhere to retreat to find it again. We were not allowed to play on any ground connected with the Board, nor could we play for our clubs, so there was no Shield cricket, no club cricket, nothing. We trained like hell but playing against a World side or the West Indies without any match practice was tough.

I ended up taking Western Australia to court on grounds of restraint of trade. I wanted to play cricket in between the World Series games but they had banned me from all Western Australian clubs, even though I was captain, coach and professional at Melville. On the day we were due in court, Bert Rigg arrived to represent the WACA. He was president of my old club, Perth, and a man whom I did, and still do, love very much.

They believed totally in what they were doing and I believed in what I was standing up for. Everyone else was waiting for this case before decisions were made on all the other players who had played for Packer. Back-court proceedings were held and the WACA settled with us 20 minutes after we should have started our day in court. The judge came out and told me I could play club cricket.

Kerry Packer backed me all the way, paying all my costs. I appreciated his support as I had supported him from the start, and I was still heavily involved in the administration.

In the one-day matches, I took 23 wickets at 12.56 and in the Super Tests I took 23 wickets at 16.82, including 7–23 against the West Indies. I remember that one plainly, rare for me, and not because of the score but because I had three days off before the game. Usually, I would have practised or run but instead I went to see my accountant Kim Butler in Newcastle, New South Wales, and all I did was some swimming and light jogging on the beach, and generally relaxed. It meant I came to the game so refreshed. I had never gone so many days before a big game without touching a cricket ball. My rhythm was fabulous.

When we batted, I copped one on my fingers from Andy Roberts and I didn't know if it was broken or not. I kept it taped up and when I bowled I kept looking at it, thinking to myself, 'You guys are going to suffer for the pain.' They did.

There was a very acrimonious series final against the World XI at Sydney Show Grounds because of the antipathy between Tony Greig, their captain, and Ian Chappell. We felt towards the end that Greig's game had diminished. Greig was carrying on as only he could, always pretty pleased with himself. We went for his throat to try to make sure he made no runs and took no wickets. He was probably at the end of his career but didn't realise it, and we were getting at him on the pitch.

It was a real quick bouncy wicket, which accounted for two low first-innings scores, and it remained a tight game until Barry Richards scored a second-innings century and turned it round to help them to a five-wicket win.

After that, WSC went off to the West Indies, which is a great spot to tour from almost every point of view as the people love their cricket and are always very sociable. Generally, we were treated very well in the Caribbean. But some of the hotels were not great in those days, and there were social problems, especially in Jamaica where we simply could not go out of our hotel because it was deemed too dangerous. We were even told not to go out in cars as people were being attacked at the traffic lights. To be told that is enough to make anyone nervous and it didn't helped when Gary Gilmour, with whom I was sharing a room, woke me in the early hours of one morning, insisting he had seen a flashlight beam across our room. Then it happened again. We reached for a couple of bats and opened the window on to the balcony, only to be greeted by the whooshing of helicopter blades – the police checking on our hotel as well as the others. What a relief!

In the first match in Jamaica, we bowled the West Indies out for 188 in their first innings. They trailed us by 62 runs when they came in again, but Clive Lloyd scored 197 out of a 226-run partnership with Andy Roberts, who made 89 before being run out. It was an amazing partnership and very annoying for us; but for them the game would have been ours.

Over the years, Andy nailed us a few times with the bat. He wasn't stylish but he was straight and was in behind the ball. Once he got going, he had lovely timing and hit the ball well with genuine shots. There was no real flair but he was very efficient and could handle the bat well, just as Joel Garner could.

The tour was going quite well but there were some problems. In Barbados, for instance, the West Indies were in trouble against the pace of Thommo and me. We had each taken three in the first innings and I snatched another three in the second. They steadied the ship after losing a couple of early wickets but then Roy Fredericks was out lbw. The crowd picked up on his unhappiness at the decision and went mad. They were behind wire netting but they started throwing bottles over the fence, full and empty, to show their disappointment, and it resulted in a field of broken glass.

We stayed out there for a while, but when officials tried to clean up, more bottles were thrown, forcing us back inside the pavilion. We managed to resume eventually and quickly took another wicket, which started more bottle throwing. That was the end of a match we were going to win but we couldn't return to the field to finish off the game. A player showing dissent caused all that. It was a Caribbean umpire as well, so there wasn't any likelihood of bias.

In Guyana, there was a riot before we started. The game was delayed by rain. The umpires kept going out to make inspections and while the square, which was raised higher than the rest of the ground, was drying well, the run-ups were a quagmire. The crowd were becoming increasingly restless and vocal, and so the umpires asked the two captains to accompany them on the next inspection. Ian couldn't see the point but, nevertheless, he and Clive Lloyd did as they were asked. When the umpires decided play was still not possible, it became clear what a smart move it had been – the blame was deflected to the two captains. Suddenly, in the eyes of the crowd, Ian Chappell was the rogue, certainly not their own man.

The fans started pushing the fence until it collapsed and they swept on to the field. Both teams were locked in the dressing rooms with tables stacked against the doors, but the mob started fires by the all-wood pavilion and, understandably, Douglas Sang Hue and the other umpire feared for their lives. Max Walker was running around taking photographs and later, at sportsmen's dinners, he recounted the story about us cowering under tables. If truth be told, after he had taken his pictures, he pushed people out of the way to get the safest position. Good on ya, Tangles!

The riot police eventually arrived and fired tear gas to clear the ground which finally stopped the rioting, but we still needed armed protection from the fans as they rushed the bus taking us back to our hotel. That was the most frightened I have ever been in a cricket setting.

Remarkably, the next day you would hardly have known anything had happened and we played out the match over three days. It was just a case of crossed wires and Chinese whispers that caused it. Also Ian and Clive were seen leaving the ground during the day for a meeting, and the crowd thought they were walking out on them. To add to the situation, the fans had been in the ground since six in the morning, drinking rum in the hot sun, and their brains were probably singed. It was a very nasty riot.

The fifth and final Test, in Antigua, was drawn. I took six wickets in the opposition's only innings, which gave me 23 wickets for the series, the best in either side. Viv's dad was the curator for the game, and there were just two innings with lots of runs. The St John's ground is small and when you consider that they hold their carnival there with all the bands and the heavy wagons carrying them, they have remarkable wickets. They must roll it so much. They flatten it out and with the small boundaries it makes for lots of runs. Why wouldn't you have one of the best batting grounds in the world when you have one of the world's great batsmen coming from there in Viv Richards? But it doesn't make for great cricket. They like to see lots of runs but it is not good for the game to have one-sided affairs.

In my 15 Super Tests, I took 79 wickets at an average of 23.97 – which was about my average for all Test cricket. If they had counted in my Test record, it would have taken me to 434 wickets from 85 Test matches. That averages around five a Test match, which is about my average anyway. They say after 30 to 40 Tests, you establish an average or a strike rate which hardly changes at all from then on with very few exceptions.

There would have also been 20 more 'caught Marsh bowled Lillee' added to our statistics. Richard Hadlee claimed if it had not been for WSC I would have gone on to amass 500 Test wickets. It is conceivable but not relevant.

While it doesn't bother me, I hope the quality of the cricket will be recognised one day, and those averages can be included in players' lifetime bests. The wickets I took in World Series were hard come by and the standard as high as I ever played. The averages made in establishment cricket during that time were achieved against much softer opposition.

If people say to me it was only World Series Cricket, I know they do not understand the game. It was the toughest cricket I ever played in my life. Tell the guys who regularly faced Andy Roberts, Garth Le Roux, Joel Garner and Wayne Daniels this was Sunday Cavalier cricket. There were no easy sessions, never mind easy games, and no respite.

I was at the coal front and I have no regrets. Sometimes, afterwards, I wondered whether I should have done it and become so involved. I was thinking of the friendships which were broken, the fights between players and administrators, but then I look at the positives. The fact that cricket is played the way it is today, the advent of full-time professionals, the revamping of the game, the greater involvement of the spectators, the added colour was all down to WSC. The most telling factor of all was that players and administrators started to think more as one, and realised each had their part to play, and they could work together. The only way I can see a chasm opening again is if the Players' Association, as strong as it is, becomes too heavy handed and reverses the roles.

Before World Series, we had asked the Board where all the gate and television money was going. They said back into cricket, but most of the associations were manned by two staff and volunteers, so they were hardly paying out huge amounts in wages, and some of the grounds were trusts. The players were paid a pittance and the umpires weren't paid much either. The word is that a lot of the money was invested in bricks and mortar. We were earning it and not seeing any of it. The transition was difficult but the entire Packer era helped change the face of the game and certainly helped future cricketers.

So often it is the bad side of Packer we hear about but there is a compassionate and a loyal side to the man, which endeared him to me. In 1985, when the family went on a trip around Australia, Austin talked to Packer to see if we could stay at his hotel at Perisher, as we had never tried snow skiing before and were keen to give it a go. Packer said to contact Colin McCrae who would look after us. He gave us a suite when we were expecting just a room. Everything was laid on. Adam and Dean couldn't quite believe it. At one stage, Adam sat in a bubble bath with a bottle of champagne from the fridge, making out he was pouring himself a glass as in the height of luxury. The boys had never experienced anything like it in their short lives. We told them to enjoy it while they could – it was another world, maybe one to aspire to but not to expect.

I don't know whether the ACB or Western Australia knew how deeply involved I was with Packer. Certainly I was pushed a lot as the face of World Series by the Packer publicity machine through advertising and promotions. Whether it indicated that I was as involved as I was, I still don't know.

It was a huge relief when it all reached a satisfactory conclusion. When the two hit head on, I really thought there would never be a coming together. As negotiations proceeded, Packer insisted that whatever deal was made with the ACB, the players would not suffer any recriminations.

However, I suspected that at any opportunity we would be weeded out. I take my hat off to the authorities because it didn't happen. I was surprised but I appreciated it. The amalgamation was quite smooth, apart from the way the State selectors picked Kim Hughes as captain of Western Australia when the current captain, Rod Marsh, had been very successful in the job. We didn't like it but we accepted it.

It happened during the 1979–80 tour of Pakistan. We were in Faisalabad (or, as Rod called it, Faisala-very-bloody-bad) for the second Test, and there was nothing to do except play cards and have a few beers when we weren't playing cricket. I wasn't particularly keen on playing cards but I liked to be around the team.

One day, during a card game, I was talking to Kim Hughes. Before we went to Pakistan, I had made some press statements about being 30 and reassessing my playing position, saying I was playing series to series, according to my physical and mental condition. Kim asked me what my plans were for next year and I said I would look at it after the tour. He persisted, asking if I was likely to play or not. He was pressing me so hard I asked him why, to which he responded, 'Because I am captain of Western Australia next year.'

You could have dropped a pin in the room and heard it, it went so quiet. I looked at Rod and back at Kim. The deal had been done behind Rod's back. I can only imagine how gutted he must have felt; not one among the half a dozen Western Australians there felt good about it.

Kim Hughes was officially appointed in June, a long time before the season. Rod was asked if he would be vice captain but he flatly refused without going into the reasons why. I thought it was big of him when he could have caused a real fuss, which would have been unsettling for the team. They asked me next and I said I wouldn't do it either because I also knew the background. Then they went to Bruce Laird, a top bloke and great mate, who didn't like making waves. He did not know what to do; he was deeply hurt for Rod and knew others were upset. He wanted the best for Western Australia and he also wanted to make sure that the team did not fall apart. He asked me for advice and I told him I couldn't pass a reasonable opinion because I was still so upset about it. But I did tell him that whatever he decided it would make no difference to our relationship. He was grateful and took the job on. It was a complete compromise.

I never disliked Kim Hughes; no one could dislike him as a man. I was, however, bitter towards him because of those underhand dealings. I don't blame him for taking the captaincy; I blame the authorities for the way they went about it.

To my knowledge, Kim had never captained a side before he was made captain of Australia for the second Test against Pakistan in Perth in 1978–79, after Graham Yallop picked up an injury, and the following series in India. From the start, I was not happy with it but I accepted I had to try and do the right thing as a team member. There were a few incidents which I didn't think were great moves from a captain. I felt I'd reached the stage where I could make my own decisions, or at least be consulted or encouraged as leader of the bowling attack. I lost confidence in Kim as a captain and, in the end, I felt he would not listen to the senior players, preferring to do things his way and take all the responsibility.

However, my disagreements with him were exaggerated, and more was read into them than should have been. I clashed much more with Greg Chappell without it being reported or becoming public knowledge.

I believe the whole situation was an unfortunate result to the Packer era, but I don't think much of it was Kim's fault, just circumstances beyond our control. I rate Kim Hughes as a top bloke and friend – and always will.

CHAPTER THIRTEEN

Tempers, tantrums and an aluminium bat

I t was during the WSC tour of the West Indies that the Board offered Packer a deal. We heard about it via Lynton Taylor, Packer's assistant, but before he agreed, Packer wanted to know whether or not we were happy to go back to the ACB or preferred to stay as we were. He was prepared to listen to us if we wanted to keep going. He had proved himself honourable so we had no doubt he meant what he said.

From the players' point of view, the whole idea of WSC was to gain a better deal for cricketers, and the deal as presented to us achieved that. We had a show of hands and everyone except a couple agreed to go back. The two who declined knew full well their Test careers were over and they would be going back to the relative obscurity of Shield cricket. No one could blame them for that. We were all given the option of a straight yes or no.

During the second year in World Series Cricket, I felt I was a fairly complete bowler and on my day I could get a five-wicket haul if everything went right. After two years out of official international cricket, I wanted to prove I was still there at the forefront.

Once back together, the first Test series – from December 1979 to February 1980 – was against the West Indies and England, three matches against each, played alternately. It was an interesting concept and something Packer's people had insisted on. He wanted the best of both worlds and he had it with the best West Indies side and the traditional enemy, England, although they did not play each other. For me, it gave me respite from playing against the same batsmen all the time, while it stopped them having the opportunity of getting on top of you.

The Frank Worrell Trophy was up for grabs against the West Indies, and in the first Test in Brisbane, Viv Richards, in particular, took us apart. He scored 140 before I had him caught behind by Rod Marsh. His was one of four first-innings wickets I took but the game petered out to a draw after we topped 400 in our second innings on a good wicket at the Gabba.

I wasn't bowling particularly well on the unresponsive pitch and, annoyed with myself, I bowled an off-spinner off three paces. When I went to do it again, Greg Chappell called from the slips, 'Hey, hold on a minute. Are you bowling fast or slow?'

I glared at him and shouted back, 'Spin.'

Greg humoured me and changed the field accordingly, with Marsh standing up to the stumps. I was not impressed and, off three paces, hurled down a very quick bouncer which Alvin Kallicharran ducked and Rod had to fend away with his gloves. Greg was straight down the pitch to me. He told me to bowl fast or spin and to make up my bloody mind. I went back to my long run, the field changed again and Greg let it rest until teatime. Then he collared me to ask what was going on. I told him he couldn't tell me what to bowl.

'I have never told you what to bowl,' he responded.

'You did out there.'

'No,' he snapped back. 'You told me what you were going to bowl and I set the field for you. You could have killed Marshy. If you had broken his hand, what does that do for the team? Therefore, would you carry on in a reasonable fashion and not like a spoiled schoolboy.'

I was suitably chastised. I did it out of frustration and it wasn't the first time. Once at The Oval, Dickie Bird refused to change a ball which had gone completely out of shape. I walked back with the old ball, moaned again and Dickie said no again. So I signalled to the captain that I was going to bowl a spinner – that was all a bowler could do with such a ball. As I walked back after bowling a dot ball, Dickie said, 'That is the best off-spinner I have seen bowled all season.' I cracked up. In his own inimitable way, he had defused what was becoming an awkward situation.

Apparently, Greg wrote of the latest incident:

From a shy, gullible bloke when I first met him, he developed into a supreme ego. It is not a criticism. Most of us are the same.

Dennis was such a strong-willed bugger and such a good bowler you had to accept that occasionally he would get pigheaded. The adrenalin would pump so fast he would go over the top. Usually it was because he was angry with himself or the batsman. When he was that intense he became irrational. The trick then was to have him channel that anger towards the batsman but if I got it wrong he would divert that anger towards me.

He was right, which just shows how smart Greg was – probably helped along by Rod, who also read me very well. I'm not sure about the supreme ego, however!

It would have been a simple thing for the relationship to break down, which would have created terrible problems, but he never allowed it to happen. The more I played and the more success I had, the more I thought I knew what I was doing and the more input I demanded. I see now it was wrong, but I was encouraged by Ian, and because I was captaining and coaching sides from the age of 21, I felt I had the background. I suppose I crossed the line from time to time, trying to assert myself when I shouldn't have done so. The captain must always be the boss. I plead guilty to the charges. I wish I hadn't been, but it was part of my personality.

At the end of one season with Western Australia, I realised that during the course of the year I had gone over the top on several occasions. Before the start of the next season, I spoke to the captain, John Inverarity, at a barbecue. I told him I knew I had crossed the line a few too many times, and was anxious about the effects of that, not only for me but for the team as well.

'From what I have seen and experienced,' John butted in, 'it has worked for you and for us nine times out of ten, and often ten out of ten. Leave it to me. I'll come and tell you if it's becoming detrimental to the team or to you.'

I had gone cap in hand to apologise and offer to change my ways, but he didn't think it was necessary. I was not damaging either my reputation or that of the team. I had great respect for him. It showed there were always two sides to every issue, and two sides to me.

The 1979–80 Test series is especially remembered for the infamous aluminium bat. It all began during the time of World Series Cricket when Graham Monoghan, an A Grade cricketer from Western Australia, and I started up an indoor cricket centre in Perth. However, because I was playing for WSC, teams in Perth were advised by the WACA not to get involved with my ventures. There weren't many indoor cricket centres in the town and ours was one of the best, but the WACA's intervention stifled our projections and we had to change our thinking. We began coaching schoolboys during the holidays, but fell far short of our budget.

At the end of the week's coaching, we would take the boys over to the oval opposite the centre and play on the park, putting into practice all we had talked about. It gave us all a breath of fresh air, having been indoors all week, and the boys loved it. Then one day, the rain absolutely belted down, so we decided to pull the nets back and play the game indoors. The kids loved it, we enjoyed it and the penny dropped – maybe we could get some teams organised. We decided to give it a go and started indoor cricket. It was so successful we set up another couple of centres including one in Wagga Wagga, New South Wales.

We were messing around one day in the Perth indoor centre when Graham brought in a strange bat made from a piece of aluminium staircase, which was smaller than a bat's width. He had cut it off at blade length and got a mate to weld on a bat handle with a couple of rubber grips around it. I hit some balls and it went really well. Apparently, he got the idea from seeing baseball players using aluminium bats in the States.

We asked Comalco, the aluminium manufacturers in Western Australia, to design a mould, extruded aluminium through it and out came a bat at the other end – well, almost. We trimmed it up, put on rubber grips and that was the birth of the aluminium bat. All very simple.

We started to manufacture them and were soon approached by bat manufacturers in England who offered to take it on and pay us a licence fee and royalties. We thought if it was that good, we should do it ourselves and make all the money. That was our biggest mistake.

The bat was not designed, or made for, first-class cricket. At half the price of a willow bat, we thought it would be useful for schools cricket, nets and for underdeveloped countries. We thought it would be especially useful in England where bats were often ruined from moisture penetration and lack of oiling – a A$200 bat could be ruined in a season while ours would last forever.

People have asked me since why I used it in a Test match – it was a marketing ploy. I'm not ashamed of that. If Duncan Fearnley or Gray Nicolls wanted to promote a new design or style of bat, they had top players using it in Test matches for maximum exposure. That happened when they brought out the scoop, the drop shoulders and the holes in the back of the bat. My best marketing tool for the aluminium bat was to use it in a Test match, and it certainly attained total exposure – although, in the end, the ploy backfired on me.

I checked with the authorities before I used it in Brisbane and they told me there was nothing in the laws to say I couldn't use an aluminium bat, so they couldn't stop me. It looked like a normal bat but with the first ball big Joel Garner bowled to me from the Cricketers' Club end, it

Previous page: On the point of delivery – and I want that batsman out!

Left: Getting ready for my debut for Western Australia in 1969.

My first wicket in a Test match in England: Mike Smith is LBW.

Dennis Amiss just kept on finding ways of getting out to me during the 1974–75 Ashes series. Here Ian Chappell takes the catch in the fifth Test at Adelaide.

My father, and mate, Keith surprises me at Lord's in 1975. His first trip in a large bird.

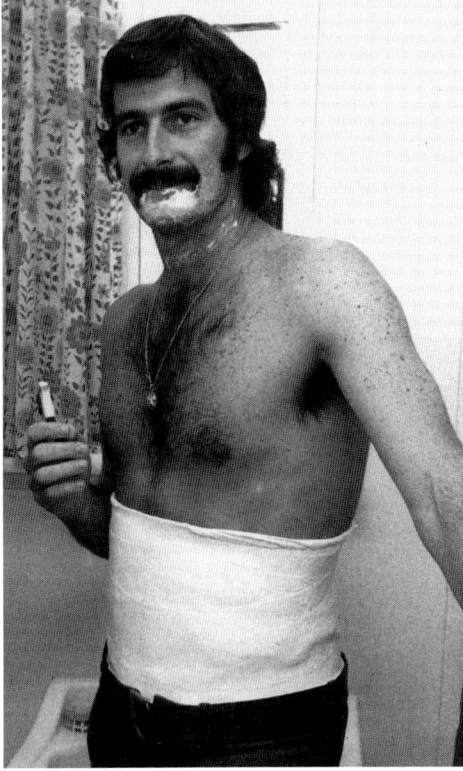

Throughout my career I had various injury problems. Here, being the first cricketer to be diagnosed with three stress fractures to my spine, a plaster cast was the recommendation.

Former Australian player Craig Serjeant, myself, and running coach Austin Robertson Snr going through a high-stepping drill. I owe him many wickets.

Checking the pieces after knee surgery in 1983.

I always worked hard on keeping fit, even if the gatekeepers weren't too impressed with my efforts.

GETTY IMAG

Mike Brearley and I begin a heated discussion about whether I could use my aluminium bat during the first Test at Perth in December 1979. He won that argument; I got him out.

More controversy. Showing Gavaskar why he is out durin the third Test in February 1981. He eventually had to g but he nearly took his partne with him.

Having committed the ultimate faux pas in asking the Queen for her autograph, she had one sent later and it takes pride of place in our house.

Left to right — sleepy Bruce Laird, me, Greg Chappell, Kim Hughes, Ian Botham at a Test match in Bombay. Botham and I would some years later be accused of causing mayhem in a dressing room.

Waving to Richie Benaud after breaking his Australian record for the number of Test wickets in Februar 1981 at Melbourne. I think Greg and Rod were as happy as I was.

Not only did I enjoy bowling at Lord's, I enjoyed batting there, too. Here I am on the way to 40 in 1981.

It is heavy, but worth it! The Sheffield Shield won b WA in 1983–84, and the joyous captain celebrates beating Queensland.

GETTY IMAGES

went 'Clangggg!' and Desi Haynes at short-leg shouted, 'Hey man,' and hit the ground laughing. He was prone for 30 or 40 seconds. I was out for a duck and there were no complaints – nothing was said, nothing was written.

Two weeks later, we played the first Test against England, in Perth. Again, I asked the WACA if I could use it and was told they would rather I did not but there was nothing they could do to stop me. I practised with it in the nets, and Greg tried it out but did not think much of it.

We batted first and struggled to make runs. The score was 219–7 when I went in. I faced a couple of balls and the bat clanged as before. Then I hit one which ran down to the boundary where it rolled into the concrete drain. When it came back this old ball was in a rough state, as you would expect after 200 runs. Mike Brearley complained to the umpires O'Connell and Weser that the bat was damaging the ball and he did not want it used.

I was annoyed because the bat was enamel coated and our tests showed it did not damage the ball. There was a Mexican stand-off with the umpires saying I must change the bat while Brearley refused to let his bowlers bowl to me. I stood there for some while before deciding that discretion was the better part of valour and grumpily making my way to the pavilion to change bats. As I walked in, great mate that he is, Rodney Marsh said, 'What's the matter, mate?' I told him I couldn't use my bat.

'Are you going to let them tell you that, when it's not against the laws?' Rod was winding me up but I didn't realise it.

'You're damn right,' I said, and promptly turned on my heel and walked back out to the middle, carrying the offending instrument.

I got back out there and waited. I regret now holding up a Test match for so long but, at the time, I was determined I was in the right and I was being set up. The steam was beginning to blow from my ears.

Rodney Hogg came out with a new bat from Greg but I told him to buzz off. Hoggy said later, 'I could see myself on national television, before a packed ground, and Dennis hitting me between the eyes with his metal bat.'

Then Greg came out, grabbed the bat off Hoggy and marched towards me. Then I knew I was in trouble. Greg wouldn't allow me to use the bat for the sake of good relations and the game itself. Not happy at being pushed into a corner, I threw the bat in Greg's direction, hoping to make him jump. It went some 30 metres and, if there is a funny side to this unhappy story, I now hold the record for throwing an aluminium bat the furthest in a Test match, and I know it will stand for ever.

Greg admitted later he used the situation to wind me up, knowing I would be bowling soon afterwards, intending to let me use the bat for one over before replacing it. It worked, because I dismissed both openers without scoring.

Some funny stories came out of the episode, including a telephone call from a bakery claiming to use the bat as a ladle to lift the bread in and out of their ovens and asking could they order 10 of them. In fact, we had sold thousands by then, junior and senior models. At the end of the Test match, I got each side to sign the bat I had used, and Mike Brearley wrote, 'Good luck with the sales.' But we did not sell one single bat after that because they were banned; the rules were changed to state that bats must be made of wood.

Of course, the aluminium bats could still be used in a schoolyard but not in a proper school match. We weren't left with any stock because we made the bats as they were ordered, producing 50 or a 100 at a time, but we were left with a hell of a lot of extruded metal. We sold that for scrap, making one cent in the dollar.

I can still source a few of them, and I have been offered up to US$3,000 per bat by someone in India, so, who knows, there may be some money in it for me yet. I hope so. I had an offer for the original bat five years ago but until the slate is clear I won't sell it. I told the guy it would cost him A$50,000 to clear my investment and he pondered for a minute or two before saying no.

England and the West Indies approached the game very differently. The West Indies went for everything while England played more of a chess game. It was a well-known notion that the first thing England tried to do was not lose a Test match, though they failed here. That's what they tried to set up, and then they might go for it once they were in a winning position but with the thought that they could always save the match. It worked for them in bygone days, but now most countries play for the win most of the time, led by the current Australian side. But you have to have a decent side to do that.

The West Indies turned us over by 10 wickets in the second Test at Melbourne with Holding, Croft and Garner whipping us out for 156 in the first innings. I bowled 36 overs as the West Indies made 397, Viv Richards top scoring with 96. The same three, with Andy Roberts chipping in with three, bowled us out again, for 259, leaving Greenidge and Haynes to knock off the handful of runs required.

However, we bounced straight back in Sydney, bowling out England for 123 and 237, and that score was achieved only thanks to a classy not out 98 by David Gower. Geoff Dymock took seven wickets in the match and I had half a dozen as we won by six wickets. But despite the easy victory, we were still rolled over by the West Indies at the Adelaide Oval.

I took the wickets of both Richards and Lloyd in my first-innings haul of 5–78 but not before they had steered the West Indies to 328, with 76 to Viv and 121 coming from Clive's bat. They put the game out of our reach with a second-innings total of 448. Viv and Clive were among the runs again but, this time, they played second fiddle to Alvin Kallicharran, who made a century. Their quartet of fast men, Roberts, Holding, Garner and Croft, sorted us out for a miserly 165.

The difference in the quality of the opposition was further underlined in our final match of the double series at Melbourne in February where we clinched a 3–0 series success against England. I was back among the wickets with 6–60 in the first innings and 5–78 in the second as we won by eight wickets.

In the end, I felt it was a good series and I had bowled as well as ever, taking 35 wickets in the six matches. I was very happy with the way I was bowling. It was really working for me.

While I respected Viv Richards but did not socialise with him, I could not help but like the smiling, casual approach of David Gower. Apparently, the feeling was mutual for David wrote:

Of all the fast bowlers I have faced – Roberts, Holding, Hadlee, Marshall – I would have to place Lillee as the best. He no longer had the blistering pace of his early years, but he was a better bowler. Given the combination of his natural talent and a ferociously competitive nature, he was as complete a fast bowler as there can ever have been. Dennis, like most Australian cricketers, was never short of the odd word, but what I particularly liked about the guys of that era – the Chappells, Marsh, Thomson etc – was that what happened on the field mattered not a jot off it. You could be smacked in the ribs at five minutes to six, and at five past the first two people into the dressing room to apply a cold beer to the bruise (plus a few more internally) would be Lillee and Marsh. In terms of the Test batsman versus Test bowler contest, Dennis and myself formed something of a mutual admiration society, and I am very proud of that. It is always nice to have earned the professional respect of an opponent you yourself regarded as one of the best to have ever played the game.

We hoped most cricketers world-wide regarded us in the way Gower expressed. We played hard, uncompromising cricket on the field, but that was all gone once it struck six o'clock.

I don't think I have ever known anyone with a better attitude towards cricket, batting and life than David. He thought life should be lived to the full and I don't think it mattered to him if he scored four, 40 or 100. Whenever he was on the other side, he was always interested in a chat and came into the dressing room for a beer. What's more, he was one of the best players I have ever seen albeit an underachiever in my opinion. He could have been even better. He regularly looked as though he was going to take us apart only to get himself out. I rate him as one of the great batsmen. He played me very well, certainly as well as any player I bowled to. I rated him highly in all areas and now also as a great friend with whom I try to catch up whenever I'm in England. He's a nice guy, smart and happy-go-lucky, and I'm not surprised that he has done well in television.

CHAPTER FOURTEEN

Trouble in store

We arrived in Pakistan very soon after, wondering what was waiting in store, having heard a lot of negative stories, particularly about the umpires. We weren't disappointed. We were warned the umpires would be biased and there would be bad decisions and we would just have to rise above them. To me, that was pretty negative but word was it could cause problems not to accept them.

Our liaison man, a former Pakistani Test player, accompanied us everywhere – he was on the bus, in the dressing room, at team meetings, everywhere. I was comfortable with that, as were the rest of the boys.

The opening Test was staged at the National Stadium in Karachi and warning bells began to ring as the match got under way. Good lbw decisions were being knocked back, not one or two but six or seven early on. We had been told Javed had been out lbw only a couple of times in his entire career in Pakistan, a remarkable statistic under any circumstances.

I must have had Zaheer out several times. He was badly out of touch but must have realised that as long as he kept his pads in front he would be fine. It was a nightmare because the wicket was so slow it wasn't carrying. Having a batsman caught in the slips or behind was almost impossible. I bowled pretty straight, and I couldn't see how I was going to get a wicket. This was rammed home to me when I went without a wicket in back-to-back Test matches. The wickets were weighted against Geoff Dymock and me.

The other side of the coin was that Bruce Laird was also having a bad time, playing with little confidence, and in the second Test he was quickly given out leg before for just six with only eight on the board to what can only be described as a very ordinary decision. Let's say we thought he was unlucky.

During the afternoon, I went with Bruce to the nets. We took it seriously and I was even excited when I got a ball under his bat and hit the wicket, but the way it was going, if that had happened in the Test match, the bail would not have fallen off.

I was so frustrated at having appeals turned down that, finally, I turned to the umpire and asked how I was going to get a wicket. He looked me in the eye and said, 'If you knock the wickets over, Mr Lillee, I will have to give him out.' I thought what a fine gesture! We lost the first Test by seven wickets without a single leg before wicket being given to us while they had three crucial decisions and a fourth when, just to rub it in, I was given out lbw to Iqbal Qasim.

We drew the second Test in Faisalabad after the first day had been wiped out and we scored 617 thanks to a double century from Greg Chappell and 172 from Graham Yallop. Me? I was out lbw to Wasim Raja.

Pakistan were happy to bat out what was left of the match, scoring 382–2 with a run-out and, incredibly, an lbw to Dymock. He took opener Haroon Rashid's wicket. Rashid, who had batted number 11 for the WSC World XI the year before, had made 21. Greg used all 11 of us as bowlers in that match, even Rod Marsh, who bowled 10 overs. Maybe I was on tour for my wicket-keeping ability!

When we arrived in Lahore for the final match, we saw they had prepared two wickets at the Gaddafi Stadium, one quick and the other an absolute road, flat and slow. The first turned like a top and the second was designed for a draw. We didn't know which one was to be used, so we put out a story that Ashley Mallett was on his way, to try to get them to show their hand. They still wouldn't say, but they checked the flight manifestos to see if Mallett had arrived.

Two nights before the Test, Greg Chappell and I were invited out by a lovely family to a top-class restaurant where I had a very hot curry. Afterwards, they recommended a lassi, a drink like a milk shake made of curd, to settle my stomach and quench my thirst. Greg had one, too. They were huge and I drank mine but Greg just sipped his and left it. So I drank that as well.

The effects of the meal, or the lassi, hit me within a few hours of getting back to the hotel. Greg was very concerned and somehow got hold of a doctor in the early hours of the morning. He gave me a few jabs and sat with me until 7 a.m., when I began to pick up. The doctor was confident I would be all right so he left.

Wherever we went, fans rang our rooms to talk to us and while it was annoying we did the right thing and chatted when we had the time. Because I was ill, Greg had blocked all phone calls so that I could get some rest, with the Test match only a day away, but somehow a call got through. Greg answered it but the caller was speaking so quickly he couldn't understand what was being said. He was unhappy anyway because the call had woken me up, and he put the phone down. But the caller was persistent and came back through two or three times until Greg was so frustrated he threw the hand-piece to the ground, but as he did so he heard the words 'doctor' and 'Lillee'. He tried to catch the phone in mid flight but failed and the doctor was cut off. We never heard from him again. He probably still thinks what rude buggers we were, after all he had done for me. I just wish I could explain to him what had happened. If you happen to read this, Sir, thank you and many apologies!

The great irony was that Greg and I had cooked up a plan whereby I was carried back to the hotel claiming a recurrence of the back injury.

Greg claimed it was a top acting performance, worthy of an Oscar, in our bid to get them to use the fairer wicket but it was wasted on the audience. They used the other wicket anyway. It seemed, having won the first Test, Pakistan weren't too bothered about winning another and were happy to go for another draw.

But they waited until the last minute on the morning of the match to announce which wicket it was to be. Finally, manager Fred Bennett, having listened to all of their excuses for not saying, demanded to see the top man. He was told he was sick with a cold and that was why no decision had been made.

I was just about well enough to take my place and, fortunately, was given an extra couple of days' rest as we batted first, mounting up 407–7 declared, with a brilliant 150 not out from Allan Border. I did not have to bat but I bowled in the evening of the second day. Any chance we had of forcing a result disappeared when they scored over 400 with Majid Khan making an undefeated century.

I wasn't the first nor was I the last to fall sick on the sub-continent in those days. A lot of players went down with bad stomachs on tours of India, Pakistan and Sri Lanka. I was just one of many, so it was nothing new to play while or after being ill. Cricketers had been doing it for years. Regularly you would see players rushing from the field heading for the toilets. Ill or not I still bowled 42 overs in that innings and took my first wickets of the tour, opener Mudassar Nazar, Iqbal Qasim and Wasim Raja. As a footnote, there were three lbws out of seven wickets in our first innings while we, once more, did not get one. The series split was 10-1.

It was tough but Pakistan was not all bad. I liked the different culture and I got on really well with Majid Khan. He was immediately friendly and went out of his way to talk. He even helped me to buy some carpets. He is a genuine person and remains a great mate from the game, as do Wasim Raja and Imran.

The whole tour was an eye opener for me. I'd never seen armed guards along the road before, but there they were on the way to Faisalabad. We arrived at our quaintly named Hottel (correct spelling)

Ripple after a long flight and a long bus trip. We were all starving after a few jars the night before and the boys all rushed to the dining room, even before checking in.

I had a bad feel about the place. It wasn't like a hotel as I knew them, more like a boarding house. The dining room was filthy, so I went to investigate the kitchen at the back. It was an open-air lean-to with rubbish all over the place, including mice droppings and spilled cooking oil. I rushed back to the dining room and told Fred Bennett not to let anyone eat anything. He came and looked, as did a few of the boys, but some couldn't face it.

Fortunately, a very wealthy industrialist lived next door in a huge house and when he heard of our problems, he said we could make use of his home for meals and to relax whenever we wanted. It was almost like a palace, with a brand new kitchen and lounges. To reach it, we had to walk 70 or 80 metres from the hotel, around a wall, but he didn't want us to be inconvenienced so he knocked a hole in his brick wall so we could have quick and easy access. We had employed a chef, Zeb, and he was commissioned to shop and cook for us at the mansion, using all fresh produce. The industrialist was exceptionally hospitable and made our stay reasonable when it could have been a nightmare.

Rod Marsh and I roomed together. There was no toilet in the room, just a hole in the ground. This was a problem for us both as Marsh's knees had gone and mine weren't too good, so we asked for a box to sit on. They brought in a huge box with a hole in it – the perfect answer.

But after three days, there was dreadful smell in the room. Neither of us was prepared to say anything until we traced the smell to the hole in the ground. There shouldn't have been a problem as it flushed but we discovered the box was not centred over the hole and rather than being flushed away everything was settling on the concrete around the edge.

We suspected a certain joker named Mick Malone had moved our box while we were out, but we could never prove it. It just shows how bad the rest of the place smelled that it took us three days to notice.

While we were there, I went pig shooting with my mate Majid, out on the border. That is a night I will never forget. We hunted in the dark, spotlighting the pigs with big torches. When we reached the border, I was sitting next to Majid and as we pulled up at the border post, I found a rifle pointing through the passenger window straight at me. The guard had come from nowhere and I was stunned. Majid said something to him quickly and, thankfully, the guy relaxed. The trip had been arranged in advance but this sentry had not been told and did not know to expect us.

While the Pakistan visit was interesting, to say the least, I never played in India. I coach there now and I am forever explaining it wasn't because I did not want to go or pulled out of tours, it was just the way it happened. In 1969 I wasn't in the side; in 1979 I was playing World Series Cricket and in 1985 I had retired. I visited in 1980 on the way to England for the Lord's Centenary Test. We stopped off and watched India play England in a one-off Jubilee Test in Bombay; the conditions would have been nice for me because there was a bit of swing, movement and some carry. I know not all the wickets are like that but some would have suited me, just as they did the West Indies pace attack of that era. I would have loved to play in front of some of the most avid supporters to be found anywhere in the world.

We arrived in England from the short visit to Pakistan in August, looking forward to comparing this game, celebrating 100 years of Test cricket in England, with the 1977 Centenary Test in Melbourne. The lead-up was fantastic. At the formal dinner, Ashley Mallett and I sat either side of an old colonel who must have been in his late 80s. He had so many stories to tell and he fascinated us. He had been coming to these dinners for 40 years, he said, and as the food was served he flicked his fine linen white napkin over his shoulders, tucked it into the back of his shirt collar and flicked it back to cover his beautiful beige suit. We watched in amazement and Ashley said, 'Excuse me Colonel, hope you don't mind me asking, old boy, but shouldn't it go on your lap?'

'Yes, Mallett,' the Colonel answered, 'but in all my dinners here I have never had anything spilt on the lap, but I have had those darned waiters spill stuff on my shoulders regularly.'

We just cracked up. We took to him instantly, watched everything he did, and talked to him as much as we could. When coffee was served to him, the Colonel took the coffee cup, placed the saucer on top and then took four teaspoons of sugar into the saucer and stirred it around. He then placed the saucer to one side and started to drink his coffee. This time it was me who had to ask.

'Do you mind me asking, why did you do that?'

'Certainly,' said the Colonel. 'The doctor told me I had to cut down on my sugar and I am cutting down, even though I like it.'

It was obviously psychological but I still don't know whether he was kidding us or whether he was serious. There were several others things he said and did during the dinner that suggested his actions went with the twinkle in his eye. He was just so eccentric I am sure they were his party tricks.

The lead-up was just as good as it had been in Australia but the game was not. It was played on a flat wicket and interrupted by rain. At one stage umpire David Constant was jostled as he came off the ground because the members thought the cricket should have carried on. It was on, off, on, off and very frustrating for everyone – but it was a bit rough to blame the umpire for the weather.

Centuries from Graeme Wood and Kim Hughes saw us to 385–5 declared and put England on the back foot. Kim Hughes' 100 was one of the best I have ever seen from the point of view of sheer class, timing and occasional brute force. It was topped off by Kim hitting Chris Old back over his head and on to the pavilion roof. It is still regarded as one of the biggest hits at Lord's. I took Graham Gooch's wicket twice and also clean-bowled David Gower, and Lennie Pascoe had five in an innings, but any hopes we had of victory disappeared at the hands of the rain. Geoff Boycott batted throughout England's second innings for 128 not out from a total of 244–3.

Fortunately, apart from the incident with David Constant, the game was free from controversy and I managed to avoid getting into any trouble. Certainly, that could not be said about New Zealand's visit to Australia in November 1980.

The rivalry between the two countries has always been very keen, despite great ANZAC tradition. To us, they appeared to have something of an inferiority complex. I suppose we were sending A teams over there until 1977, which probably had an effect. Before 1980, they were willing to soak it up and learn. They were friendly and we mixed well, but this particular series soured it.

With New Zealand being our geographically closest cricket-playing neighbours, I got to know and had the opportunity of watching a number of them. From previous years I liked Ken Wadsworth, who unfortunately died of cancer as a young man. He was very competitive and a good wicket-keeper, with a bit of chat as you expect from the man behind the stumps. Headley Howarth was a handy bowler. Dayle Hadlee was totally different from his brother Richard, and Mark Gordon Burgess was a nice enough guy and a good player.

One of my favourite people from anywhere was John Wright, a great mate. If I held a party, he would be one of the first I would invite. He was a good, workmanlike player. His opening partner, Bruce Edgar, was quiet and didn't mix in too much but was a good bat. Lance Cairns and Bobby Cunis, against whom I never played in a Test, were tough uncompromising competitors. They were all great blokes. I also got on well with Geoff Howarth, Ian Smith and the Crowe brothers. The only Kiwis the Australians seemed to love to hate were Glenn Turner and Richard Hadlee, who rubbed our guys up the wrong way.

As a cricketer, Richard Hadlee was a tremendous. I didn't think we got on particularly well when we played – we were always at each other – but I once read a very flattering comment Richard had written: 'When things were going badly wrong, I'd think what would Lillee do, and the answer was always that he would not give up.' If people in cricket thought no more of my game than that, it would do for me. I believe he was right – it was the main thing which contributed to my success, more than skill, pace or anything else.

Hadlee was special because he was super skilful, the first true professional I saw in Test cricket. He was prepared to bowl away swingers on the off stump, over after over, with the occasional inswinger or cutter, the odd bouncer and a very rare yorker. He was also concerned about conserving runs. Before him, I did not notice many other fast, swing bowlers who worried too much about that. He was the first to be mechanical – and I mean that as a compliment. Yet when he started off, he was very erratic; if he hadn't changed, he could easily have faded out of the game at the top level. He was smart enough to realise it when he went to play county cricket. He shortened his run-up and learned to bowl at the off stump on a good length. I would put him up there with the very best fast, swing bowlers, Terry Alderman and Kapil Dev included, as well as Bob Massie for his short career.

His batting was very handy, sometimes explosive and demoralising. I enjoyed bowling to him because he gave me a chance – but he got me a few times as well. He could tear an attack apart on his day with his big hitting.

Glenn Turner, on the other hand, I didn't get on with as a bloke or rate as a batsman. He rarely made many runs against us, and you can only rate a player on what he does when you play against him. But then I never rated Sunil Gavaskar either, and yet he has proved to be a great batsman. The only way I could judge a player was on the way he batted when I bowled to him.

During that 1980–81 series, the day came when we all fell out. We had won the first two Tests quite comfortably, by 10 wickets in Brisbane and eight wickets in Perth, thus clinching the three-game series. I was enjoying myself with eight wickets in the first game and seven in the second before we headed off to Melbourne for the dead rubber of the three.

We were all still very focused because the game was against our local rivals, and when we batted first we ran up 321. I contributed a nice little 27 before being bowled by Lance Cairns. They were solid in their reply, finishing just four short of our total, and I didn't take a single wicket in my 21 overs.

It was only thanks to Greg Chappell's 78 we made any sort of total in the second innings, and then it was only 188, leaving the Kiwis just 193 to win. Again, I didn't get much of a return as they stumbled to 128–6 at the close and the game finished in a draw.

But any friendship which might have been kindled during the series disappeared when we played the third final in a triangular one-day series on Sunday, 1 February. We found ourselves roundly criticised, not only by cricket fans around the world but even by politicians.

It was a typical one-day match with New Zealand chasing 236 to win. They were 221–6 when Trevor Chappell stepped up to bowl the last over to Richard Hadlee, in front of 52,000 at the MCG.

We felt we had it in hand even after Hadlee hit a four off the first, leaving them 11 to win. He was out lbw off the second ball leaving them on 225–7. Ian Smith was next man in and he hit two twos off the next two balls only to be bowled off the fifth ball – 229–8. So there was one ball left and a six needed to tie the scores. Former All Black rugby player Brian McKechnie came in, a strong man with a strong nerve as he amply displayed when he kicked a last-gasp penalty against Wales at Cardiff Arms Park for a 13–12 victory. Captain Greg Chappell was well aware he was big enough and strong enough to hit the ball over the fence. Greg said to Trevor, 'How are you at bowling underarm?'

Trevor looked at him sideways and answered, 'I don't know – why?'

'Well, you're about to find out.'

Trevor thought about it before eventually agreeing. Greg told umpire Don Weser what he wanted to do. Weser went to consult his fellow umpire Peter Cronin and then told the batsman what was about to happen. McKechnie looked up in astonishment and said, 'You have got to be joking.' But Greg wasn't joking. Even Rod Marsh was taken totally by surprise and mouthed towards Greg, 'No mate, don't do it.' I still vividly remember Rod crossing his arms, head down, clearly unhappy.

But the captain instructed Trevor to go ahead and roll the last ball of the match down the wicket. McKechnie blocked the rolling ball and threw his bat away while skipper Howarth ran on to the pitch to protest as booing broke out round the Melbourne ground. As the Australian team walked off to the jeers of our own fans, a little girl ran out and grabbed Greg by the arm. He thought she wanted an autograph but she just told him he was a cheat. We had won but the dressing room was totally silent while there was pandemonium in the Kiwis' dressing room.

Australians love to win but everyone was dumbfounded. On air, Richie Benaud looked for an excuse and suggested Greg had his maths wrong and meant for me to bowl the last over.

When Trevor was about to bowl, I didn't know what was going on. I could see instructions were flying around but I was too far away on the boundary to appreciate the decisions being made on the square. When Trevor bowled underarm and the game was over, my immediate reaction was relief, even though I knew straightaway it would cause trouble. I thought it was the right thing to do to ensure we won the match. On reflection, I quickly realised it was not right for cricket.

I know Greg still regrets his decision, but there was nothing to say you couldn't do it. It transpired that the underarm delivery in Australia was still legal even though England had banned it two years earlier along with declarations in the limited-overs game – now there's one we didn't try.

Trevor Chappell suffered for it but he didn't attract the flak which came Greg's way as captain because it was clear to everyone watching from the stands and on television he had made the decision.

What would I have done if I were in Trevor Chappell's place and a bit player in the team? Would I have said no? Would I have feigned injury? No. In any case, he did it for his brother.

If it had been me, I would have said no way. My attitude would have been if you don't think I'm good enough to bowl a ball and not be hit for a six, then don't ask me to bowl. I would have flatly refused and been very cross at being asked but Greg would not have asked me because he would have known what the answer would be.

Greg was in trouble and I went to help him. I began to wonder just how much the heavy schedule of matches had affected his judgement. Some players were staying in Melbourne that night while others were leaving for Sydney.

'It could be a good idea to get out of the hotel early,' he joked. 'There could be a few bombings tonight.'

'You've got to get out of town because there's going to be trouble with the press. I'll come with you.' I was not joking.

As a friend and a team-mate, I knew how tired he was and he needed looking after. There were all sorts of ramifications. I organised a James Bond-type escape out of the tradesmen's entrance and away to the airport. When Greg got on the plane, you could have heard a pin drop as everyone went quiet. Greg eventually sat down two or three seats in front of Douggie Walters.

'Excuse me, Greg,' said Douggie.

'Yes, Douggie.'

'I have only one thing to ask, Greg.'

'Yes, Douggie.'

'When I was at school, my teacher told me the game wasn't over until the last ball was bowled.'

Well, Greg turned back quickly while the rest of us tried to stifle our laughter. Typically, Douggie was trying to extract a little humour from the situation.

The sad thing is I am sure it has affected Greg ever since. It certainly made him just about the most unpopular man in New Zealand, especially as there had been another incident with him earlier in the game. The Kiwis claimed a catch by Martin Snedden, a brilliant diving affair off Lance Cairns, only for Greg to stay at the crease unsure whether the catch had been grounded. Both umpires claimed to have missed it because they were checking the crease for short runs. There was no third umpire, of course, and the benefit always went to the batsman. Greg went on to top score with 90.

But we were all unpopular in New Zealand. At a reception held for us when we went there for a three-match Test series a year later, a senior New Zealand politician said that the yellow shirts we wore for our one-day internationals matched the colour of our spines. The recriminations were huge. Wherever we went, the New Zealanders abused us.

Trouble, it seemed, pursued us whomever we played and next waiting in line was India. We had already beaten them in Sydney by an innings in the first Test. Len Pascoe and I took four wickets apiece to bowl them out for 201, a score surpassed by Greg Chappell on his own as we scored 406 and then bowled them out again for 201. This time I shared the wickets with Jim Higgs as he took four and I took my match tally to seven.

The Indians were much more competitive on an easy batting track at the Adelaide Oval. We scored over 500, but this time in reply they scored 419 while I toiled through 34 overs for my 4–80. We still had a good chance of getting another result with a quick declaration at 221–7, but India held on for a draw, although they were struggling on 135–8 at the close. Pascoe took three early wickets and I weighed in with two.

But the series blew up in Melbourne in a tight game India won by 59 runs to tie the three-match series. It was in this match that I reached the landmark of 250 Test wickets, overtaking Richie Benaud's Aussie record of 248.

Despite a century by Viswanath, we again had the Indians in trouble with our pace, bowling them out for 237. Lennie and I took seven wickets between us. Our 419 put us in the driving seat, with Allan Border scoring 124.

Then came the trouble. India started well with Sunil Gavaskar and Chauhan sharing an opening stand of 165 before I trapped Gavaskar right in front for 70. I jagged one back a bit, it whacked him on the pads, we appealed but he stood there. Gavaskar claimed he had a nick on to the pads but we were sure it was clean, as was the umpire. The only one to think there was a problem was Sunny who, up until that day, had never scored runs against me to speak of. I know from what his team-mates told me he was desperate to score a hundred against me; it was frustration at getting so close to his goal which made him blow up.

In temper, he spat the dummy right out of the pram, whacking his bat against his pad, claiming the ball had hit his bat first. He was promptly told in which direction to go, and insisted his opening partner, Chetan Chauhan, left the field with him in protest. Fortunately for the sake of cricket, the team manager was waiting for the pair when they approached the pavilion, and he ordered Chauhan back to the middle and Gavaskar into the pavilion.

We were bemused. I was upset at times but it never changed the umpire's decision, and I never grabbed my fellow bowler and walked off the field. We had a good chuckle that someone should go to such extremes after being given out.

I know he was a great batsman but as I have said I cannot rate him among the great batsmen I bowled against. It would be like me rating Dennis Amiss, who, I have no doubt, was a wonderful batsman, but I cannot include him as a great because he did not make runs against Australia. I have to be honest and say the Indian I ranked as the best player against us was Viswanath. He made runs against us and regularly at that. I rated both Amiss and Gavaskar as of medium quality only, and I have never changed my mind.

Although I took another four wickets, taking my total for the series to 21, they reached 324, leaving us around about 150 to clinch the series. But we were bowled out for a miserable 83 in under 50 overs.

How could such a collapse happen? Generally, it was a flat track, which was useful for the first hour or so, a real old-fashioned Melbourne pitch. From what I can remember, it was hot, around the 100-degree mark, which baked the pitch, and towards the end of the second last day, it began to deteriorate. The old ball was keeping low while others would jag alarmingly. It was a typical last-day wicket in those days.

Kapil Dev was off the field with an injury for a lot of our first innings and again for the start of our second, when we had to bat for a few overs before the close of play. A little left-armer, Karsen Ghavri, who bowled medium pace swing very accurately, got a couple of wickets. One crept along the ground and got Greg Chappell; the other reacted strangely to get Jeff Dyson, and we were two wickets down for 11 runs. Doshi then picked up Wood for 10 and we were in deep trouble. It became even worse the next day when Kapil Dev reappeared and bowled his heart out, beautifully, taking 5–28.

At the end of it, and for one of the few times in my life, I was sarcastic to a fellow player, and a great one at that. I just said to him, 'Congratulations on the win. Well bowled, and could you leave the name of your doctor for me so I can get hold of him at some stage.'

Kapil, typically, just said yes and I'm sure he didn't know I was being sarcastic, probably still doesn't. Call it sour grapes. For most of that match we were in total control and, in the end, the wicket did beat us. But that's cricket.

CHAPTER FIFTEEN

Gambling on the Ashes

It appeared controversy was following me wherever I went. In July of the same year, 1981, we not only lost a Test to England in very odd circumstances, but also there were suspicions we might have thrown the game to win a 500–1 bet.

It was a strange series altogether. England had been struggling after two hard series against the West Indies, having hoped the charismatic Ian Botham was going to turn it round as captain. It didn't happen and, after bagging a pair in the second Test at Lord's and with England one down, he resigned (or was he pushed?). Indeed, there were many who questioned his future international career as his form in the West Indies was so poor.

On the face of it, England were on the ropes after a succession of bad results, and we fancied ourselves as we went in to the third Test at Headingley on 16 July. We won the toss and batted first, scoring 401–9 declared. Jeff Dyson scored a century and Kim Hughes 89 before being caught and bowled by Ian Botham, one of his six first-innings wickets. Clearly, he had been written off too soon.

In response, we bowled England out for 174 in 50 overs with just three of us bowling. I took 4–49, Terry Alderman 3–59 and Geoff Lawson 3–32. Naturally enough, Kim Hughes enforced the follow-on and with England on 135–7 by mid-afternoon on the fourth day we had already packed our bags when it flashed up on the scoreboard that England were 500–1 with the on-course bookmakers to win the game.

I said straightaway that in a two-horse race that was a ridiculous price and I was going to have £100 on it. I was quickly talked out of it. It was suggested I would be better off putting the money on the bar for a celebratory drink later that night. I forgot about it for a while, but later I thought I just had to have a bet on a two-horse race at those odds and I decided a tenner would be all right. During the tea break, I asked Peter our coach driver to put the bet on. He was a lovely fellow who joined in everything we did. I told him to take a ten-pound note out of my wallet.

I told Rod Marsh what I had done and suggested he did the same, but he brushed it aside and said it was a waste of money. Then he thought about the odds and shouted down to attract Peter's attention, holding up five fingers to show he wanted to put on a fiver.

Peter, in the meantime, thinking it a waste of time and money, was debating whether to put the money in his pocket to return to us at the end of the day's play. But then he thought what would happen if the unimaginable happened and England did, indeed, win. He had a cold shiver at the prospect of handing Marshy and me our £15 back and saying he hadn't put the bet on. He thought everyone would accuse him of pocketing the money. So back he went to the Ladbroke's tent and put the money on.

The wicket was doing a bit at the time and they were still not in front. Fast bowler Graham Dilley and Ian Botham were at the crease with only Chris Old and Bob Willis to follow. I ask you, what could happen?

I'll tell you what happened. Botham went on to score 149, Dilley 56, Old 29 and even Willis, who scored only two, helped Botham put on 37 for the last wicket to give England a fragile lead of 129. Big deal.

A great innings from Both? Let me tell you it was a bloody lucky innings. We dropped him countless times, nicks went over the top and there was lots of playing and missing. I get sick and tired of people saying it was one of the greatest innings of all time. Even Ian agrees it was not and admits there was an awful lot of luck. He had nothing to lose and just threw the kitchen sink at everything we tossed at him. According to the record books, Botham scored 45 runs off the 24 balls he received from me and I expected to get him with virtually every ball I bowled. He just went for it and it came off. Good luck to him. He chanced his arm and it worked. But great? No.

What was great was Bob Willis's bowling in our second innings. That was the greatest one-off sustained effort I ever saw from a fast bowler in the entire time I played cricket, with the crowd roaring him on. To me, it was Willis's match, despite the superhero thing about Botham. I'd like to point out the next two innings he played, and the way he bowled, made it clear this was Botham's Ashes series, but not as a result of that one innings. So the next time someone comes up to me and says, 'Wasn't Ian's innings at Headingley great?' and I say, 'No,' perhaps people will understand me a little better.

The undoubted man-of-the-match was Bob Willis. He was at his best with final figures of 8–43 off 15.1 overs and, remember, we were 56–1 at one stage, chasing that total of 130. I reckon I would still have got 500–1 at Ladbroke's on an England win then.

What people have to remember is we had been having bets on our games ever since Ladbroke's opened their tents at cricket grounds. It was a natural thing for us to do. It was all very innocent and there was no suggestion of losing a match or a betting coup. For instance, in 1972 at Headingley, when Ladbroke's first had a tent at a game, the entire team had a bet on how many wickets would be taken in a session.

We didn't even think of the bet until we were sitting in the dressing room afterwards, flattened by the defeat, having thrown away the Test match. Peter, I think it was, said, 'What are we going to do about this money?' Suddenly it hit – we had lost the game but won some money. We didn't want to know about it. Later on the tour Peter came back with the £7,500 less tax.

I can say here and now I would have gladly have given every penny back to win that match. It was just the odds were so ridiculous we had to have a go. It was the age of innocence as far as on-track betting was concerned in cricket. Of course, the next thing that happened was a number of journalists discovered we had put a bet on.

I have been asked about our bet several times since the gambling problems beset the game in India and other places. My answer is if I had known the result in advance through a set-up, does anyone think I would have had just £10 on it. I would have put my house on it!

As for Botham, I fancied I would get him on the hook, as we had done often in his career. What's more, he was out of form. Headingley was a small oval and his top edges were carrying all the way. If I'd been smarter, I would not have bowled him so many short balls; I should have thought it through better. But even then, we all thought it was only a matter of time before he skied it. How wrong can you be!

Everyone was so sure it was going to end on the fourth day that both teams were packed and ready to move on. If I recall correctly, we had even checked out of our hotel. It was just one of those games when the impossible happens.

At the end of the tour, Rod and I gave Peter, who had never been out of England, a return ticket to the Gold Coast along with accommodation and a set of golf clubs. The rest of the team chipped in to boost the kitty and thus most of our ill-gotten gains were disposed of. In fact, quite a lot of it was spent in bars around England.

I can understand why in today's climate we would have been hung, drawn and quartered, but in today's climate, no one would have put on a bet through Peter or anyone else.

In those days, there were never any thoughts of setting up matches. In today's more cynical age, I can understand the suspicion. About that 1972 bet while playing Yorkshire at Headingly, for instance, someone might wonder did we drop a catch because we had taken the number of wickets in a session we wanted; or, indeed, did someone get themselves run out because it was the one wicket we needed in that session to win the bet.

The answer is, of course, a categorical no. On that occasion, our bet was five wickets in a session and we had them five wickets down with 10 minutes to go. I went to pick up our money but was told the bet ran to the end of the session and it was exactly five, not six or seven or any other figure.

As I came out of the tent, I told Bob Massie on the boundary and he said no worries because there were only five or six minutes to go. I continued to the pavilion but before I reached it there was a groan and applause. A wicket had fallen and who had taken the catch on the boundary – Bob Massie.

This is why I say it was an age of innocence. The irony of the situation was that if anyone on our team was likely to drop a catch it would have been Bob – sorry, Bob.

When spread betting became popular in England, myriad bets were available, from the time of the first toss of the coin onwards. Anyone caught fixing a match in any way at all should never be allowed to be involved in cricket again – coaching, playing or anything else. It's just downright dishonest. However, I do not agree the so-called selling of information to bookmakers is so punishable. These are the conversations cricketers have been having with cricket fans since the game began:

'How's it going?'

'Fantastic.'

'What's your team going to be?'

'Oh, Billy Bloggs is going to be twelfth man.'

'What do you reckon you will do on this pitch?'

'Greg will probably bat.'

'What's the pitch like?'

'It's a bit of a green top, we should do all right on it.'

'Is Joe Soap going to be fit?'

'Yeah, he passed a test last night, he should be fine.'

It might have been one person, or three, and while it was totally innocent, you can see the degree of information offered. That's where you have to be careful now. Some of the guys who were accused of providing what seemed like trivial information were naïve in thinking they were going to get a couple of thousand dollars just for chatting. However, I also know about the fanatical people in India who would pay thousands of dollars for Indian players to go to their homes for dinner. Players hear about these things and think, silly buggers, if they are prepared to give me a couple of grand for telling someone the team, then fine. If the amounts quoted were true, it's nothing compared to their earnings, contracts and, indeed, their careers.

In contrast, when one of the players came to Shane Warne and Tim May in Pakistan and asked them to bowl badly, they went straight to the management.

What I'm saying is that any cricketer knowingly giving information to someone who is trying to organise a result, or a four off a second ball, or to contrive a toss, in other words anything that could change the course of the match, should be banned.

For a long time, betting was the culture of the dressing room. Imagine day after day of rain in England, sitting in the dressing room with nothing to do. Watching the racing on television, and having a bet, was a good way of passing the time and, of course, we had a few who liked a bet in the Australian teams, as did most teams.

Oddly enough, I wasn't that keen. I only bet a few times. Even now, when I own horses, I don't bother much about the betting side of the sport. My money is hard earned so I rarely gamble. Nowadays, I might put a little bit on if I fancy a horse, or if Dad comes up with three horses he likes, we might have A$15 on them between us. A big bet for me, even on my own horse, would be A$100.

You could say I punted by the way I played my cricket, but I knew I had trained and worked hard, and was ready. So I would try something that was not the norm, such as pitching a little leg-cutter on leg stump or an outswinger on leg to Viv Richards when usually he would crucify you. That, to me, was a gamble.

When the gambling story broke recently, I was not too shocked. My head coach, T.A. Sekar, at the fast-bowling academy in India had told me three or four years earlier there was betting going on at games which were rigged. I told him it was rubbish. To me, it was bulldust. So he named places, matches and players and I listened in disbelief, but he assured me match fixing was big on the sub-continent. Even so, he didn't convince me.

When eventually it came to be public knowledge, he told me of other games which had been fixed. This was a guy who is as honest as the day is long. His information came from the chat among the players. Obviously, gambling was around for a long time before it came to light because he told me of games going back to the early nineties in India, Sri Lanka and Pakistan.

When I heard about Hansie Cronje, I was doing my exercises while watching an early morning programme on television. I immediately said to Helen I did not believe it. It was like being hit by a truck while crossing the road. I believed his integrity was beyond reproach, just from the way he played the game, the intensity of the guy, the commitment. Then there was his Christian background and the fact that he married into wealth – it all shouted not him.

I was never privy to the whispers and stories because when I stopped playing I also stopped going into dressing rooms. I followed the game from a distance but I did not go to the dinners or try to hang on to it. For four years after retiring, I kept right away from the inner sanctum of the game because, basically, I had had my fill of the administrators, journalists and so forth. I needed to walk away. We also had two young boys, Adam and Dean, who needed their father around.

I don't know how I would have handled it if that sort of thing had been going on while I was playing. How would you keep a team together when you think there might be a cheat in among them? When everything you have worked towards for your sport, this full-on endeavour, this love of your country, this love of winning – how could you play a game thinking there may be one or two on your side who were trying to undermine all those things? If you suspected players in the other side, you would leave the field wondering whether all the wickets you took or runs you made were legitimate. It would wreck not only the spirit of the game, but the game itself.

That spirit was still there in England in 1981. The series was as unpredictable as it was good, and before Botham and Willis set about us in Leeds it seemed to be going nicely our way.

In the first Test at Trent Bridge in the middle of June, England collapsed against the pace attack of Alderman, Hogg and me when we bowled them out for 185. But we did even worse, finishing six runs short in the face of sustained hostility from their pace quartet of Dilley, Willis, Hendrick and Botham, with only Allan Border scoring a half century. However, the wicket and weather suited us because Alderman and I took five apiece in the second innings to hurry England out for 125.

Even then we struggled before eventually winning by four wickets with Trevor Chappell, on his debut, holding the ship steady after Graham Dilley took four wickets.

The second Test at Lord's, when Botham bagged his pair, was altogether different and although Geoff Lawson took 7–81 when England batted first, England reached a respectable 311. We put on 34 more than that in our first innings and I played my part with 40 not out in 107 balls.

A draw looked the most likely result as England declared at 265–8, leaving us no time to reach the required total, and a draw it was. There was a warning for us as they took four wickets and we needed opener Graeme Wood to shore us up with 62 not out in the three hours left for play.

Then came the Leeds Test and the whole series was thrown into the melting pot. England won by 18 runs, despite the batting efforts of Bright and myself at the end. He scored 19, our second top score, and I scored 17 off just 15 balls as I tried to hit us to victory but we had no answer to the destructive powers of Bob Willis.

From then on the series came alive, especially as far as England was concerned. The whole atmosphere of the series had changed. Suddenly, Mike Brearley was leading from the front, and from being a beaten team, England started believing in themselves. They won the next Test in Birmingham in just four days.

We thought we had recovered our lost composure when we bowled

England out for 189 in the first innings and then responded with 258. I was feeling good about it, having taken a couple of wickets and scored a steady 18 before being bowled by John Emburey.

We were again the favourites when Alderman, Bright and I bowled England out for 219 and this time there were no heroics from Botham as I had him caught by Rod Marsh behind the wicket for three.

We needed the low total of 151 to win, but Botham tore through our bottom order to finish with 5–11 off 14 overs as we went from 87–3 to 121 all out. This time there was no doubt Botham had won the match for England and deserved his man of the match award. He took his five wickets for one run in a spell of 28 balls.

So it was on to Manchester and the fifth of this six-Test series when again we let the advantage slip and once more it was Botham who took advantage of the situation.

Certainly their 231 first-innings total was nothing to be scared of as Terry Alderman and I shared eight wickets, but again England hit straight back and bowled us out for a miserable 130 with Willis taking 4–63 and Botham 3–28 off his 6.2 overs.

Not to worry, we thought, we would come again and, sure enough, England were struggling on 104–5 when Brearley was caught behind by Marsh off Alderman, one of his five wickets in the innings. But then Botham got hold of us again, and in a much better display of controlled hitting than at Leeds, plundered 118 runs in a partnership of almost 150 with Chris Tavaré. The England tail wagged again and with Alan Knott (59), John Emburey (57) and a few more bits and pieces, they scored 404 and left us a target of 506.

It began to feel as though whenever England were on the ropes and in need of a hero, one would turn up. It was bewildering when we were so sure we were the better team.

We made a good fist of it, especially when Kim Hughes (43) and Graham Yallop (114) shared a useful partnership, and then Yallop and Allan Border (123 not out) gave us hope. But although he and I managed to put on 51, we finished 103 runs short of our target and the series was lost.

At The Oval, even with the series won, we couldn't keep Botham quiet. While Allan Border scored his second unbeaten century in succession, Botham took six wickets and Willis four as we were bowled out for 352. I had my best return of the series, 7–89 off 31.4 overs, but England amassed 314 thanks to a long and patient 137 from Boycott.

Dirk Wellham held our second innings together on his debut with an equally patient 103 as the middle order made sure we set England a decent target of 383, with Botham and Hendrick both taking four wickets.

I took my match analysis to 11–159 off more than 60 overs, but England hung on from 144–6 thanks to Mike Gatting, Mike Brearley and especially Alan Knott, who scored a brave 70 in almost three hours at the wicket.

It was strange we lost the series 3–1 when we dominated so many of the sessions and, indeed, the Tests themselves. I have no doubt we were the better side, but for us it was an unhappy series, apart from not winning, because of the captaincy issue with Kim Hughes.

There was an embarrassing incident at Edgbaston when Graham Yallop was struggling against Willis, and Hughes seemed to be trying to shield him from the strike. As a player in the dressing room I cringed because you don't do that to a top-order bat; he has to survive on his own and if he's not good enough, don't pick him. Happily, Graham bounced back with a century in the next match.

It was one of many small, disconcerting things which happened on the tour. At Headingley, I fancied getting Peter Willey at fly slip. When he came in, I asked for a fielder to be moved there because I knew he liked to step away and flick the short one over gully. Kim refused and said let it stand. I bowled away and, sure enough, a little while later, off it went high in the air, a simple catch for fly slip.

I asked him again for a fly slip and once again he said no and once again a ball was flicked through there. Only then, with me standing hands on hips and Marsh having a word with him, was a player moved there and, sure enough, not long afterwards we took his wicket in the way I had prescribed.

There was a series of little things like that. Again at Headingley, Kim could have bowled Ray Bright when England were slogging instead of the pace men, who ended up bowling two innings in a row because of the follow-on.

I was still on antibiotics from a bout of double pneumonia, which I picked up soon after arriving in England. I had had a sinus operation in Australia and it was freezing cold in the UK at practice. When I thought about it later, we were netting, bowling in two or three jumpers, sweating and then sitting around outside in the cold answering journalists' questions – a recipe for disaster. I remember the symptoms – blinding headaches and profuse sweating, and I passed out a couple of times.

We were staying at the Waldorf in London from where I was rushed to hospital. A doctor told me they were going to do a spinal tap to assess me. I was in excruciating pain and couldn't stand the light but the pain from the needle was even worse.

I was sweating profusely and then shivering. They were changing my sheets five or six times a day. I was in there for two weeks and lost two stone in weight. The Test matches were looming and I was advised not to play because I had lost not only weight but also energy, fitness, strength. With my system weakened, I was vulnerable to infection in the chest and sinuses, and was constantly on antibiotics. After a Test match, I couldn't do anything for five or six days.

I was not very tolerant of anyone; my fuse was short because I was not well and felt lethargic all the time. My anger was showing through, focusing mainly on Kim Hughes, even though he gave me terrific support. As the tour went on, however, it is fair to say our relationship deteriorated.

Kim had great talent and could have gone down as one of the greatest batsmen of all time. He was an impetuous player – some say his impetuosity made him – but I also saw the Kim who said to himself that no one was going to get him out, and they couldn't.

There were two sides to the guy. One displayed this amazing talent, and the other showed itself when he was made captain before he was ready for it. Naturally, he made mistakes and some of the senior players found it hard to cope with some of the decisions he made in the field because they thought they were to the detriment of the team.

There are those who said we lost that series because of the captaincy but I don't believe that now. When you are batting or bowling, you are doing so for yourself and your team, not necessarily your captain.

I went against the doctor's advice to play in the first Test, but I had to go off every time I finished a bowling spell and change my saturated shirt and vest for clean, dry ones. The authorities stopped me doing that because they claimed I was having a shower and a rest. Ridiculous. You cannot shower and change in four or five minutes. The nearest I got to a shower was towelling myself off before putting on a fresh shirt to go back out in the freezing cold.

The umpires told me they had been instructed to stop me going off the field to change. I don't know if it was gamesmanship by the opposition or the authorities leaning on me, but at one stage I was changing on the boundary or during drinks breaks.

Terry Alderman took 42 wickets in the series and the reason why I took as many as I did, even though I was not well, was because the wickets were so helpful. I was able to come down a peg in pace and let my action on the ball do the work while bowling a good line and length. I bowled more with my head than my body, placing the emphasis on thinking batsmen out, deciding where to bowl with line length and movement; it was due to circumstances rather than by design.

CHAPTER SIXTEEN

The Javed Miandad incident

That controversial year of 1981 continued to tease and torment me and never more so than in the first Test against Pakistan in Perth in November. There was a history of acrimony between Australia and Pakistan, and considerable bad blood between some of the team members, but for me, it focused on Javed Miandad.

We went back a long way. He used to stand at short-leg when I was batting to Imran Khan's bowling, and just as Imran was about to deliver, Javed would be mouthing off at me. All the slips would laugh, forcing me to pull away over and over again. Once I told him to shut his mouth, which only increased the taunts. Another time, the Pakistanis tried to slow things down, so much so that it was taking three times as long as usual to bowl an over, and I got so fed up I sat down to make my own protest. In reality the umpires should have hurried the bowlers along.

In Perth, when Javed was batting, he played a ball down to fine leg and as he ran past I made a remark about how lucky I thought he was, or words to that effect. I came to within a couple of metres of him and

I was still talking to him while turning to go back to my mark. At that point, I was struck by his bat right in my back and ribs. I tried to grab him but missed, so I followed him down the track.

I was interested to read in his version that I was supposed to have hit him from behind. I was actually leaning backwards and sort of throwing my foot out, which was called everything from a vicious killer blow to a karate kick. I was in fact off balance and pushing my foot out towards his pads, and then up came his bat as if to strike me. It was all on video for everyone to see.

The whole thing was unsavoury and should never have happened and I regret being involved. However, I did not start the physical contact.

I was pleased Greg Chappell, once again Australia's captain, defended me, arguing Miandad, while looking at fine leg, knew precisely where I standing and furthermore, when we collided, Miandad gave me a jab in the stomach with his bat handle. He said we had been niggling each other as we always did and both of us were to blame.

Richie Benaud said I moved off my line and after an exchange I kicked Javed's left pad and Javed raised his bat to hit me and I backed away. Richie observed that, as we came together again, umpires Tony Crafter and Mel Johnson stepped in.

That same season the ACB had introduced a disciplinary panel whereby Aussies sat in judgement on each other. The umpires lodged a complaint with them against me under Rule 1 of the code and sent Ijaz Butt, the Pakistani manager, a letter setting out a complaint about Javed's behaviour. The complaint about me was handed to Greg Chappell who, with Kim Hughes and John Rogers, general manager of the WACA, fined me A$200. The two umpires protested it was too lenient and the Board picked up the matter while Butt was threatening to take his team home.

I was called before ACB adjudicator Bob Merriman. I brought a couple of witnesses with me and also had a video from a different angle, which clearly showed Javed whacking me. That was all the proof I thought was needed.

Merriman was sitting behind his desk with papers spread out in front of him. I spoke first, then brought in my witnesses who told him what they had seen and that Javed had whacked me and this caused me to react. I asked if I could show the video and was told that the video machine was broken. I asked if he was going to take my word on what it showed because if he didn't, I would show it outside to the waiting press and let them make up their own minds.

At that point, he told me to wait outside the office where I sat for a long time. When I was called back in, on the desk where there had been many sheets of paper, there was now just one, which he picked up and read to me. I take my hat off to Bob because he punished me for reacting, not for causing the incident. I was fined A$120 and suspended for two one-day matches.

I was not proud of what I did; I wish it had not happened and I make no excuse for it. It was a bad example to set for my sport. I would probably have been rubbed out for a substantial period if it had not been for the video and the other facts I presented – and on the basis of the original facts at hand, quite rightly so. I owed it to my mom and dad, who alerted me to the video evidence, and to my witnesses for presenting the true facts.

I accepted the punishment but was not pleased Javed had got away scot-free. That's why I always say that there were two people involved and only one disciplined. The Aussie team stood up for me, claiming I had been judged by television replays and nothing had been done about Javed, who denied any involvement.

In a subsequent interview with Mudar Patherya in an Indian sports magazine in 1983, Javed was asked about abusive language and behaviour of players, and various other incidents, as well as the fight with me. He is reported as saying:

It happens on the spur of the moment on many occasions. Afterwards, of course, you apologise and regret that it should have happened so. When you lose your temper on the field you lose your power to think. In a way you become mad. And the most you can do afterwards is repent for it. Most of us after doing it feel very sorry and admit to having done wrong. Sometimes, of course, what one does is misinterpreted. For example, during the infamous incident with Dennis Lillee I was not to blame. I was merely going for a fast run – there was a second to be got – and looking at the other end. I was unsighted and Lillee came towards me muttering something intentionally.

Suddenly I saw him in front of me so I tried to push him away as I had to make it to my crease. He stumbled and when I was returning for my second run he kicked me from behind. After that I lost my temper. The opinion of many was that the team should have been taken off the field. But let me tell you that there were people who said I should have proceeded to hit him on the head! Personally speaking, I thought I had done the right thing in picking up my bat but not hitting him. The Australian Board later punished Lillee.

I knew all about the previous incidents and I can understand the problems with running out, backing up and all the rest. Because there was already deep aggravation over the previous series, it needed only small things to bring it to the surface. This moment certainly raised the temperature. Having said that, I still got on well with Majid Khan, Mudassar Nazar, Imran and Wasim Raja; they were a sociable bunch of guys whose company I enjoyed.

Things that happened in the Perth match started the ball rolling for some more bad feeling between the teams. The acrimony with Javed continued throughout the series. As a fast bowler, I did not mind the aggravation; indeed, I felt that it gave me an extra edge and an even greater determination to get my own back by bowling well.

We won the first Test by a massive 286 runs, even though we scored 180 in our first innings, of which I made a respectable 16. That looked good against Pakistan's reply of 62 in just 21.2 overs. I took 5–18 off nine overs and Terry Alderman took 4–36. We rubbed it in by scoring 424 in our second innings, with Kim Hughes scoring 106. Javed

Miandad led the response with 79 but Bruce Yardley took 6–84 and we bowled them out for 256.

The second Test was just as comfortable as we won by a substantial 10 wickets at the Gabba. Pakistan totalled 291 this time but again I had a decent return with 5–81. Any hopes they had of getting back into the series were dashed by Greg Chappell who scored a double century in our total of 512 and then, after early resistance, we bowled them out again for 223. Yardley and I claimed four wickets apiece. I took Javed's wicket in both innings – something I enjoyed!

Having wrapped up the series, we collapsed in the third and final Test in Melbourne where I bowled 36.3 overs for 104 runs without taking a wicket in Pakistan's massive total of 500–8. Bruce Yardley bowled 66 overs in the two days and took 7–187. We were bowled out twice, the second time for just 125 on a deteriorating pitch, with Iqbal Qasim tying us down with 4–44 off 24 overs.

It had not been the happiest of series, so I was looking forward to the contest against the West Indies who were arriving later that month, and were by now arguably the strongest side in the world.

CHAPTER SEVENTEEN

Lance Gibbs' record

It would have been especially good to break the world record for Test wickets against Pakistan after all the problems, and I should have done so in the final game. I needed five wickets and didn't take one. Lance Gibbs, the West Indian spinner, was the record holder with 309 wickets, and Channel Nine brought him over to Australia in anticipation, taking 10 days out of his life. He was left waiting in vain. Maybe it was the expectation level. I was clearly in form but did not perform.

It was an amazing let down. I can't even remember how I bowled but I do remember at the end of the game thinking I might never get another Test wicket. If I lost confidence and didn't get a wicket in the next Test, I might be dropped, and that would be the end of it.

The next game, the traditional Melbourne Boxing Day Test match, was the first in the three-match series against the West Indies for the Frank Worrell Trophy. Channel Nine couldn't keep Lance hanging around just in case I did it there so he left without having had the opportunity to hand over his crown.

We won the toss, batted, and were bowled out by Holding, Roberts, Garner and Croft for just 198 on an irregular pitch. Kim Hughes scored an incredible unbeaten 100 out of that meagre total.

There was time for them to go in, and we had them struggling at 10–4 overnight. I took the wickets of Des Haynes, nightwatchman Colin Croft and Viv Richards, but after that we were made to struggle and once again I was assailed by negative thoughts as Clive Lloyd, Larry Gomes and Jeff Dujon held us up and began to put on the runs. I thought I had equalled the record when Gomes nicked one down to the off-side to the safest pair of hands in our team, Greg Chappell. He dropped it. What if I did not get another chance? Fortunately, I got Dujon, to bring me level with the record.

It was some time later, when the ball was getting old, that I angled one across Gomes who, in what felt like a slow-motion replay, hit it straight to Greg Chappell. This time he pocketed it. The record was mine. All of the team congratulated me and someone from the crowd came out and draped me with a boxing kangaroo flag, I was so emotional I even went to the wrong part of the field as it was the end of the over.

I went on to take the wickets of Andy Roberts and Joel Garner in the innings to finish with 7–83 off 26.3 overs.

I didn't think much about it for a long time afterwards because it was on with business as usual. It was only after I retired that I thought a bit more about the meaning of the record. I was lucky it came while I was still bowling well. It has meant more to me since I stopped playing.

At the time, winning was more important than personal records and we were in a good position because they were all out for 201 with just a three-run lead. But, after a great start between openers Laird and Wood and a fine innings from Allan Border, we collapsed to 222 all out with Michael Holding ripping through our late order, me included, taking 6–62.

It left the West Indies needing just 220 runs to win but Terry Alderman struck quickly with the wickets of Bacchus and Viv Richards and we were on our way. I added three wickets to my first innings haul;

Yardley took four, Alderman two and Lawson one as we bowled them out again for just 161.

In Sydney, the West Indies were all together more solid and made us toil for our wickets as they scored 384. Once again, Michael Holding pinned us back, taking another five wickets, as we were bowled out for 267. It remained nip and tuck, and outstanding bowling from Bruce Yardley with 7–98 held them to 255, leaving us with an unlikely 373 to win in four sessions. We were grateful for Jeff Dyson's not out 127, which steered us to 200–4 and the safety of a draw.

The West Indies levelled the series at the Adelaide Oval. I was struggling with a groin injury and bowled only 4.5 overs in the first innings and four in the second. A bowler light, we struggled and the visitors won by five wickets despite brave innings from Bruce Laird, Allan Border and Kim Hughes, giving us a second-innings total of 386. So the series, which had started with so much excitement for me, ended disappointingly.

Within a few weeks, we were playing our old friends in New Zealand – it was our third series in just over three months. Rain wrecked the first Test. There was no play possible on days one and four, culminating in the inevitable draw.

In the next Test, New Zealand beat us by five wickets at Eden Park in Auckland. Bruce Edgar was our main tormentor, this time scoring 161 in 516 minutes before being caught and bowled by Yardley as they answered our first-innings total of 210 with 387.

Hadlee, having experimented with a short run-up in our first innings, was back on his longer run and took five wickets in the second. Lance Cairns, with three, gave him great support as they bowled us out for under 300 again, leaving themselves just 104 to win. Although we shook them up with three wickets for 44, they coasted home to a five-wicket win.

Hadlee, who went on to break my record for the number of Test wickets, took six wickets in the first innings of the third Test at Lancaster Park in Christchurch, but not before we had scored 353, with Greg Chappell contributing a superb 176.

This time we whipped the Kiwis out for 149 with Thommo taking four, me three and Terry Alderman two. New Zealand followed on and although I was unable to bowl for their entire second innings because of a knee problem, we bowled them out for 272, and coasted home by eight wickets, levelling the series.

My knee had been playing up before the tour started but in Christchurch the cartilage went and I couldn't carry on. I had just nailed Coney and was keen to get Martin Crowe. I hardly managed to reach the pitch off a short run but bowled a nice little outswinger, he got a touch and we walked off together. I put my arm around him to console him for getting out to such a gentle delivery – not to mention to give myself much-needed support. It also gave Rod Marsh his 300th dismissal.

Although the season was nearly over, I was out for a long time, missing our series in Pakistan the following September and October, returning for England's visit at the end of 1982. Meantime, I had an operation, which did not work. I did all the pre-season and, although it was sometimes touch and go, I was getting through Grade games and even a couple of Shield games, but I was depressed, particularly when I played against Rick McCosker in the New South Wales game. I didn't bowl well; he made runs and suggested I should retire.

I played in the first Test against England anyway, but it was not right and I bowled mostly off a short run, just getting through. I took 3–96 in 38 overs in England's total of 411. Derek Randall scored a bright 78 and Chris Tavaré a lot slower 89, spending an hour and a half on 66.

Another ton from Greg Chappell saw us safely through the first innings with a total of 424, but any hope of a result in our favour disappeared when Randall, man of the match, followed up his first innings with 115. I took just the one wicket, David Gower's, but still bowled another 33 overs in their total of 358. Willis took two quick wickets but there was not enough time for a result.

Ian Botham reached a couple of milestones in the game, but that was not what made the headlines. During England's first innings, Terry Alderman dislocated his shoulder in a disgraceful incident. It happened when England reached 400. Some spectators, two waving Union Jacks, made their way to the middle, clearly the worse for drink. As we were leaving the square, one of them made heavy contact with Terry, who chased him, brought him down with a rugby tackle and in doing so severely dislocated his shoulder, putting him out of the game and out of cricket for some time.

When Terry went down, Allan Border and I chased after the guy who had hit him and we held him down until the police arrived.

Spectators had started to get physical towards players by this time; they grabbed your hat, your bat, anything they could reach in their search for souvenirs, and I had been whacked several times. It was getting out of hand. It reached a climax some years later during the World Cup in England when there were a number of invasions, which were truly dangerous.

It's like when streaking first started. It was funny at first when a guy jumped over the stumps and made everyone laugh, and it produced a good photograph. But then it became monotonous. It took your concentration away and interrupted the games, and apart from that, it could very well have been dangerous. These exhibitionists wanted to get close to the players and slap them on the back.

I suppose it all began a long while back with the West Indian fans running on to the field to give their favourite players money for any major achievement with bat or ball. They ran straight off and caused minimal disruption but perhaps the problem developed from there.

Years ago on the sub-continent, stands were set alight, and even in the West Indies a local umpire's house was torched. I recall many odd announcements in 1973 in the West Indies, including one asking for a spectator to hurry home because his house had burned down.

It was serious enough in Australia when Terry was hurt. Fighting broke out in the crowd and the police made more than two dozen arrests, mainly English fans. Greg took us off the field for a quarter of an hour while things settled down, but the batsmen, Willis and Taylor, stayed in the middle at the request of the umpires.

One of the outcomes of that incident was the ACB issued a ruling banning players from retaliating. The previous instruction had read: 'Players must not assault or attempt to assault an umpire, another player or a spectator. This code does not apply to any players' conduct towards any spectator trespassing on the ground.' The concern was about players injuring themselves as Terry had.

The selectors were prepared to gamble on me for the second Test but I decided to go with the Shield side to try out the knee against Tasmania. At Launceston, it totally gave way. I flew straight from there to Sydney where my orthopaedic surgeon, Dr Merv Cross, took one look and operated straightaway.

That was the end of my series against the Poms although I played in one or two of the one-day games. The only good news was that we went on to win back the Ashes 2-1. The operation was a success but the knee needed a lot of recovery time and rehabilitation. It was a major renovation and I doubt there is much left of the cartilage. When Dr Cross explained what was wrong, I had never heard of anything like it before. It was pretty rare and not even he knew how it was going to react under the pressure of fast bowling.

After weeks of hard rehabilitation, I played in the one-dayers just to let the other bowlers know I was around and still nipping at their heels. It may have been a bit of a mercenary or selfish attitude but I did it on purpose because I didn't want those guys to think I was going to fade away.

My next Test appearance came five months later in April 1983 in a one-off game against Sri Lanka in the Asgiriya Stadium in Kandy. Sri Lanka were feeling their way to full status and quickly saw how tough it was going to be. Kepler Wessels and David Hookes both finished a handful short of 150 while Graham Yallop was out two short of his century as we declared at 514–4.

I celebrated my return with a quick wicket, taking two as the home side totalled 271. I took the other opener for my sole wicket in the second innings as we won by an innings and 38 runs.

I had done all the hard work to get my knee right, but I was still struggling with it and not doing myself full justice. I didn't know whether it was going to be totally right ever again, and so I suppose I decided to play as many games as I could before being put out to grass.

While we were in Kandy, a movie crew were shooting scenes for *Indiana Jones and the Temple of Doom*. We met the director and were invited to the set to meet the star, Harrison Ford. He must have wondered what the hell was going on and just who we were. Fortunately, there were a number of British guys there who were able to explain.

I was rooming with Rodney Hogg and the night before the match he was up all night being sick. He bowled 12 overs in the first innings and just three in the second. There were often such heroics on the subcontinent because of the food problems and some of the players came back with long-term sickness which affected them for the rest of their lives.

Bruce Yardley came back from Pakistan with some bug in the lining of his stomach which took a year to get rid off. He felt drained and tired all the time. I'm sure some people didn't understand how difficult it could be and why some players would not tour there. These days it's a totally different scenario, with excellent medical facilities and nothing to be compared with the rough and ready past.

CHAPTER EIGHTEEN

The beginning of the end

The next stop on the ever-growing international circuit was the World Cup in England in 1983. I was dropped for one of the warm-up one-day series against England, and then I was told I was not playing in our first game, against Zimbabwe. In the nets on the morning of the game, I vented my anger by bowling for a good hour flat out and giving the lads a hard time. About 10 minutes before the start, while still letting them fly, I was suddenly informed I was playing. I was livid, having spent all that energy bowling my guts out in the nets.

I was ready to quit during the Prudential World Cup in England because I could not see a future for myself in the team; but the more I thought about it, the more I wanted to quit on my terms, when I was ready, and not be pushed out by someone else.

The Cup started badly for us when we were beaten by Zimbabwe at Trent Bridge. I had taken out both the openers for a total of 55 but they went on to score 239–6 off their 60 overs. We finished 13 runs short despite a 50 not out from Rod Marsh and 76 from Kepler Wessels in 130 balls. We lost to the West Indies by 101 runs and, coming on second change, I again took a couple of wickets.

After a comfortable win over India, in which I did not play, we gained our revenge against Zimbabwe at Southampton where I was back opening the bowling and conceded just 23 off my nine overs. Then we were well and truly taken to task by the West Indies at Lord's when Viv Richards scored 95 off 117 balls and I finished with 0–52 off my 12 overs. I was not alone as Thommo was 0–64 off 11, Hogan 1–60 off 12 and Trevor Chappell 1–51 off 10.5.

However, it was me who was axed and, for a while, I took it personally. Australia didn't even reach the semi-finals. I might well have quit then except for the remarks from Kim and from the Australian press, all of whom seemed to be writing me off. I wanted one last fling. The odd thing is if I had not been dropped during the World Cup, I would probably have quit at the end of the English summer because I was not 100 per cent fit after my knee operation. They do say a lot of the game is in the mind and I was determined to be ready for the series against Pakistan in Australia in November 1983 – if selected.

Before the start of the season, Kim Hughes was in touch to say he wanted to talk to all the players and could I be at the WACA at a certain time. From the way he said it, I assumed it was a team meeting and everyone would be there but when I turned up, it was just me. I thought to myself, 'This is interesting.'

I listened to what he had to say, which was basically that I was getting older, couldn't bowl as fast and was suffering with a bad knee, and so he saw me as a first change bowler. I'd be used in a supporting role, bowling 18 to 19 overs and achieving around 2–30, 2–50 sort of figures, tightening things up after the opening bowlers' first spells.

I listened, not very impressed but not saying a lot. I asked, 'Are we talking about Western Australia or Australia because I wasn't aware they had announced the Australian captain yet?'

He was quick to say it was Western Australia and I answered that, if he was finished, I would go. I jumped in my car, drove home, got into my joggers and did a punishing 12-kilometre run. That signalled the start of a training routine which was as tough as I had ever put in. I pushed myself, putting in the extra effort, very much as I did after my back injury, but this was a mix of a long and a short training programme.

I felt I had something to prove and, more than that, I didn't want someone, be it a selector or a captain, to tell me where I fitted in. It was pride and maybe it helped me get through the season as well as I did.

In the first Shield game, Kim threw me the ball and I let it go past. He said, 'Oh, you're on.'

'Things have changed then,' I said. 'I thought I was bowling first change.'

He had seen enough of me at Grade cricket to know I was bowling extremely well and so ate humble pie.

Sometimes you need a little kick in the guts and maybe I can thank Kim for giving me the spur I needed. I had reached a stage in my career, with my knee injury and everything else, when I needed the sort of push he had given me.

But the pressure did not let up, the press were starting to hammer me and I began to wonder again whether my career was coming to a hasty conclusion. It was annoying because I had trained hard and the knee was beginning to feel a lot better. I had done a lot of gym work on the legs, a lot of running, avoiding the roads, going instead along the beach and on golf courses. I built the muscles up to support the knee in just the same way I had built up the muscles in my back. It was not 100 per cent but it was now stronger than it had been since the first operation.

The build-up to the Test series went well for me. I took wickets in the Shield competition and felt very good. I was selected for the first Test, and Kim was the captain. There are lots of things I don't remember about my cricket, and I constantly have to check the scorecards to confirm almost all of the facts, but I do remember the match in Perth because I was so happy to be bowling really well and without pain. I was finding the edge and beating the bat and even though I took just 1–26 off 13 overs, I was satisfied.

We had an excellent start to the series, winning by an innings – which made me feel even better. A massive second-wicket partnership between Kepler Wessels (159) and Wayne Phillips (141) set us up for a total of 436–9. We then bowled Pakistan out for 129 with Carl Rackemann taking 5–32. In the follow-on, Pakistan struggled to 298 with Rackemann adding a further six wickets to his collection.

I didn't take a single wicket in the second innings but felt very good about life as we headed up to Brisbane where Zaheer Abbas won the toss and decided to bat. I waited for Kim to throw me the ball to open the bowling – but it never came. He opened with Lawson and Hogg and the first change was Rackemann. These were the guys who took the wickets in the first Test so I could easily accept it, but I did feel I was owed a little word before we went out rather than not be told at all.

I stood in the outfield for the first session, shortened because of the rain. After lunch, Lawson and Hogg carried on for another shortened session. They were staying fresh and still bowling and I was boiling inside. When I was finally thrown the ball, I bowled the biggest load of rubbish ever seen at the Gabba because I so wanted to do well. I bowled with stupid emotion instead of my head, trying to prove I was still a good bowler. I didn't get a wicket. Lawson took five, Hogg two and Rackemann three. I was left with 0–33 off eight overs, bowling up the hill and against the wind.

It did not help when, after bowling them out for 156 in the first innings, journalists informed me they were going to write that this was the end of my Test career. I decided to call a press conference, mainly because I did not want the speculation to drag on for days.

The manager agreed and there seemed to be press from everywhere. I said straightaway that I had two things to say and both were questions. The first was who had the best first-class bowling average that year? The second was who had the most wickets in first-class cricket that year? They looked at me blankly, so I told them it was me. I said I was bowling bloody well. I told them to go away and come back when they could tell me who had the most Test wickets at Adelaide, Melbourne and Sydney, the next three Test venues. 'That,' I said, 'is all I have to say,' and off I walked.

In their second innings, Pakistan were 82–3 when rain finished the game. I had bowled just two overs for 10 runs and no wickets. Lawson, who took one wicket, had opened the bowling with Hogg while Rackemann had come on first change again and had taken 2–31 off his eight overs.

For the third Test, I was originally nominated 12th man. There was no announcement but someone had whispered in my ear that I would be carrying the drinks. However, the in-form Rackemann was injured playing against New South Wales and I was pulled back into the side at the last moment. It was a reprieve and I showed what I felt when we batted first with a nice little knock of 25 after Wessels and Allan Border had both scored tons in a final total of 465.

It was a good batting track and Mohsin Khan, Qasim Omar and Javed Miandad all scored centuries as Pakistan piled on 624. I came on as first change and finished up bowling more than 50 overs and taking six wickets in an inevitable draw.

Melbourne provided another beautiful flat track for batsmen. Pakistan won the toss and batted first and I opened the bowling with Geoff Lawson for what was sure to be another long session. Sure enough, the two of us bowled 38 overs apiece and both of us took two wickets as Pakistan made 470.

A massive 268 from Yallop killed the match off as we replied with 555, but there was time enough for me to have another bowl – indeed, another 29 overs with 3–71 to show for it.

I felt I had made my point as we set off for the fifth and final Test in Sydney, defending our narrow 1–0 lead. The press and the commentators were all raving, but I was coming to the conclusion it would be a good idea to get out before they got me. I thought of all the other things: my family, the run-ins with authority, the injuries and everything else, and I told Greg Chappell and Rod Marsh this was going to be my last Test.

Greg asked me when I was going to announce it and I told him I would wait until the end of the match. He promptly went out, without telling me, and announced two days into the game he was going to retire. That was fine by me because, as a former captain, he deserved the first announcement. Then Rod said if the two of us were out, he was also going to quit – but after the one-day matches.

During the game, Richie Benaud said this was the best he had seen me bowl, and I took that as confirmation that it was time to call it a day. I thought to myself if this was the case according to the doyen, I could not do any better than quit at the top.

It felt good. I was back opening the bowling and went through 31.2 overs in their first innings, taking 4–65 as we bowled them out for 278. We replied with 454–6 declared, and Greg showed he intended to go out at the top as well with the top score of 182.

We all but clinched victory when we bowled Pakistan out again for 210 and I had another long session with 29.5 overs. I looked up at the scoreboard at one stage with five wickets down and I had not taken one. I could not let that happen and I finished up taking 4–88, including a wicket with my last ball in Test cricket, having Sarfraz Nawaz caught by Wayne Phillips for 20. We cleaned up the match and the first five-Test series against Pakistan with a 10-wicket win. It was a good series win because Pakistan came to us in prime form with Abbas, Mudassar and Miandad all scoring lots of runs against India.

I had taken my wicket haul to 355 from 70 Tests and I left the SCG feeling very satisfied. I knew, at the age of 34, I had made the right decision.

It was also nice that Rod finished on a high note, taking five catches in his last innings, making his record total 355 (95 of them off me), freakishly exactly the same as me. Greg also took a couple of catches. He broke Don Bradman's run record of 6,996 and Colin Cowdrey's 120 slip catches.

We had plenty to celebrate with so many records broken and three veteran players retiring. None of us had talked about it but we had all been thinking the same. When I put my hand up, the others decided this was the end of an era.

We had a splendid evening; all the players were there and a lot of mates. There was not a sad moment, not a tear, just a lot of fun. People joined in, there were slaps on the back. I suppose we ate but I cannot remember where or when or even if we did. In fact, I'm not even sure where we ended up but it was a great send-off with the usual bulldust and a lot of bragging and sending each other up.

One incident summed it up nicely. When I arrived at the pub where we had arranged to meet, I pushed my way through the door and someone came up behind me. It was Geoff Lawson and he said, 'Excuse me, weren't you Dennis Lillee?'

CHAPTER NINETEEN

Retired – or what?

After my farewell Test against Pakistan I saw the season out with Western Australia.

Life was suddenly fun with all sorts of invitations and a lot of goodwill. I even had a tilt at horse racing on pacers or trotters, taking on Ian Botham. I know now I was never destined to be a driver because he beat me. The event at Adelaide's Globe Derby Raceway was in aid of a charity for crippled children. Ian won on a horse called, would you believe, So Sensitive, while I finished three yards behind on Beau Lincoln. The challenge was there and I guess we had a side bet, but I'm sure he cheated by getting the guys to give me the lame horse.

Ian is just fantastic fun and great to be with. He is uncomplicated, lives life to the full and never brags about his cricket. Like me, he doesn't believe in holding on to it once you have finished. In fact, we rarely talk cricket.

I liked the way he played, the way he enjoyed life and, above all, his enthusiasm. A measure of a person is the way the Australian cricket public takes to them, and they took Ian to their hearts. They loved to hate him, but loved him all the same. I would always seek him out for a drink, even though some would avoid him because of the obvious consequences of coming out second best in any session – I often did.

It was unfortunate he never got on with Ian Chappell. It went back a long way and was well documented. I don't know the full story, only that accusations flew about between them after they played against each other in club cricket when Botham was in Australia on a scholarship. There were two totally different sides to the story, each backed up by their friends. I don't care much who was right or wrong, and I'm not silly enough to try to act as a peacemaker between those two tough characters. It strikes me as a clash of two very similar personalities, neither of whom would ever back down, or admit they were wrong.

Early on, we all knew the two Ians did not like each other at all, and it was not helped on one occasion when Chappell was angry Botham had got him out with two bouncers. Chappell hit him for four from the first and Botham went round the wicket for the second ball. Chappell turned his back on it and took a run. As he went up the other end, the umpire was signalling a dead ball. Ian Chappell argued he was taking evasive action and hadn't deliberately taken the ball on the body. That was when he called the umpire an incompetent fool. He didn't use bad language because he had been warned and just served a four-week suspension for bad behaviour.

I became involved once when the English version came to the wicket and the Australian version told me he would be expecting a bouncer so to bowl him a yorker. I bowled the first one short and was hooked for six; the next ball I heeded my captain's advice and trapped him leg before wicket with a full-length ball. As usual, the captain was right and I was such a slow learner. It took me being hit out of the park to realise he was right once again.

Chappell had no respect for Sir Donald Bradman, who was involved with the ACB and sat on the Disciplinary Board. Perhaps he was influenced by his grandfather, Vic Richardson, who couldn't stand the Don. Whenever Vic was asked what he thought of him, he answered, 'He was a very fine bat.'

Ian was so much for his players. He realised some people had given up lucrative business careers to play for their country. In my case I had given up my cleaning business to pursue Test cricket, and he didn't think the financial renumeration for Test cricket was fair. This was pre World Series Cricket, of course, and he took it upon himself to go to the Board, with advice from a former senior player in the game whom he admired and respected, and who had experience with the Board previously. This senior player told him to make an agenda on what he wanted to put to the Board on behalf of the players because in his experience many of the things brought up were never minuted. Points five and six were about finance and about the way cricket was going with more and more Tests being played but with the players still being paid the same as they were 10 years earlier. Ian put forward financial proposals. Apparently, on the first four points there were no comments from the Don, but when point five came up, he moved forward in his seat and said, 'Don't be silly, sonny,' and quickly dismissed any questions pertaining to finance.

Ian had another brush with the Don over his brother Greg. It was suggested Greg should go to India to gain experience against spinners to round off his batting education. You faced quick, hostile bowling all the time in Australia and, Ian believed, India was the place to go to play against the great spinners. He put it to the selectors including Sir Donald Bradman and the Don replied, 'We have got to look after him. We don't want him going to India and getting sick.' Ian couldn't believe that, coming from a man who had never been to India in his life. Of course, some did get ill in India but it was strange to make that decision about someone else's career.

The Don clearly did not like India, and maybe even had a phobia about it. When the team stopped off in India on the way to England, he wouldn't even get off the boat even though the Indian cricket fans adored him and couldn't wait to meet and greet him. All they wanted was for him to touch the ground on the dock so they could say the great Don Bradman had been to India. It's a sad story and strange he felt so strongly about it.

Personally, I had no fears about India or anywhere else and there were plenty of invitations to continue my cricket in retirement, including lots of charity games. I was invited to play in a World XI against England at Jesmond two or three seasons after I had quit, and Helen and I were treated superbly. We were promised the earth and it was delivered. We had six-star treatment with the very best hotels for two weeks and everything laid on. It was an ideal opportunity to see more of Europe and England. We decided we would spoil ourselves by taking the Orient Express to Venice after the game, and it was one of the greatest trips of all time.

In Jesmond, we had a couple of heavy nights with dinners and a few drinks afterwards with Botham, Gower, Lever, Lamb and Allan Border among others.

The day we had to perform, I must have bowled quite well. My body needed a lot of warming up so I had worked quite hard in order to bowl as quickly and as well as I could. I must have knocked over a few guys despite not having touched a ball, other than the odd game, over the previous year or two.

Allan Border was impressed, especially as I had not had a lot of practice; he told me it would be great if I got back into shape because the Test side were not bowling well or to his plan. The seed was sown in his mind and the next thing I knew I had John Cornell and Austin Robertson asking me if I would consider a comeback. Allan was getting at them and would not give in. I said emphatically no. I was enjoying a great lifestyle and spending time with my family and friends, something I hadn't been able to do previously.

Over the next few weeks, every time they had any business with me, John or Austin mentioned Allan had been on the telephone again. After the fourth or fifth time, they began to wear me down and I said I would give it a go, but if anyone asked me I would emphatically deny I was considering playing Test cricket again. I knew getting fit wouldn't hurt and I could always pull out before embarrassing myself if it did not feel right.

I trained so hard I finished up too lean. When I played, I always had a 36-inch waist and weighed 87kg but I got down to 34 inches and was a lot lighter. In trying to prepare properly, I had overdone it, probably because I didn't want to make a fool of myself.

I approached one of the State selectors, Alan Edwards, and told him in confidence about Allan Border's plans and asked what the policy was for selection for Western Australia these days. He said they picked on merit and it had nothing to do with youth. I told him that was fine and I was not looking for any favours. I knew I would need to bridge the gap between Grade cricket and State cricket after such a long absence, let alone the last step, Test cricket.

So I played Grade cricket and took more wickets and at a better average than I had ever done. One mistake I made was to bowl off my old run-up. That was a bit too ambitious, and very tiring.

At 38, I was just bowling outswingers, not trying yorkers or off-cutters, because of lack of confidence more than anything else. I was going for line and length, but it was successful and I took plenty of wickets at 12 or 13 apiece, which was unheard of for me.

The start of the State season came and my name wasn't mentioned or considered, which was fair enough. Western Australia had won the Shield the year before and those who had won it deserved another chance. I decided to keep playing and wait my turn.

I kept taking wickets in Grade cricket and, eventually, someone was injured for the State – and they picked another guy. That was fine because the bloke they brought in had had a couple of games the previous season and deserved his chance. But when another fast bowler was forced to drop out and I wasn't considered again, I began to think the worst. There was no false modesty because my season's results were far better than anyone else's in contention, and they were backed up by a very long record.

Needless to say, I was angry and I went to see Alan Edwards at his home. I got on very well with him and I was able to lay my cards and my averages on the table, and ask why I was being overlooked. He gave me no real answer so I rang John and Austin and told them there seemed to be a blockage in the system because Alan was hedging.

It was all extremely frustrating, and during all this time Allan Border had not called me to find out how I was coming along or anything, though there was a full schedule of internationals keeping him busy. On reflection, I had previously heard from high up that Allan had been told I was not wanted in the team, but I had dismissed it as gossip. But there was a blockage which could not be passed with both the State and Australia. I did not know it then, but I know it now.

At the time, however, I carried on, keeping my promise to Allan. When it was learned I was playing Grade cricket and taking wickets, a couple of States were interested, but I was happy to stay in Perth and not unsettle my home life after so many years on the road.

Brian Davidson, the Tasmania captain, eventually got on to me with an offer of a big contract, sponsored by AAMI, to play the last five games of the Shield for Tasmania. Still unaware how strong the block was on me, I thought if I could play some Shield cricket and take wickets, I could prove a point. I had done the hard work, so why play just Grade cricket and waste it? I wanted to show Allan and the others I could do what he had originally asked me to do, and put the ball right back in their court.

There were hassles from the start of my short time with Tasmania, right from day one when I was up at five o'clock to travel to Melbourne on the 6 a.m. flight and then on to Hobart. My first game was the next day and I had to get three States to rubber-stamp the switch. Western Australia agreed and sent me a best of luck message via Bert Rigg, who added his own good wishes. Tasmania faxed the other two and they agreed just before I boarded the aircraft, but I didn't know that at the time, so it was all fairly tense. I slept for 50 minutes on the trip and heard the good news when I arrived.

It was straight off for a practice session and to meet the players, and then dinner. I was highly nervous as the new adventure progressed. I received lots of telegrams and the next morning went through the customary interviews and then suffered a delayed start. Our opponents were South Australia. We lost the toss and batted first on a pitch which had a wet patch. I would have loved to bowl. The ball seamed all over the place and we did well to score 111 on a difficult track.

My first ball back was to Hilditch and he was promptly in the scorebook as caught Richard Souel bowled Lillee. It was a dream come true for both Souel and me. The wicket settled down, the wind changed around and I no longer had the benefit of the wet patch, but I soon had Bishop caught in the covers. Hookes and Phillips, uncomfortable throughout, survived until the end of the day.

I felt I bowled well despite South Australia topping 400 in the first innings, but we were soon in trouble in the second knock. Apart from a good partnership between Taylor and Faulkner, we batted badly. Afterwards, I talked to the team about positive attitudes and learning from the game.

I was staying in Hobart with Brian Davidson and his wife Carolyn. I had played against Brian many times over the years and we got on well. On the way back, we discussed the organisation of Tasmania cricket and I said I thought it was too decentralised and that the players were too negative. We stopped at the Oaklands pub in the middle of nowhere with a population of around 300 to ask the owner to get us a snake for the game against Queensland because Greg Ritchie was scared of snakes. Obviously I'd retained my ability to plan ahead.

I was missing Helen and the boys a lot but enjoying the cricket, especially when we came up against Western Australia. We were competitive and I bowled well but without success although I was pleased with my form. Geoff Marsh, playing for WA, felt Tasmania was improving with my involvement, which was very encouraging.

For our next game we travelled to South Australia and showed a new approach, scoring 590 on a flat track. Then we dropped Hookes three times before he had reached 20 and lost the opportunity for a surprise first-innings win.

It was during that match that my troubles returned to haunt me. I was reported for using abusive language by umpire Tony Crafter after a caught behind when the player hung around. I told him to buzz off – or something similar. The umpire said nothing to me on the field or after the game. It was an official, Ray Sutton, who told me I had been reported. My disbelief was shared not only by my team but by South Australia as well.

There had been all sorts going on. One South Australia player had given two fingers to the crowd when he was being barracked for batting slowly; another said to one of our players, 'Get f***** now,' after he completed his century. Some of the South Australia players told a teenager in our side where to go in no uncertain terms. There were insults flying around and slow hand-clapping from the crowd.

But the important factor as far as I was concerned was there was lots said but only one person reported. According to the umpires, they heard nothing else untoward from any other quarter during the game.

The Tribunal Chairman did not want to know about any of the other incidents because they had not been reported. I told him he was quite right, they hadn't been, and told the rest of the panel they were guilty of double standards. I further told them they could all take a jump, left the room and refused to take any further part in the pantomime.

I put my side of the story to an appeal panel. I'd gathered my witnesses but was told they would not be needed as my word would be enough. I asked again why the others had not been reported. The Chairman repeated that the umpires did not hear anything from anyone else. I told him they were liars. He started reading the statement, saying there was no change to the charge and at that I stormed out. The appeal was only window dressing. It was typical ACB. Usually I would have said 'not happy – but guilty' but this time I was angry and felt badly done by, especially when cricket writer Allan Shield told me the umpire was supposed to have informed me if he was going to report me.

It left a sour taste, and Graham Halbish, the ACB chief executive at the time, came to Melbourne airport when we were on our way back to Tassie and advised me not to go to the press over the incident. I found that strange. He was obviously worried and, on reflection, I should have gone straight to the papers and told them what had happened, but I didn't. I went fishing with some friends in Tasmania, even though I was still tired after my long spells in Adelaide over the previous two days.

Our coach called a long training session instead of giving us all a day off. The bowlers, especially, deserved and needed a rest. The next match against Queensland started the next day and we bowled. I lasted seven overs before my hamstring gave in through tiredness after the Adelaide marathon, confirming my body had needed rest the day we practised.

Tasmania went on to win the match and the next one, too, a McDonald's Cup game. They were improving all the time, with a much stiffer attitude. It gave me a great feeling but I was very down because of the injury.

Once my Tassie commitment was over, I went back to Western Australia and applied to play for Scarborough. I needed another clearance but was told it would only be considered if I paid the fine for a ridiculous incident in the Launceston dressing room.

Ian Botham and I were having a drink in the dressing room, together with my sponsor, as we often did at the end of a game. There was the usual friendly banter. Botham would have a dig at my age and tell me I couldn't do the things I did as a young man. It was all in jest and good fun. One comment was, 'I noticed that your arm is made of gello these days.' I answered that I would accept a challenge from him at any time.

'OK,' he said. 'Right now,' and pointed to a spot on the dressing-room wall. We were in the home room which was due to be done up the following week. Ian threw a beer can and hit a plaster crack in the corner of the wall and said, 'Beat that.'

I took my turn, missed and hit the end of a fluorescent tube, which came crashing down. It was all a big laugh, not least of all with the sponsor, who was enjoying the banter and the ribaldry between two old campaigners.

The next day he went back to the ground to ensure the glass and cans had been cleared up in the dressing room and to see what, if anything, should be done. He arrived as the curator was sweeping up the glass and throwing the empty beer cans in the bin, along with the usual after-game rubbish. The sponsor offered to pay for any damage but the curator was relaxed about it all and said he had a spare fluoro light and, in any case, the dressing room was being renovated shortly and the bottle had done little harm.

About a month later, I was slapped with a report. I was totally shocked and telephoned the sponsor. I asked if I could read the report to him to see if he recognised it. They were claiming I had ruined a wall and various other things, and enclosed photographs of a can with a little beer spilled out on to the floor. There was another picture of the same thing from a different angle – it was just amazing. They showed the crack in the wall and the honour-board damage which were already there and the broken glass from the light, and claimed there had been thousands of dollars worth of damage done.

The sponsor couldn't believe it because he was there with us and had been back to check the damage the next morning. He knew it was a wrongful accusation and was amazed Botham and I were being charged thousands of dollars for repairs. He offered to come to the tribunal with me to tell them what he had seen before and after the incident, but when I rang him with the date a week before, and offered to pay his fare to Brisbane, he told me his boss had forbidden him to attend.

Botham, in typical fashion, didn't care and paid his fine with a shrug of his shoulders, but he wasn't an Australian and wouldn't have to live with the reputation. I felt it was another example of victimisation. I told them if they wanted a donation to ask for it. If they wanted someone to pay for the redecorations, why didn't they just ask me for the money rather than drag me through the dust. I thought afterwards it was small-mindedness to say that, but what the hell. At the time I was furious.

Nothing was done or said about the dressing room until Botham was in court a month or so later on another matter. If there was to be a report, the rules stated we should have been notified within 12 hours of the incident. Had that been done, we could have taken them back to the room and shown them what it was like and exactly what happened.

Ian had been arrested over events which took place on the plane coming across to Perth. He needed a landowner in Perth to stand bail for him, and I jokingly said, 'You have to be careful, there's only one landowner you know in Perth.' I took Ian a few beers and bailed him out and, in fact, I still have the bail papers as a souvenir of someone who was in more trouble than me.

My son Adam, who was then 11 or 12, wanted to come with me to the East Perth lock-up and when I asked him why, he answered, 'Because I want to be able to tell my mates I saw Botham behind bars.'

I was very agitated by all these things, but time has made them seem a lot less significant, and the anger I felt then has, to a large degree, dissipated.

Until the injury, I worked hard for Tasmania with a best of 6–99 against South Australia. In the return game, they scored over 600 and I bowled more than 55 overs over two days and took 4–165. I was 38 and had not played for three years! For my age and taking everything else into consideration, I was happy with the way I bowled. I wasn't as quick as I was in the middle of my career, but I was about the same standard as the Test bowlers at the time. I was treated really well by my new team-mates. There was no disdain or backbiting and, what's more, the media were also excellent. Maybe this was a nostalgia trip for all of us.

I certainly wasn't hobbling in; I was running in well. The media asked me if I was interested in playing for Australia again but I fobbed them off, as I had still heard nothing from Allan Border or anyone else. At the same time, Australia began to improve and that, allied to the pressure on Allan, kept me well away from the Test scene.

I knew by then it wasn't going to happen and the door Allan had tried to open had blown closed. All he wanted me to do was to play for a year, stand at mid-off or mid-on, support him in the dressing room, help the team's attitude and set an example by the way I trained and bowled. In other words, he wanted me to help with the overall schooling of the young guys coming into the team. I had been badgered into coming back when I was quite happy in retirement, and then I never heard anything. I didn't think I deserved that, but I felt no animosity towards Allan and the team. I wanted them to do well.

It wasn't long before I received a telephone call from Stephen Coverdale, Northamptonshire's chief executive. I had always wanted to try county cricket. I felt fit and strong and it wasn't as if they were asking me to play every game, just to cover for Winston Davis. The idea was that when he needed a break, I would play one or two matches and then he would be back for three. It sounded the ideal set-up for me at my age. The contract was very good and it gave me the chance to play county cricket in a relaxed manner, without too much expectation.

They were so professional and I was kept in touch about the developing situation with countless telephone calls from Stephen Coverdale. Gestetner, an Australian firm, said they would set up fax machines and other communications so I could have regular contact with home and business. In addition, my mate Allan Lamb played for Northants and it began to sound more and more interesting.

I travelled via India for the start of the 1988 season and picked up a sinus problem and a chest infection. To make matters worse, I was scheduled to play as soon as I arrived, against Terry Alderman and Gloucestershire in a four-day match. It was a tough debut as I had no energy and was suffering breathing problems related to the infection.

Northants organised a house for me. John Inverarity and his wife Jane were in England at the time, and I cooked a meal for Jane and her auntie when they were passing through on their travels around the country. John roasted me for showing off and putting pressure on him, and when I took him out for dinner, he had the nerve to say I should have cooked for him.

Invers watched me bowl against Leicester and was pleased with the way the ball was coming out, even though I had no wickets in the first innings. It was then that disaster struck. I turned to field the ball and all my weight came on to my toes. I went over on my ankle because of the long sprigs in my boots and I heard a loud cracking sound, followed by excruciating pain. I could hear people in the crowd laughing until they realised I was in real trouble and was carried from the field. I waited for two and a half hours in the casualty department for an X-ray. They didn't even have any ice to stop the swelling.

The X-rays showed I had cracked a bone and torn all the ligaments, not strained, torn. I was taken to an orthopaedic surgeon who had looked after the brilliant motorcyclist Barry Sheene after he had been badly injured in a crash. He told me they would have to operate, as there was a 30 per cent tilt. I didn't want to upset him but I wanted a second opinion. I called Dr Merv Cross, the surgeon who had done my knee operation in Sydney. I told him what had happened and he said not to let them operate. I explained everything to him and he said he understood it was a third-degree tear, which was the worst. He said if they operated it would be the end of my season and the ankle might never be right again.

I went back to the doctor and told him I didn't want the operation. He was a bit put out because he thought he was doing the right thing.

When I explained the whole thing to Steve Coverdale, he spoke to the committee and they gave the OK for me to go home if I wanted to. It was a terrific attitude and made me even keener to complete my contract. He also told me how my arrival had doubled their membership, helping Northants tremendously.

Dr Cross told me a certain type of physiotherapy and strapping had a 90 per cent success rate, and a quicker recovery time than an operation. That meant a shorter period of time out. He explained the operation was the last resort.

I contacted Don Gatherer, the English rugby union physio, a top bloke and a great physio, and told him what Merv had said, and he agreed to give it a go. Don was marvellous and I owe him a big debt of gratitude. I drove an automatic car with my left foot to see him twice a day. It was very dangerous and I don't recommend the practice to anyone, especially as the trip took an hour each way.

We worked together and I was playing again in just under eight weeks, wearing a brand new ankle brace from America. It allowed up and down but no sideways movement. It was all very one-dimensional and I was still wary on the ankle, lacking confidence; for many years after retiring from the game, it remained that way.

Northants were a good-looking side. They had Allan Lamb, Rob Bailey, Ned Larkins, the captain Geoff Cook, spinner Nick Cook, wicket-keeper David Ripley who was a promising youngster, Richard Williams who had knee problems, Alan Fordham, David Capel and, of course, Winston Davis. It was a good team on paper but somehow it never quite gelled because it was missing that vital killer instinct.

In one way, I was disillusioned by county cricket because players did not seem to get the right sort of pleasure out of winning, or the feeling of disappointment at losing. The expression and the attitude in the dressing room generally never changed. It was one beer, a shower, change and then off. I tried to change it and suggested a few beers after a win, but it was quickly pointed out that the players had to drive, either on to the next game or home to see their families first. I understood, but I didn't like it.

Nevertheless, I had a wonderful time, particularly with my old mate Allan Lamb, with whom I got on fabulously, and, with our influence, a few of the others gradually joined in the after-match socialising. Eventually, it wasn't so much Northants but the other teams who didn't seem to want to mix. It was more like a job to many of them, rather than playing sport. I had never experienced this before. I was surprised and have to admit I was pleased I hadn't played county cricket all my life.

I was treated really well. I was welcomed by the committee, the players, the fans, everyone; people couldn't do enough for me.

I have to admit it was pretty lonely in the house. Helen and the kids came over in the school holidays but I rattled around it when I was there by myself. I must say I enjoyed the touring most because I had company and my meals were cooked for me, but who wouldn't! It was when I was injured the boredom came, living on my own in the big empty house.

I played a few games in a row right at the end of the season. I wanted to complete my contract after the faith Northants had shown in me.

The first couple of games back, I don't think I bowled at all well, but I could feel it coming back, and when we played against Essex and my old foe Graham Gooch, I was feeling good. Here was a guy who had done so well but he was a dour bloke, so I told the boys I was going to shock him.

I bought an old man's mask with long grey hair and put it in my pocket. When we went out to bowl, I reached the end of my mark and put on the mask. Gooch hadn't noticed a thing as he went through his usual routine. Halfway through my run-up I could see how startled he was while Lamb and the others in the slips were killing themselves laughing. He pulled away and complained it wouldn't be fair if he was out while I was fooling around.

He was out soon afterwards anyway, and I showed I had not lost my sense of humour, remembering having bowled apples and tennis balls for a bit of fun and a release of tension. You had to liven things up now and again, especially in the county game, which could become a little sleepy. I expect they thought I was a mad Aussie with my occasional antics.

There was a bit of fun at Worcester, too. They made 362, Northants 191, and we walked back out behind our skipper Geoff Cooke, closely followed by Phil Neale and the Worcestershire team. Phil said to Geoff, 'You're batting.'

Geoff replied he hadn't been informed of that and, as far as he was concerned, Northants were fielding. Phil had assumed we would follow-on but had said nothing. Geoff was right to the letter of the law, and was probably a bit indignant no one had bothered to tell him.

They asked the umpires for direction, but they passed the buck back to the captains. Phil asked Geoff to bat again but once more our captain said that, technically, the Worcester captain was wrong and should bear the consequences.

There was massive confusion. The rest of us sat around as the umpires, captains and the Worcester secretary got in touch with Lord's for a ruling. Richard Williams, tongue in cheek, asked how many wickets they should forfeit since so much time had elapsed between innings.

I enjoyed my time with Northants and had some good figures now and again, including six in my first match against Gloucestershire. Terry Alderman, playing for them, did not have such good figures in that game. I felt very good about that because he was in the prime of his career. It was a great confidence builder for me.

Northants wanted me to do another season but I declined. They were very understanding and asked me to come back over as coach, which I did for three months, but I realised, during the season, it was not a feasible role. We had a great time and I did a lot of work with the young bowlers, but you cannot work with fellows who are bowling day-in and day-out. All I could do was talk to them whereas my main strength at the time was showing them what to do and how to do it.

While I was injured, I asked the county if I could coach any young fast bowlers. I would stand there on crutches and coach them for a couple of hours a day, but after about three sessions and seeing about six guys, it came to an end. I wondered what the problem was and was told that there were no more up and coming fast bowlers.

'In Northampton?' I asked.

'In the entire county,' was the reply.

I knew then there was a problem. They were bringing in guys from the Northern Leagues, including Simon Brown who went on to play a couple of games for England.

I learned a lot of things about county cricket; the system was festering at the time and just not working.

In each county I went to, the pitches were being prepared for that county's strengths. I found it distasteful and a big problem for English cricket. Some of the pitches were terrible, including Edgbaston, while the Test track at Notts was as green as anything for Rice and Hadlee. It was no coincidence that English Test cricket was going through a bad spell. I could see that county cricket was going to suffer long term.

Batsmen were going in and just getting the quickest runs they could before the pitch got them; and from the bowling point of view, they didn't have to bowl a line and length and work to get guys out. They knew they only had to put the ball somewhere near a reasonable length and the pitch would do the rest. Then, when they were promoted to the Test team and played on good pitches, they were in trouble and found wanting. England cricket went through a bad time partly as a result of the pitches in county cricket.

Added to this, there were too many overseas players, too many teams and too much cricket. It was short-term gain, but all it did was help certain counties and force the hand with other counties. This had a detrimental effect on batsmen and bowlers.

The one-day game meant a lot of negative bowling with little swing, fewer spinners, and few real quicks. England had three one-day competitions. Other countries were improving while England were on a decline. They passed somewhere in the middle. They were even passed in the one-day game, which was mind-numbing with players often going through the motions. When you play so many games, you can lose two or three and it doesn't matter.

But for me, it fulfilled a dream of playing county cricket and being able to assess what was going on. It was not something I would have considered at that age except for the circumstances. It was worth going over and having a look from a coaching and playing perspective.

Back home in Perth, Barry Shepherd, who recently passed away, put forward the idea to the WACA of having a pipe-opener to the Australian season with a similar flavour to Arundel, which I always loved. He approached the Midland Guildford Cricket Club and they, in turn, approached me and asked if I would play to try to get a crowd for the first match at Lilac Hill. Their gutsy endeavours used almost total voluntary labour from the local club and townsfolk, but it needed something other than two teams having a practice game.

I enjoyed it so much I carried on playing that one game every year. As I reached my late 40s, I kept saying to myself I would like to play one game of top-class cricket at 50, survive and not be an embarrassment.

Our eldest son Adam had started to play a bit of cricket and, as the magic age approached, I thought it would be great to play a game with him before I finished, so I asked if he would like to play at Lilac Hill. He was playing third and fourth grade and this would be against a touring side, Pakistan, but I reminded him they are only club cricketers when it's all boiled down. It took him 24 hours to decide and he told me he would love to.

I remember, after Adam had played three games of fourth grade, he rang to tell me he had his first five for. I was delighted and told him I never had a five for in fourth-grade cricket. He thought he had one over me and was thrilled until I told him I had never played in fourth-grade cricket. He loved that.

His first A Grade game was against my old club, Perth CC, and he rang to say he had another five for in his first game. I told him how great it was and that in my entire first year in A Grade, I did not take a single five for. He hesitated and asked, 'Is that like the fourth-grade story?' In fact, it took me many games to chalk up a five-wicket haul in one innings.

We practised together for the Lilac Hill game and I did my usual two months of solid running, sprint work and bowling to prepare for my one game a season. This would be my last. They asked me to carry on but it was hurting too much.

I was nervous going to the game because I didn't want to embarrass myself. I picked up Adam on the way and said to him I would understand if he felt nervous because I did, too. He said, 'No, actually I'm not. I can only do my best so I'm not nervous or concerned.'

I always insisted on bowling downhill with the wind at my back in those games, but when Adam played I gave him the honour. I felt he could do with any help he could get, having played only in lower grades. But the way he bowled, he showed no sign of nerves at all, not in the least bit perturbed. He bowled beautifully and with the two of us bowling together, we had them struggling on 24–5 after eleven overs. I had the nerves for both of us.

The Pakistanis were not at all happy the game was taken seriously and I understand a complaint was lodged that this was supposed to be a practice match. That was a red rag to a bull. Did they expect us to go out and bowl them half volleys? I have never seen a batsman not try, so why should a bowler, especially a 50-year-old and a third-grade one?

I bowled eight overs, four maidens, and took 3–8 while Adam also took a brilliant catch off my bowling. He ran in from the fine-leg boundary, suddenly realised the ball was going over his head and arched up and to the side to take a wonderful catch. He was very excited about it. He said he overran it because in third grade cricket they didn't come so fast.

I told him, 'It was a good job you caught it, otherwise you'd have been walking home.'

For me, the remarkable coincidence was I took a wicket with my last ball in a Test against Pakistan, and then I took a wicket with my last ball against Pakistan in my final game at the Lilac charity match. I also have a feeling I took a catch with my last ball in Shield cricket for Western Australia. Maybe I'm dreaming but if not, that was some hat-trick. It's freakish there should be such coincidences in life, very spooky.

I enjoyed my involvement with the annual match, calling in friends to play to add to the attraction for the spectators. The odd thing is that, as a player, I did not get on with Midland Guildford Cricket Club. Their nickname around Perth was 'Monkeytowners' because they were seen as very parochial, steeped in tradition. But they were really hard workers who put everything in whether it was for the club or for Lilac Hill. It was one of those things that I loved to hate them, but it was nice to see the real feel for their town and their team.

I am patron of the Lilac Festival now. No one has explained to me what a patron is supposed to do, so I try to keep everyone happy at the game by visiting as many of the sponsors' tents as I can.

One of my great mates said to me in the bar, 'It's awfully disappointing, isn't it.'

'What is?' I asked.

'Missing one of the eighty sponsors' tents.'

'Why is that such a bad deal?'

'Because it was Veuve Clicquot.'

'Right,' I said. 'We start with them next year.'

That's the sort of day it is.

CHAPTER TWENTY

Lillee the coach

The odd thing is when I stopped playing at 34, I never thought about going into coaching until I had an approach from New Zealand. I was asked to help some of their young fast bowlers in their mid teens. I agreed because I thought it was a way of keeping in touch with the game. It was also a good opportunity to see if coaching was something I wanted to do.

I suppose I was fortunate because I was handed a good bunch of players, including Andrew Caddick, Chris Cairns and Danny Morrison, and thoroughly enjoyed the experience. The coaching was interesting and I did a couple of years with New Zealand.

Then I received a letter from India's former wicker-keeper Syed Kirmani. He told me Ravi Mammen, another former wicker-keeper and a friend from schooldays, had a great idea about producing fast bowlers for his company and for India, and would I talk to him. Ravi was head of the Madras Rubber Factory, a huge corporation in India which produced tyres, one of the biggest companies in the southern hemisphere.

Ravi telephoned and we established an immediate rapport. I told him to send me a letter outlining what he had in mind, and on the way to England to play county cricket for Northamptonshire, I called in to see him for a further chat. As a result, I more or less agreed to set up a fast-bowling foundation from scratch. There was no written contract and the deal was sealed on a handshake. It's the only time I have ever committed to a contract on just a handshake.

We used the Madras Cricket Club ground and appointed a local coach. They had someone in mind but I was adamant it would have to be someone of whom I approved and who had the enthusiasm to do what was going to be a difficult job. They went for T.A. Sekar, who had played two Test matches against Pakistan in the early eighties, but I knew little about him.

So many youngsters came for coaching in those early days. They were not evaluated properly before I saw them and many were sons of important men or were there because of favours owed. At first it was a shambles, but at least it was a well-organised shambles. Explaining the philosophy of fast bowling and showing the technique to all of these kids, many of whom I knew would never bowl fast, was very hard work. Within three or four visits, I told MRF I wouldn't coach these boys any more. They were to be put straight back on a train home. I told them it was wasting their money and my time.

Fortunately, my first impressions of Ravi held good. We also discovered a mutual liking for rum; Old Monk was his favourite and he used to import Bacardi for me. Over a fairly big rum intake one night, I told him of all the shortcomings I'd found, that it was going to be hard work, expensive and it may take as many as 5 or 10 years to see results. I expected him to cancel the whole exercise but I wanted to tell him the truth. He was untroubled by my alcohol-induced revelations.

The press were a lot harder; they were looking for instant results but I told them there was no chance of immediate success.

During my first few visits, the boys bowled morning and afternoon for 14 days straight. Now that alone, as I told them, meant they would not be able to produce fast bowlers because they would wear themselves out, or bowl within themselves if they were sensible. There would be no way of telling where the potential lay.

Virtually no one had ever done any fitness work, such as swimming, aerobics, bike workouts or running, and there was no such thing as a gymnasium for strength work. They bowled six days a week, for at least two hours a day. This was how they had always done it in India, so I had to change the entire approach. I held meetings with our coaches and the MRF executives and told them the kids would bowl afternoons only; if I saw them getting tired, I would give them a day off.

I brought in fitness experts from overseas and set up a gym with an instructor to show them how to use the weights. We employed a sprinting coach, a fitness guy and a dietician, and had a doctor, a physiologist and an orthopaedic surgeon on call. That was our infra-structure; it was huge and was costing a fortune.

But they had faith in what I was doing. We changed the entire way in which fast bowlers were trained in India and brought it more into line with Australia and other parts of the world. In Australia, we were leading the way with research in to fast bowling and had done so for a long time. Frank Pyke, Darryl Foster, Bruce Elliott and others had progressed the art and moved it into the twentieth century.

Teaching a new technique was also a problem. The trainees would do it with us, and do it very well and effectively, but next time I saw them they had gone back to square one because their club coaches were changing them back. It took a little while to twig what was happening and I didn't blame the coaches. They were earning their living and had no access to the new research. The only way I could get around it was to coach the coaches.

So, within a year or two of starting up, we invited the coaches to come to watch the sessions. We had about four turn up the first time. Maybe there was resistance; maybe they were embarrassed they were not up with the latest developments. I don't know.

Ten years down the track, once the youngsters were succeeding and going back to their clubs and helping to coach the kids, we began to progress. Over 100 people turned up to one of our seminars and we couldn't get everyone in. Now we hold seminars every couple of years and every one is fully subscribed. We hold the seminar in the morning, and there's coaching in the afternoon.

Another problem we came up against was the slow Indian wickets. We could have a guy bowling really quickly, but back with his State or his club, the wickets were so bad he bowled six overs only, to open up the event before the spinners came on.

My good friend Papa Vasu, a former coach, was so on side it helped. He told me, 'Dennis, you are trying to change a whole culture here. Historically, potential fast bowlers have been ribbon cutters.' Traditionally, it was a case of getting the ball a bit dusty and rubbing off some shine to help their great spinners get a grip.

Every chance I had, I mentioned to the press they must come in line with the rest of the world with good cricket wickets, rather than wickets which assisted only their spinners and their batsmen. I think this is just gradually being rammed home and there are signs of change.

I have never worked with a more ethical group or a more supportive company than MRF. T.A. Sekar has developed into as good a fast-bowling coach as I have seen anywhere in the world. He has a couple of university degrees, and admits he knew nothing about fast-bowling coaching when he started. He learned quickly and is now doing a fantastic job, along with the other support staff in general.

MRF are still as excited about the project as ever and there are two factors keeping me going. One is that we have opened the Foundation to the world. I was getting so many requests to coach but I couldn't do any more, so we welcomed other countries' fast bowlers. At this stage, we do not charge a fee and all they have to find is their airfare.

The other factor is personified by a youngster named Tinu Yohanan. We inducted him as a teenaged athlete who had never played cricket before. He was 6ft 4ins tall and had a terrible action, but after four years of coaching he was picked to play for India – proof you can take the raw material of a good athlete with cricket ability and turn him into a fast bowler.

We now have MRF trained fast bowlers at every level, with some who have played first-class and Test cricket going into coaching, which means the scheme is bearing fruit for India in the longer term. That is very satisfying after my early promises to MRF.

When we started there was no fast-bowling history or base in India; even Kapil Dev, a great swing bowler, was not genuinely fast. To have helped start it on an upward trend has given me immense satisfaction. What we have done is to develop the entire structure to encompass strength, fitness and the mental side of fast bowling and, of course, technique. Hopefully, down the line, we can encourage the authorities to develop better pitches. I'm still doing it, still loving it and still without a written contract.

Vinoo Mammen kept the school going after Ravi died of a massive heart attack at the age of 39. I lost a great friend and the company lost a great chief executive. Vinoo, who wasn't much into cricket, told me he wanted to keep the foundation going in memory of his brother. Even though he runs this massive company, he turns up regularly at practice. The ultimate compliment was paid a couple of years ago when Vinoo said to me, 'Our company is today better known for its fast-bowling foundation than for its tyres.' I'm glad the publicity has helped the company. Sadly, the founder and chairman of MRF, Mr Mammen Mappillia died only recently. He was a great man who keenly followed the Pace Foundation's progress through his daily attendance at the MRF office right up until he passed away. At least he saw Ravi and Vinoo's dream bear fruit. Vinoo has recently been elected as chairman, so the company is in top hands.

I would love to have a similar fast-bowling foundation in Perth but it would take a monumental company to be able to afford to take on this commitment. However, we have most of the infrastructure and I am going to set up a fast-bowling academy with the WACA. There has been a dearth of local fast bowlers for some time and we want to put that right because Western Australia, with hard, fast wickets, has always produced fast bowlers.

From a personal aspect, my involvement with MRF convinced me coaching was something I enjoyed and I continue to enjoy the opportunities which have arisen to keep up my involvement with the game.

Late in 1985, it was a case of poacher turned gamekeeper when Australia slumped after five players departed the international scene. We were thrashed by an innings in the last two Tests against England and then lost to New Zealand by an innings in Brisbane.

The ACB chief executive Graham Halbish organised meetings between selectors, officials and the skipper Allan Border in a bid to improve team performance. Remarkably, they called on me to help them out, something I was delighted to do.

I began by concentrating on the bowlers, but became involved in all aspects. Drawing on my own experiences, I talked about the importance of attitude and the application of skill. I was careful to praise the players rather than knock them down, and emphasised the importance of teamwork to bring out individual skills, but I was always careful not to usurp Allan's role.

I liked Allan. He was the first in Australia of what we call cricket journeymen – a full-time cricketer at a time when most players had other jobs. He was a professional and did everything asked of him. You had to respect him for his gutsy attitude. He was a dogged player who could also play some very good shots, bowl a bit and was a top fielder. In other words, he was a very good cricketer and a good team person. I got to know him as an opponent in State cricket and as a team-mate in the Test side.

Bob Merriman, the team manager, was particularly pleased with my contribution, even though the last time we met was in a Tribunal. He was once quoted as saying that, despite the problems, I had always accepted the role of the team, including the importance of the manager. He went on to add, significantly, 'He demonstrated the importance of team spirit and tradition – a point that some other senior players have not fully accepted over past seasons.'

Australia won the next Test against the Kiwis. I was in Goondiwindi, some 700 miles from Sydney where the match was played, doing some promotional work, and as soon as we heard the result, I telephoned to congratulate the team. A few people heard me making the call and realised the players had said come down and join the celebrations.

Everyone chipped in and three or four of us flew down on a private plane owned by one of the farmers. We arrived around midnight and got back around 7.30 the next morning. It was a whirlwind trip and the players appreciated the effort.

In the early nineties, Merv Hughes was getting towards the end of his career and Craig McDermott was nearing 30. Some handy players were coming along, but few who were really quick, or ready for Test cricket. Of more concern was that many of the promising young fast bowlers around the country were breaking down. There seemed to be many more back problems and other injury problems than there had been in the past. By nature, fast bowlers have injuries, but back injuries were increasing and getting out of hand.

The ACB asked me to address the State squads and the Test bowlers. I agreed but I also wanted to look at the 17- and 19-year-olds because I wasn't sure I could help those who were already in State teams to advance to the next level. I wanted to look at the next five years down the track. They agreed and we set up the Pace Australia programme.

There was an improvement, and a few of the guys who came into the Test side because other players were injured did not disgrace themselves at that level, which had not always been the case in the past. I suggested we look for depth in order to cover for injuries, and in the future there should be seven or eight guys playing Shield cricket who would not be far off the mark if called up for Test duty.

At present, I feel we are in good shape. A lot of fast bowlers have come through the Pace Australia programme. Andy Bichel, Jason Gillespie, Brett Lee and Glenn McGrath form our Test attack and there are some other very good ones in Shield cricket, competent enough to play at Test level. The idea was to keep up strength at the next level so these guys could come in and do a good job. It also gives them an understanding of all facets of fast bowling, as they are the coaches of the future.

Before Pace Australia, there was not a lot of understanding of the mechanics of fast bowling. As far as coaching technique is concerned, I suppose I was in the right place at the right time. Each state now has a permanent fast-bowling coach to follow up work with the Board's programme. The infrastructure is there and I believe I have done a reasonable job so far.

Coaching holds a great fascination for me these days, and the more I am involved, the more I want to be involved, especially where fast bowlers are concerned. With Pace Australia, my main concern is to work on technique and the mental approach to fast bowling. I leave the fitness and strength side of things to the experts and talk about what's needed to make it to the top level and how hard it's going to be to get there and stay there.

Of the current crop of McGrath, Gillespie, Lee and Bichel, who all came through the Pace Australia programme as well as the Academy, Glenn McGrath is clearly the number one. He is a great machine, but he was very raw when I first saw him as an 18- or 19-year-old. If you had asked me then if I thought he would make it, I would have said, 'Are you talking Sheffield Shield or Tests?' I thought he might have a chance of playing Shield cricket, but that was by no means a certainty. Test cricket was way out of his reach. So there's a guy whose work ethic has not only allowed him to reach the highest level, but has made him one of the greatest fast bowlers of all time.

Jason Gillespie seems to come back stronger after injuries. He's got more of a surprise element about him than the other three because of that whippy action. He tends to swing the ball a bit more than the others, and to slip in a delivery which slides on to a batsman a lot faster. In other words, he's a breakthrough bowler.

I have seen Brett Lee come through from a 16- or 17-year-old kid when I thought he had technical problems with his action. I mentioned it to him but he wasn't too worried; all he wanted to do was run in and beat everyone in front of him. He has also gone through injury problems and come out stronger for it. The best is yet to come from him. He is a superb, attacking bowler.

Andy Bichel is a real workhorse with a terrific attitude. He will bowl until he drops – one in a million. In any other era he would be a permanent first-change bowler and would have a Test career lasting more than 10 years. It's unfortunate for him that there's such extreme talent ahead of him and he gets a game only now and again. He should have played a lot more games for Australia. Currently he is bowling superbly.

What the authorities are concerned about most at the moment is over-bowling teenagers. In the past, the coaches over-bowled the bigger, stronger boys, as evidenced by too many injuries in that age group, or players who abandoned pace to become hack medium pace bowlers. The ACB set up the Pace Bowling Technical Group to look into the problem, and a lot of research has been done. One result is the experimental introduction of over limits in matches, and ball limits in the nets. Now the ECB is doing the same. Let's see if that approach works, rather than allowing kids to bowl for two hours in the nets and over-bowling them in games when they are too young. It is at least a positive initiative.

CHAPTER TWENTY-ONE

There's more to life than cricket

Just after I first retired, the family went on a four-month trip around Australia in a four-wheel drive vehicle. We had never camped together, nor had we been four-wheel driving, but we decided to go and see a little of our country.

We started putting bits and pieces together for the trip, but left the major things to the last minute. Then a week before we were due to set off, my manager signed me up for a television commercial and I had to fly to New South Wales and film from Tuesday to Friday. We had arranged to leave on the Sunday and we still didn't have a tent or a car. So I rang up a mate and asked him to select a suitable vehicle for us to go travelling round Australia, not a new one, but a good one with a buy-back price. He said later, after the trip was over, that it was the most nerve-racking thing he had ever done, finding one with all the right specifications and then hoping it wouldn't break down on us – and he owned a car dealership. He needn't have worried because not a lot went wrong with it, apart from the odd flat battery.

I got back from making the commercial on the Saturday and we went shopping for a tent for the four of us. The boys were then aged 10 and 12 and I told the salesman it had to be a good family tent. Everything was going in or on the roof of our newly purchased Toyota Land Cruiser. The first night out we stayed in a motel and the second night we put up the tent. With four of us in it, we could not move without treading on a mattress. I thought three months of this was not going to be good.

Arriving just after the sun was setting at the beautiful Monkey Mia, near Shark Bay on the north-west coast, we were told by the site owner we could pitch camp anywhere. I looked around for a quiet spot, away from all the other campers, and noticed a tree on the beach, all on its own and very beautiful. That was the place. I drove the four-wheel drive over to it, pitched the tent, and for the next six hours we were slapping and scratching because of the sand flies. It was very difficult to sleep.

We got up early, packed everything on top of the car and as I started to back out, it got bogged down in the soft sand. Some people were sitting up on the ridge watching, and one of the guys came down to help in his four-wheel drive. The man had two strong arms but two stumps where his legs should have been. I reckon they sent him on purpose to show the townie you don't have to be able-bodied to get out of a place like that. I am totally indebted to him for his help, but I'm still convinced we were set up.

It was like 'National Lampoon' holidays with us cast as the Griswald family. It was brilliant, though, terrific for the family. The boys were learning all the time, which was good because we had taken them out of school for this trip of a lifetime. We organised them to write diaries and they started with a flourish, two or three pages a day, but this gradually diminished to two or three lines a day. They became restless with the schoolwork, and were much more interested in what we were doing and seeing.

There was a strong feeling of camaraderie on the road. We helped a couple of people out of problems and, in return, we were helped whenever we had problems. The main one came right up in the north-east in the Gulf of Carpenteria. We were trying to make the next place, which was an hour or so away, but we had left late and got back to the river crossing at the worst time of day, almost nightfall. We had been told someone had to walk in front of the vehicle through wash-aways to check the depth of the water, and to make sure there were no rocks to damage the car, but I remembered the route we had taken coming in. So I took the right instead of the left-hand side of the watery track, and sank to the floorboards of the car, in fact past them.

There were no trees around to help us winch the vehicle out, and we thought it unlikely there would be another car along because it was late. We thought we were well and truly in the manure.

They say to keep your motor running, otherwise water flows up the exhaust and is sucked into the engine. If we nodded off to sleep and the engine cut out, or if we ran out of petrol, we were stuck. Anyway, it would have been difficult for us all to sleep in the cramped vehicle and the marshy landscape was not conducive to bedding down under the stars. The children were getting hungry and fractious. We were hundreds of miles from mechanical help and it was scary to think what might happen.

Fortunately, as dusk descended, someone came along out of the blue and pulled us out. We were saved from a hell of a predicament.

Our rescuers were typical of the lovely people we met. Travelling around the country was one of the best things I have ever done. There were no commitments, no obligations work-wise, no story to do for a newspaper, no commercials to film, not even any calls to the local radio station. This was just pure adventure for the family and me.

We had arranged to meet John Cornell in the Northern Territory, where we planned to go to Kakadu to see the location for the film *Crocodile Dundee*, starring Paul Hogan. But everywhere we went we were delayed by friendly people wanting to chat, even in the outback.

One night we camped in a caravan park in the remote north-west town of Halls Creek in Western Australia where, unknown to us, they held a Stockmen's Ball once a year – and this was the night! Next day we pulled out and went to buy some petrol in the township. I was standing at the petrol bowser filling up, with Helen and the two boys sitting in the car. Suddenly, four huge guys appeared. Now I'm fairly big but all of them towered over me. They were built like brick outhouses. They surrounded me, stopped and just stared. I was nervous because of the family in the car, and also there weren't many people around. The only thing to do was to go on the attack and act brave. I picked out the biggest and said in a gruff voice, 'Yes mate, what can I do for you?'

'Jesus Christ, it is boys,' he said. 'How you going, DK? It's great to see you!'

Before that moment I had all sorts of images of what they were going to do to us. For once, it was a great relief I had been recognised.

I had stopped playing only about a year or so earlier, and I was still pretty recognisable, with all the facial hair and the mop on my head. So I made a momentous decision to shave it all off, moustache, stubble, hair, everything. It's ironic now, I suppose, as nature has got rid of it all anyway.

Sporting my new look, I decided to surprise Cornell. I rang him up and told him to expect us. When he answered the door he just said, 'Yes?' probably thinking I was some sort of freak. He couldn't believe it; he didn't recognise me at all. He immediately rang Paul Hogan, who was staying in the same hotel complex, and said he was coming over. We went up to his room, knocked on the door, and when he opened it, he looked me straight in the eyes and said, 'Hello Dennis, how're ya going?' You could have flattened us with a feather – so much for my disguise.

Even being in such confined quarters together, we all got on. The boys were a bit difficult in the early days, but a quick slap on the behind when the first monumental argument wouldn't stop and they settled down to life on the road. I explained to them we were in the car for three months and I wouldn't accept any arguments, which would make it unbearable for all of us. After that I only had to touch the brakes and things settled down. It was a bit like Pavlov's Dog but It worked. I think the boys loved the whole concept of the trip, learning to muck in, pitch the tent and the rest of it, and it gave them, particularly Adam, a great love of nature and the outdoor life.

We travelled approximately 28,000 kilometres around the circumference of Australia, including Tasmania. It took longer than the three months we'd allowed, but I had to be back in Perth for a mate's wedding because I was best man. I left the car and the family in Melbourne, where my brother and sister lived, flew back, did the necessary, and then carried on to finish the trip.

How many people get to know their own country? It was a fantastic trip and we enjoyed it so much Helen and I are planning to go again, but this time we will take much longer and see everything at our leisure.

When I stopped playing, I had to work because the sport, as much as I loved it, had hardly provided me with a pension.

I've been involved in many business ventures over the years, including the contract cleaning business I joined when I left the bank and helped to build up from employing 40 people to 440. When I returned to cricket after my back injury, my partner offered me a consultancy, but I thought it would be unfair because I wouldn't be able to give it my all; and if I tried to do too much it would not be fair to my family. So I decided to get out. I took back my initial borrowed capital interest and, after having worked extremely long hours and very hard, I walked away with virtually nothing. Two years later, I believe the business was sold for around A$2 million, half of which would have been mine if I had stayed on. That's life. It was more important I was doing what I wanted to do.

After a time out of work, my brother-in-law suggested I went to see a friend of his in the car-selling game. I told him I didn't want to sell cars. However, Rod Slater, the proprietor of Eurocars, didn't want me to sell cars; he wanted me to be his Promotions and Advertising Manager. Now that was something different, but I had to tell him I had no experience in that area. He said he would teach me, and he did. I enjoyed myself immensely and worked hard to repay his investment. In the end, a downturn, along with bans on French imports, hit the business hard. I was the last of his unskilled staff and he sat me down and told me that, because of the problems, he would have to let me go. I was disappointed but there were no hard feelings; I completely understood the circumstances.

I had just secured a job in television with a three-month contract and very good money which eventually carried me into the Packer era. Since then I have been self-employed.

I'm involved in Superstars and Legends, a retail venture selling memorabilia old and new. It was initiated by Mike McCabe and based on the American franchise Field of Dreams, to whom a percentage is paid. After eight or ten years, Superstars and Legends have around 14 stores. When they first started up there was nothing like it in Australia. I helped to recruit the people the company needed and became a shareholder and advisor.

The generation who were young when I played are now in the 40s and 50s, and with more disposable income, they are able to buy things to remind them of those early, developing days. There was no marketing then – no caps, no shirts, no T-shirts, in fact little to buy other than scorecards and bits of trivia. I remember someone doing Thommo and Lillee T-shirts and they expected to sell hundreds of thousands but, according to the guys who set it up, they sold just a couple of thousand. That has changed now; I could probably even sell my aluminium bats. I take a back seat these days as it is a big operation run by the best people.

I am employed as an ambassador by Sony Music and have just finished with ABB, the big engineering and construction company, basically to help with clients at dinners and staff functions, and also to help with advertising and promotion.

I do a few after-dinner talks, coach in India and Australia and, more recently, Helen and I have come up with a new coaching set-up which I can continue with at my leisure for many years to come.

Early on, we dabbled in some renovation work. Helen and I would buy a run-down house on one of the better streets in a reasonable area, with a view to resale or rental. We'd rip up carpets, scrape walls, fix ceilings and redecorate. We couldn't afford to employ contractors so we did it all ourselves, with very little expertise in the beginning. We did it with the first house we bought and took it from there.

I am on the Board of Governors of the Sony Foundation, which is a charitable organisation set up by the Sony companies. Its aim is to contribute to the advancement of the Australian community by assisting young people and fostering their talents. It directs money to worthy recipients under 25 years of age, be they facing major challenges, from disadvantaged backgrounds, or gifted and talented individuals.

I endorse the Dennis Lillee Sports Foundation for People with Disabilities, which is a fund-raising arm of the Western Australia Disabled Sports Association. In addition to supporting disabled athletes, they run a variety of programmes for all skill levels with myriad sports and recreational opportunities. I'm also patron of 'Walk for the Cure', an unusual fund-raising effort for the Juvenile Diabetes Foundation of Western Australia.

All this time I have stayed in Perth, the remotest capital in the world, and I know I made the right decision to stay with my roots. The smartest move in terms of business would have been to relocate in Melbourne or Sydney because the amount of time spent away from home is horrendous and has been since I was 20. But I have never found a place I like more than Perth. I've been to a lot of wonderful places but the remoteness of Western Australia has been an advantage. People don't ask you to do trivial tasks at every turn just because you are so accessible. It takes up to five hours to get to the other major cities, and that's an expensive air trip, plus the cost of accommodation. That always sorts out the wheat from the chaff; only those with real purpose follow through.

The people of Perth are blasé; they let you get on with life and don't treat you much different from anyone else. The oddity is that the reverence seems to have become more noticeable as I have grown older, and I believe it's because people think I was a lot better than I actually was. People still come and ask me for autographs for their seven-year-old child. I'm never sure how true that is and often wonder as I sign if it's a little trip down memory lane for the parent doing the asking. I don't mind.

I was introduced to house husbandry when I came back after my stint as a coach in Northampton. I flew in at about 2 a.m. on the day Helen was going to start her two-year, full-time university course. She had been going part time for some years but this was an opportunity for her to complete her studies. Five hours after I arrived home, jetlagged and shattered, Helen woke me up to say, 'It's all yours. Today is washing day and you need to strip all the beds and wash the sheets, pillowcases, bedspreads, towels, tea towels, everything.'

'Fine,' I answered, 'but how do I switch on the washing machine?'

She had to write it all down and by the time she returned home that evening, I was still doing the last bit of washing and housecleaning.

Along with this, I was still working and if I needed to go away on business interstate, I would prepare food and freeze it for Helen and the boys. I must say it was a shock to the system.

I'd told my mates I would be having cups of tea and lunches with the ladies in the street. Two months down the track, my mates were ringing me up at seven in the morning and saying, 'Have you looked outside – it's a great drying day! Get the washing done and come to lunch with us!'

I can tell you that not once in those two years did I have a cup of tea with a neighbour, and if I went to lunch it was only about half a dozen times. I even had headaches for the first three weeks!

CHAPTER TWENTY-TWO

Western Australia

I was very fortunate to play for Western Australia in a great era. We won four Shields out of six between 1971 and 1977 and, for good measure, beat touring sides England, Pakistan and the West Indies. We won the next year, too, but by then I was playing World Series.

Every season, we played eight home and away games against each of the other States – South Australia, Victoria, New South Wales and Queensland. Whoever gained the most points during the season won the Sheffield Shield. A bonus points system was introduced later and disappeared again, which I was glad about because I didn't feel it helped in the preparation for Test cricket. What it did do was help some average cricketers look good.

Western Australia had six players in the Australian team for most of that time. We expected to win every game in Perth and we pretty well did. It was a matter of how many matches we could win in the eastern states, where the wickets were very different from ours. We reckoned if we could get maximum points at home and one or two away wins, or even a few first-innings only wins, we could win the domestic trophy. It helped that the Test players were in the team most of the time which is different today due to heavy international commitments. When I first started, there were times when there were no tourists in Australia, and all the Test players who were fit and available played Shield cricket. It was commonplace then.

I remember in 1971, Geoff Boycott playing for the MCC in Perth. I bowled him a lifter and turned the peak of his cap around by hitting it. The look on his face was worth all the hard work I put in to the delivery. They say the way I bowled in that game against the MCC, and their uncertainty, was the telling factor in my being selected against them for my first Test match. I doubt whether I would have made the same impact at that stage of my career at any other ground in Australia.

I loved playing at the WACA. The spectators were usually very quiet and restrained, but often changed when I bowled. The chant started up when the lads had got a lot of booze inside them, and as I came in off my full-run up, they would start up, 'Kill, kill, kill, kill, kill.'

When I started playing, the WACA's southern end had open grassland and a little brick building probably no bigger than 12ft wide – a bit like a set of toilets. In fact, it was a bar, with five or six guys serving from kegs of beer, and every so often you could hear a great hissing noise as they speared a fresh one. It could be pretty disconcerting when you were batting. The opposition always claimed it happened just when I was running up to bowl; knowing how parochial Western Australia fans are, they might have been correct.

I was determined to be friendly with the cricket supporters because I was taught a lesson myself when I was young. One of my heroes at the time told a group of us kids to disappear when we asked for his autograph. I don't know why he did it – and I'm sure he had a reason – but from that moment on I thought that if I were ever in that position, I would never knock anyone back. It was unusual for this particular overseas player because he was usually very chatty and friendly, but on this occasion he snapped and it left a bad impression. Later, when I got to know him, I didn't tell him and I would not reveal his name now because I still like to believe it was a one-off. I remembered it, though, and even if I didn't have time, I would apologise and tell the kids where and when I would sign if they still wanted me to.

The youngsters liked us because we would smile, say hello and talk to them off the pitch, and then on it we were so young and combative and played to win. They enjoyed that and felt part of it.

Because of this, I was disappointed with the response to my joining World Series Cricket. When I came back afterwards, I tried to put as much of the nonsense over what happened in the background as I could, and got on with my cricket and my life. I put my bad feelings to one side. It was hard but I certainly made peace with the players although I remained very cool towards the officials. I didn't make a real effort or go out of my way for them; I just did the things I had to do. There was a chasm, and I felt it was justifiable to have a cooling-off period with them and some of the press after being ostracised during that time. I had no qualms about it.

Now I'm fine with the WACA, and I help them out when I can. I'm patron of the WACA museum and head their fast-bowling academy. I have some very fine friends around the board and I'm more relaxed with everything than I was for a time after the troubles.

When the WACA said they would like to name a stand after Rod Marsh and me, I was surprised and delighted, and only too pleased to accept without feeling anything of a hypocrite. Later, when my mates suggested we all hang out in my box in the Lillee and Marsh stand, it dawned on me that I had no box. It would have been a nice gesture if I'd had somewhere to sit in the stand named after me. Even so, it was a wonderful honour. To start with, it was the butt of a few jokes because it was called the R & I Lillee-Marsh Stand, sponsored by the R & I Bank. Mates used to say they had heard of R & I but who was this Lillee-Marsh fellow. Now it's just called the Lillee-Marsh Stand.

The defining moment of my cricketing life came at the WACA on 11 December 1971 when Western Australia played the Rest of the World in the game arranged to fill the gaps left by the banning of South Africa from world cricket. Taking a lot of wickets against quality players, even though the pitch was helpful, was a boost for my confidence. They were good conditions and I was able to exploit them. I wasn't really sure at that stage exactly where I wanted to go, except I knew I wanted to achieve maximum results with what assets I possessed. That performance gave me the confidence to keep on trying. To bowl out a team of that quality for 59 was something which left a big impression on a youngster. Some said it only happened because it was a green wicket, but it wasn't like the Miracle Match pitch because we made 350 on it and pitches don't become a green top as the game goes on. Maybe it had sweated a little overnight but I remember it gave me good pace and lift. There were other guys bowling at the other end and you still have to bowl well whatever the conditions. What really suited me was it was fast and bouncy and I was bowling bloody quickly. I don't even think there was much movement in the air or off the wicket.

John Inverarity and Graham McKenzie were Western Australia's representatives in the Australian team to tour the UK in 1968; prior to that, the Test team had just the occasional Western Australian. We were considered the Cinderella state, with some guys who should have played but did not, and a few who justifiably felt hard done by.

This was a coming of age and no one could complain about us having six in the squad for the UK in 1972 at a time when Australia was struggling. There is no doubt it was a turning point for Australian cricket. Western Australia had a fitness regime, which other states did not have at that time. We prided ourselves on being fuel for each other and for each other's success. We would have regular get-togethers, as families and as a team, and this was not done in other states, as far as I know. It was the beginning of Australian teams developing a close bond, talking about comradeship and team spirit. I have no doubt it started with the influx of Western Australia players. That may sound a little parochial coming from me, but when it's analysed properly, I'm sure others will agree. That, combined with a captain, Ian Chappell, who was a born leader of men, made it an amazing era of change for both Western Australia and Australia.

On the subject of captains, John Inverarity was one of the best, if not the best, captain I have played under together with Rod Marsh and Ian Chappell. However, out of the three of them, the one who made some amazing decisions based on his feel for the game was Rod. He could set up an ambush or turn the game around when it was going the wrong way. Invers and Ian often consulted him during games, and had he been given the opportunity to captain Australia more, he would have been one of the great captains.

They were three different sorts of blokes. As captains, Ian let the game flow a lot more and would pull in the reins when he felt it was drifting. He wouldn't make changes for the sake of it and would, in most cases, leave it up to the bowler and the players in general. For example, Ross Edwards, fielding in the covers, asked Ian should he be a bit squarer, to which Ian replied, 'Listen mate, you're the expert cover fielder. If you think you should be squarer – go!' That typified Ian whereas John would set his field and you would stay there.

But that didn't mean he wasn't always trying new things. One story shows both what a competitor Ian was, and how he would try everything and anything to gain an advantage over his opponent. It was during a tour of England, when we had been the guests of a friend and the plan was to take in some golf the next day. Most of the team went back to the hotel while the golfers sat and talked, eventually getting around to the question of whether there were many homosexuals in sport and, in particular, in cricket.

The conversation moved on to other subjects until suddenly it was three or four in the morning when Ian Chappell looked at his watch and decided it was time for bed if he was going to play golf in the morning. Rod and Ian played golf against each other for sheep stations – or so one would have thought!

Ian and Rod were shown upstairs to the spare bedroom where they were expected to share a double bed as all the other beds were already occupied. Ian hesitated but then both said no problem. Ian quickly grabbed the duvet, rolled it up and put it between the two. They both lay down but Ian had some trouble dropping off and, having thought of the earlier conversation, he leaned over the rolled up duvet and grabbed Rodney fair and square between the legs.

It was reckoned Rodney rose two feet in the air horizontally and floated there in shock before descending back to the bed. Rod swore out loud but Ian just turned over and went to sleep, leaving Rod lying awake all night wondering if it was going to happen again. Rod didn't get a minute's sleep, which suited Ian down to the ground with the golf match coming up in a few hours' time. Rod, however, even without his beauty sleep, whipped him again. Ian's attempt at gamesmanship had failed miserably.

Invers, a headmaster, was much more of a precise mover, working out what should be done in the period – what are we going to try, how do we get this batsman out and things like that. Rod leaned towards that style rather than Ian's. Rod would be making slight changes from behind the stumps even when he wasn't captain.

Initially, I liked to be told where I should be bowling but when I gained confidence and experience, I had my own ideas and hoped the captain would be prepared to back me. But all the way through my career, if Rod told me I should be bowling in a certain way, then I bowled that way. He was probably the only bloke whom I followed without hesitation. With the others, although they may have been in a better position than me to assess the situation logically in the heat of battle, I thought about it first.

Greg Chappell was a perfectionist who expected everyone to be as perfect at what they did as he was at what he did. He seemed not to allow for guys who played in a slightly different way, less professionally and more for fun in those amateur days.

When he had the series of ducks, he was labelled 'Chappello' by the inventive press, and that weighed on him, but it made him realise nobody is perfect and he became a better captain for the experience. It showed he was as human as everyone else in the team and no matter how good, how professional, how talented a player is, everyone could go through a horror run. He realised people were trying their hearts out and they were either not good enough, were having no luck or their ambitions were not aligned with his.

Towards the end of his bad run of scores, he asked me to go out to the nets and bowl to him. In the past when I bowled to him in the nets or in a game, he had used a very straight bat for his first 20 or 30 balls faced, hitting in the 'V' between mid-on and mid-off with no cross batted shots. Now I was seeing him turning the bat's edge on balls pitched on middle and middle and off, trying to play them to the leg side, and whereas before I never saw anything other than the full face of the bat, now I was seeing only half a bat. It seemed to me he was playing from the start of his innings like a man who had already made 50 and was seeing the ball really big. I suggested he went back to the basics he had adopted previously at the commencement of his innings.

Before that, I didn't take much notice of Greg in the nets because he always appeared to be playing well. There wasn't even a middle ground with him until his bad run.

Both Greg and Invers were big practical jokers and smart with it. They were quick-witted and dangerous to be around. I'm glad they backed off after a while; otherwise I would have been a complete mess, although I think it probably helped to toughen me up.

Ross Edwards, although playing in the days of amateur cricket, was the consummate professional. He was fanatical about fitness and demanded perfect practice sessions, not only with his batting but also with fielding. He would practise alone, throwing ball at a single stump in a hockey net. He had all sorts of catching practices worked out, and in the nets he batted as though it was a Test match, which is the only way to improve but not many did it. Even when he bowled, although it was pretty ordinary, he put everything into it.

In those early days, we were paid A$200 for playing a Test match and A$30 for the State, so none of us had much money. Ross was the guy who initiated and set up mini sponsorships at a time when they were not commonplace. He did things like organising for us to be supplied with suits, ties and shoes in return for contra work for one of the clothing stores. He would organise gear and cars and all sorts of things. He was enthusiastic and seemed to enjoy it.

I would always look for Rosco to go on a run or do some exercises. He loved a chat, liked to have people around him and took his guitar with him for a singalong whenever we toured. He was a great tourist;

you would seek out his company. His enthusiasm about everything in life was so infectious and there was nothing negative about him at all.

He came on the scene quite late, probably because he was thought of as a wicket-keeper and there were others in front of him for glove duty. As a batsman, he was an accumulator of runs with a sprinkling of top shots. It took time for the selectors to realise his worth for all the workmanlike things he did in the middle for Western Australia, and by then he had ceased to be a wicket-keeper. He saw no chance of advancement in that position, so he decided he would get into the Aussie side as a batsman and a fielder. He worked many long hours, aiming to become the best cover fielder in the side. I reckon he was worth 30 runs an innings to any team. He was always in credit before he batted.

On his day, Bob Massie was the best swing bowler I saw. He suffered badly from asthma and hay fever so his fitness work and training was minimal compared with others. He did his work by bowling lots of overs in the nets and running around the boundary while umpiring Aussie Rules football. He wasn't a physically strong person, which let him down badly in the end, but with the right conditions, he was as good as anyone.

There was, of course, his match-winning 16-wicket performance against England, and he had many great matches for Western Australia. Who knows why he didn't play more? His style was to keep pitching the ball up to try to get some swing, and if it wasn't there he did not get wickets.

Most fast bowlers used something to help shine the ball; there's no doubt about that. I used spit and perspiration from my oily skin and I discovered that if I wore a pure wool jumper which contained lanolin and rubbed the ball on the jumper, it really glossed up. From time to time, almost everyone had a bit of something hidden about their person, but generally it made a different red mark on the shirt or trousers. Some used Friars Balsam to protect their fingers, they said, but it made the fingers stickier, allowing a better grip on the ball. That sort of thing has been going on since the game started and there will always be someone prepared to try something to gain an advantage.

I was guilty of running a thumbnail round the seam to clean it, but you saw a lot of guys doing that. I suppose you do what everyone is doing and there wasn't a lot said about it in those days; it was more or less accepted. It was only when people started to use bottle tops, gramophone needles, nails and other implements to alter one side of the ball totally, causing unnatural movement in the form of reverse swing, that the authorities stepped in. Oil or salve may have only enhanced and maintained the shine but it still changed the natural condition of the ball and was wrong; but it was an even playing field at the time, and no one took a lot of notice. Reverse swing changed everything. Nowadays, the umpires often check the ball between overs. In any case, trying to tamper with it is stupid in today's game when there are so many cameras focused on the players.

It was my big complaint that some of the Aussie team did not bother to shine the ball. Thommo didn't shine it much; Lennie Pascoe gave it just a couple of rubs. I asked him what that was supposed to do and urged him to work on it, which, to his credit, he did when he remembered.

In contrast, everyone was at it in the Western Australia side. There was always someone in the covers who would work away at the ball with plenty of spit and polish, and perhaps even someone in the slips before it reached the covers.

When I first started, there were two fixed television cameras at the WACA, one at the side and one sitting high in the members' stand. Les Trueman, the secretary, came into the dressing room one lunchtime after I had been bowling from that end and said they had received a lot of telephone calls, particularly from old ladies, asking if I would stop rubbing the ball so vigorously around my crutch area. I told him I would not as that was by far the best place to shine it to maximum effect. Fortunately, for either me or the old ladies, the wind changed during the break and I switched ends. When I came in at the tea break, Les came straight up and thanked me profusely for stopping doing it, saying the calls had now stopped. I explained to him I hadn't stopped but was now walking away from the camera, with my back to it, while I was shining the ball. Realising he had made a mistake, he walked out very red faced.

Former Australian captain Bobby Simpson complained that the players from Western Australia were more fervent about playing for their State than for their country. He was wrong although maybe I gave a little bit more for Inver. His enthusiasm rubbed off on us. The teams under him were very passionate and I never knew team spirit in any team better than we had then, not before or since. I would have died for Western Australia, but I would also have died for my club side and for Australia as well.

But I gave 100 per cent for every team I played in; not doing so at every outing is an indictment of players who gave more for their country than for their state or for their club. I never saved myself for a second innings or a Test match or a tour because you never know for sure that you will be around for the next game. That is why I did it, even playing at Lilac Hill at the age of 50.

When we were playing New South Wales in the early seventies, we were bowling to knock them over, something we rarely were in a position to do against them. I was bowling to Kerry O'Keeffe who was hanging around and standing in the way of a rare Sydney Cricket Ground win. Eventually, he nicked a ball off me straight to Ian Brayshaw at third slip, a very straightforward catch which was dropped. I was very disappointed but went back to my mark and bowled another – another nick and another straightforward catch to Ian who turfed it again. I bent down, hands on my knees and yelled out the magic word at the top of my voice, and was reported for it. It was made to sound as though I had directed it at an umpire or the batsman but it was pure frustration. I know I shouldn't have done it. It was abusive language but I wasn't abusing anyone else. I was hauled over the coals for that.

On another occasion, after I had retired from international cricket, I was captaining the State side while Rod Marsh and Kim Hughes were away on one-day duty for Australia. The first session was shortened because of rain. One of the umpires asked me if I wanted to take the drinks on the hour or halfway through. I went for halfway through, which was fine. The next session was shortened again and, as the umpires had not consulted me, I assumed the same thing would apply. I had never read a rulebook in my life but it all seemed fairly logical to me. The session was about 45 minutes or so in and we were about halfway when I called for the drinks. Umpire King said he didn't think we could take drinks. I answered I was sure we could. He said in his opinion we could not because it was a different set of circumstances from the first session. By this time the drinks were at the middle and I told him my bowlers needed a drink because of the extreme heat and the high humidity after the rain, and as they were now on the field we would take them.

I was not abusive but then the other umpire, who had an officious style, came up and indicated we couldn't take drinks. When I asked why not, he replied that rule whatever number it was states if rain delays the start of a session by more than so many minutes, then drinks cannot be taken. By then it was too late and we'd had our drinks while he tried to shoo off the 12th man.

I was reported to Mick Harvey, the umpires' representative. He should have told either me as captain or the players' representative about it, but he couldn't find me and so he went to vice-captain Tony Mann, who apparently just laughed saying he would sort it out. Tony said there was nothing to answer for and I assumed that was the end of it, but it was taken to the Board. An issue was made of it and I was banned, I think it was for a month, and fined many times more than I earned for a game. It was for ignoring the umpires and disobeying them by taking the drinks. I didn't know the rules but this problem could have been avoided by earlier communication from their side.

One of the things I asked was whether they would have fined another Shield player the same sort of money when they only earn A$200 a game.

I made an unsuccessful appeal to keep playing and then went to India to play in a couple of games and a testimonial.

In March 1983, I received a suspended fine of A$1,000 after South Australia officials appealed against the failure of my team-mates to discipline me for abusive language at the Adelaide Oval.

I was bowling. I'd taken three wickets for no runs, turned the game around, and in doing so I'd damaged my knee. I limped off the field through the South Australian supporters who had just seen me end their dreams of the Shield for that season. Nevertheless, I thought I deserved some applause, especially after all I had put in for Australia on their ground, so I said, 'Why don't you clap, you bastards?' It wasn't loud and no one seemed to take any notice, with the exception of an official who either heard it or was told about it. He reported me.

I appealed against the decision after talking to some of the people who were sitting there when I passed through. I asked them if they found my remark abusive and was told, 'No! You should hear what David Hookes regularly has to say when he comes through here after he's been dismissed.' Of course, the tribunal didn't listen to me.

I had a couple of brushes with some officials of the WACA over the years and I presume there was a personality clash. It could be very sour at times. They even complained about me talking about selection in my newspaper articles. I felt it was the tall poppy syndrome and the Board were quietly saying to themselves, 'You just wait, we'll get you!' That was one of the reasons I retired.

Some of it was my own fault because I was forthright and challenging and was always ready to say what I thought, even if it didn't correspond with what they were thinking. I did some things I now regret, but if you weigh up my wholehearted approach and what I contributed to the State and the country, I believe that far outweighs the negatives.

Rodney Marsh was also in trouble a few times, so I was not on my own. He was fined in 1984 for hitting the ground and throwing his bat away in his last game, even though the umpires did not agree with such a penalty.

In a match against New South Wales in February 1981, he was fined just A$25 by the team's panel for remarking to the umpire, 'You f***** idiot, Peter, that was the worst decision I have ever seen in a game of cricket.' The umpire was a good bloke and Rod would not have said it had they not been friends who had a beer together afterwards.

They always knew where to find me, even in those latter days, because I was usually training. If any of those officials who hounded me over the years doubted my commitment to the game, they only had to watch me work out. Training hard was a religion to me and for years I trained on my own. I was even given a key to Fletcher Park, my club ground, because I was always last to leave. I never felt it strange that I was the last man away and locking up the ground. The workload was something I felt I needed to do.

If I wasn't there, I would be at the WACA where I would be lapping late again. During a season I didn't have a lot of spare time because I had a wife and growing family with whom I wanted to spend as much time as possible, but I had official training three days a week, two days with my club and one with the State. I tried to get the bulk of my fitness work done while I was there. I did train on other days as well, after I got home from work, throwing on the joggers, and going around the streets and then back home for a few exercises.

When Darryl Foster became Western Australia's fitness coach he had a very well-planned format. He was highly qualified in sports science and had some fantastic routines. For instance, on a Monday evening Ian Brayshaw and I would go on a recovery run through the forest, something which wasn't often done in those days. It was a three-quarter pace run over about five kilometres to get the stiffness out and the body going again after a weekend of cricket. Tuesday, Wednesday and Thursday were always hard training sessions during the season.

I believe our extra fitness allowed us to knock over sides in the last session. I had learned the principle of a second wind from Pop Len, and if I was fit enough to bowl as fast in my last spell as in my first, there was a huge advantage to be had. We felt other teams did not have the same fitness levels in those early days and fell away in the latter part of the game. That was a factor on which we could capitalise.

CHAPTER TWENTY-THREE

Playing the Poms

When I was very young, I used to listen to the cricket from England on a transistor radio when Australia were playing. The programmes were on in the middle of the night and, with the poor reception, it was eerie listening to John Arlott and the Australian commentator Alan McGilvray under the blankets when I was supposed to be asleep. That was normal practice for most cricket-loving youngsters.

These guys had amazing presence and were great picture painters. The games weren't on television so our images were all conjured up from their commentary as we hid under the sheets so our parents didn't find out.

It was all quite mystical for a very young kid and the aura developed because everyone spoke about Australia v. England as taking on the old enemy, the one that really counted. I guess that dated back to the days when we were shipped out as convicts with England being the mother country. I suppose it came down to wanting to show them, a master–servant type of relationship. I learned to hate what they represented.

The reception we got in 1972 when we went to functions as a team was often condescending among the hierarchy, authority and the wealthier supporters. It was almost as if they were saying, 'We will put up with you – just.' That didn't apply to everyone, of course. We were a big hit with the West End and horse-racing fraternity and lasting friendships have developed over the years. That was the good side, but in those early days, the English were the enemy and we had to beat them. You build it up in your own mind with hatred for the team rather than individual players. I didn't find it hard to build up a dislike because it was traditional; we always talked about England as the major opposition.

As a youngster, I only ever saw them on newsreels or, rarely, on television, yet the names were printed indelibly on my mind – Brian Statham, Fred Trueman, Colin Cowdrey, Tom Graveney, John Edrich, Peter Parfitt, Ray Illingworth, Bob Barber, Ted Dexter, Peter May to name but a few. There was a grudging respect for a lot of them while Fred Trueman and Ted Dexter were secret heroes. When I had to be on England's side in our childhood backyard games, they would be the first players I would pick.

When I eventually met some of those legendary players, they invariably lived up to my expectations. What a good storyteller Fred Trueman was! The first time I met him was in 1972 at Headingley when he bustled into the dressing room, made himself at home and told stories for half an hour in that inimitable accent. He was fabulous and seemed so at ease with himself and his surroundings. He was just so natural. I held him in high esteem, as I did the others. Colin Cowdrey was always trying to make you feel at home, as was the lovely Tom Graveney. I met many of the others only fleetingly.

One of my favourites was Colin Ingleby-McKenzie. He is a fabulous person and one of my 'must sees' when I'm in England. He always made me feel so welcome as a friend and fellow cricketer. He was like a mate anywhere we met, even though he was establishment and well off while I had all the rough edges of a wild colonial boy – but he didn't treat me like that. It was always equal terms with Colin. I love his conversation and his wit, and the fact that he is easy with people.

The irony is before I met him, he typified all the things I thought I hated about the English cricketer, with his wealthy background, his double-barrelled name, the fact he spoke beautifully and played correctly. It shows how we are apt to pre-judge people, often incorrectly.

Allan Lamb is a loveable rogue, a mate and someone I like being with. Lamb makes me laugh all the time and I constantly have aching sides in his company. I cannot believe his energy. When he talks, he's already thinking about the next thing. There's a lot of bluff and carry on, but he has a heart as big as a watermelon and you can see the sparkle in his eyes. He is a veritable Peter Pan with an unquenchable zest for life. He could also bat. He certainly took us on a few times and came out on top, as did David Gower – another person I seek out when I'm in England.

Of the others, I liked 'Deadly' Derek Underwood. He was more serious than Lamb or Gower, but he still enjoyed a laugh, a drink and company, as well as being a great bowler. Give him the right conditions and he was unplayable, and given perfect batting conditions, he was very hard to get away.

Bob Willis and I were probably at loggerheads most of the time because we both had fierce competitive natures, but I still enjoy his company. If I was able to organise a meal with all the people I like best, he would be at the table.

Funnily enough, Mike Brearley, whom I hated with a passion when I played against him, is another former England captain whose company I now relish. Having had a few drinks with him since we stopped playing, I find I really like the man. I still don't overrate him as a captain or as a player. Certainly he's smart and a good man-manager, but my belief is that a great team makes a great captain, and if you are a great captain with a team of ordinary players, you are not going to win too many matches. He marshalled the great troops he had at his disposal very well, but if you have a player like Botham in your side, you are halfway there. He handled him well but that was as much to do with man-management as it was captaincy.

Geoff Boycott would not be at the table. For a start, we have not sought out each other's company over the years and I'm not likely to start now; and I'm not sure many of the other people would want him sitting down with them because he may not be their cup of tea. It takes all kinds to make the cricket world and maybe the person Geoffrey is made him the cricketer he was – not my type of player and not my type of person. I don't think he was a team man. When we played against him, we felt his sole objective was to score a hundred and it didn't matter how long it took him to do so.

I did not rate Mike Denness either, certainly not as a captain, but he was a nice bloke to have a beer with. Ray Illingworth was one of the best captains I ever played against. He had a marvellous feel for the game and the way it was developing. I also liked the way he used his main strike bowlers. If they got a couple of wickets and reached the stage where they might not get another if they carried on, he would rest them. He'd shore up the game with a bowler such as Underwood or himself, tie it right down, give nothing away, while he freshened up John Snow, say, to hit the opposition again.

He was so much more professional than we were in those days. He was also hard-nosed, could bowl beautifully and was handy with the bat, even though he was coming to the end of his career when I came across him. He was a thinking cricketer's captain who could lead by example. His field placings were always carefully thought out and he read the game really well, never asking anyone to field where he wouldn't.

Tony Greig was another inspirational captain, a man to lead from the front. While there was a touch of Pom about him, he was more South African in his attitude – very refreshing after previous England captains. He was the sort of player I liked to play against and he is another I would like to have at the dinner table for his provocative attitude and to liven up the conversation. We would never be mates in the true sense of the word, but I would always be happy to have a drink with him.

Oh yes, he could also play. He bowled quite briskly and was handy with his off-breaks. He could field, and as a batsman he could take a game away from you in a session. On his day, he was a player to be feared because he was likely to get a breakthrough with the ball and then take you on with the bat and change the course of the game. He was similar in many respects to Ian Botham. Greig was a better captain while Botham was a better player who always seemed to make things happen.

John Edrich was a nice guy. He was also a top player whom I rated as one of the hardest to get out because he had such a good sense of where his stumps were and a perfect attitude. If he played and missed, edged the ball or gave a catch which was dropped, he would just walk around, chew his gum and start all over again. It was always the same routine and nothing seemed to bother him. I couldn't tell what he was thinking, judging by his deadpan facial expression.

He only played the balls he had to play, and that was a very new thing to me in those days. I had never seen anyone with such knowledge of what to play and what to leave alone. He played on length and width. It was very frustrating for a bowler like me. I used to think he was lucky when a ball flew past the off stump but I gradually realised it was skill with no luck involved at all.

I enjoyed a beer with Dennis Amiss, a lovely guy, top batsman and good company. He was steeped in cricket and deeply involved with Warwickshire, as was John Jameson, another Warwickshire opening bat.

Bobby Taylor – what a keeper – can arrive any time because he is one of nature's great, great people, just fabulous. We were born a day and eight years apart and he can share my dinner table whenever he wants, as can Mike Gatting, who could be bloody difficult to shift when he was at the batting crease. I rate him both as a person and a batsman.

Basil D'Oliveira would be one of the first through the door. As a batsman, he had such beautiful timing, and he was always at you with good swing bowling. He was also a good fielder and a lovely guy, perhaps underrated because of all he had to go through with the apartheid business. I never saw him at his best but he was still bloody good when I played against him.

Among the fast bowlers, apart from Snow and Willis, the best of the bunch was Chris Old on his day and Mike Hendrick in the right conditions. That's the problem – a lot of them were very good when the conditions suited them. Graham Dilley was great company and a very good bowler who worked hard at his game and thought it through deeply. I rate him up there with the best English bowlers I played against.

John Emburey was a very fine spinner until he started to bowl flat. Playing lots of one-day games clearly affected him, causing him to bowl more negatively.

There were many more positives than negatives about the England players against whom I played. I've kept in touch with several of them since our playing days ended. We don't call each other every week but if you hear they're around, you give them a call and catch up for a drink. A lot of the friendship was built up because of the atmosphere and the tradition of the Ashes.

When it comes to the grounds in England, I rarely think of the pitches which suited me. I think more of the feel and the general cricketing ambience of the place. Lord's had everything and a little more. After Lord's, you could raffle them from my point of view. Trent Bridge, The Oval, Edgbaston, Headingley – compared with Lord's, they were just other grounds.

It's funny to think two of my grandparents were Poms, English to the bone. Pop Len would always barrack for Australia except when we played England, even though his grandson played for Australia. I take my hat off to him because he just used to say, 'If it's England, it's England. I don't care. I barrack for England.'

England was, without doubt, the best of enemies for me.

CHAPTER TWENTY-FOUR

Down south and personal

We have an escape from Perth, a little property down on the coast of the Margaret wine-growing area, private and secluded, and the ideal place to entertain a few friends, particularly around Easter time. Several come down for the weekend, usually at staggered times so we have a chance to open up and get everything ready.

You can imagine the tricks the guys get up to when old team-mates and their wives are due. On one occasion, Bruce and Lorraine Laird were among the latecomers and we got together with the Inveraritys and the Brayshaws to hatch a plan, which involved an old scarecrow I'd found abandoned in a ditch, complete with coat, hat, and trousers on his stick. We knew roughly what time the Lairds were due to arrive, but just to make sure we had the timing right, I arranged for Bruce to let us know when they reached a certain point. It would gives us exactly an hour to prepare our little surprise. I gave him the real build-up about the kangaroos being thick on the bush road they were about to enter and sucked him into our plot.

We had a few drinks, grabbed our coats and a broomstick each, made to look like weapons, and set off through the pitch-black night. Just about the only thing we did not do was black our faces.

We parked the four-wheel drive at an angle 30 to 40 metres from the side of the road with the doors wide open, and laid the scarecrow down on the road, covering it liberally with tomato sauce. I'd remembered to bring a bottle with us. Just as we were finishing, we saw some lights in the distance, and rushed off to hide.

As luck would have it, the moon was behind clouds and visibility on the unlit back road was down to a few metres. Out of the blue, John posed the question, 'What if it's not them?'

I could understand his reservations in view of what we were planning to do, but this was an isolated road and the chances of someone else coming along at precisely the same time as Bruce and Lorraine were due was pretty remote.

Sure enough the car arrived as we dropped behind the cover of a shrub right next to the 'body'. As they slowed up at the grisly sight, we rushed out with our weapons. Invers was still unsure and stayed back in the bushes as we burst out of cover. As soon as the Lairds saw us, the foot came off the brake and off they sped, skidding on the ground, running over the 'body' and off up the road. They went about 50 yards up the road and screeched to a halt, having heard Ian Brayshaw's distinctive laugh.

Bruce was all shook up and said he saw the 'body' first and then the abandoned four-wheel drive and began to think it was a trap. When he saw two figures running out from the roadside brandishing God knows what, he just took off and to hell with the body in the road. It was only Bray's bray that pulled him up short.

Since then, I've had rubber snakes in the bed and all sorts of other tricks, but the Lairds have promised much, much more to come as they plan their revenge.

Something always happened on these Easter jaunts. One day we went out to do some sea fishing in a 12ft by 3ft river punt with a flat bottom and a flat nose, especially designed for lagoons and calm rivers. There was a six-horsepower motor on the back, which gave just enough power for calm water with four adults aboard. We chugged out of the river mouth on a millpond-still day and fished happily all morning. We must have pulled in seven dozen whiting, rock cod, herring and skipjack, and so when the wind began to get up, we decided it was time to start making our way back to base.

One and a half horsepower per person meant we were chugging along rather sedately as the wind and the weather began to whip up. By the time we reached the river mouth, instead of it being a millpond it was becoming a bit more interesting. There were 300 or 400 metres to go to the channel and, as the waves washed by, we had to pick our moment. We were about halfway through the channel when someone shouted that there was a wave coming up behind us. I had the idea of keeping in front of it and gunned the engine, but there was little or no reaction. We were badly underpowered with four adults and a load of fish on board, and the wave quickly caught up with us. With no nose on the dinghy, I couldn't steer it and we were pushed sideways by the wave and overturned.

Joan Brayshaw and Bruce Laird swam madly for safety while Ian tried bravely to get hold of our catch and rescue the supper. As it transpired, we were only up to our chests in water, but no one realised that at first. I was grappling with the boat, which was full of water and very heavy. I eventually righted it but it was a chaotic scene with fish floating everywhere, and Ian shovelling as many as he could into the bucket. Earlier, we had pulled in a two and a half foot long shark, just before we took off for home, and we were all keeping an eye out for it while struggling in the water. Another boat went straight past as though we weren't there, totally ignoring us and leaving us wallowing, but another one came along and took pity on us. We tied our boat to theirs and they towed it into the shallows.

Despite that adventure, I love fishing. Usually I find it very relaxing, even if there are no fish around. You just lose yourself, sitting there with a blank mind, chilling out. I like catching fish but it doesn't matter if I don't. I used to have second-hand boats, but now I've upgraded to a better one that will take me out five or six kilometres where I can fish for bigger ones.

I must admit to having bad luck with boats over the years; I've sunk a couple. One day after fishing for four or five hours, I pulled the boat into the jetty and retired into the house. Next morning there was an urgent call from a neighbour, asking me if I'd lost the boat. A couple of us went down to see if it had pulled a rope and floated away, but as soon as we reached the jetty, we could see it under the water. I had to strip to my underwear and dive in to have a look at the damage. A fisherman helped us haul it out and we discovered the boat had suffered stress fractures in the aluminium body, which had allowed water to enter slowly before finally sinking it. The last straw with second-hand boats!

Sharks were another problem. Before I left for my season at Northants, I was surf skiing, catching the occasional wave. The regulars knew me and used to tease me, shouting they had seen a fin and to watch out for sharks. I ignored them because I had never seen a shark down there – until that day. Suddenly it dawned on me that everyone had left the water except me and another surfer. But it was near to lunchtime, and I decided to have one more wave run before calling it a day.

I made for the major break, which was now totally unpopulated. As I waited for the wave to reach me, I looked up and saw a lot of surfers standing on the beach watching me, and one of them was making fin movements with his surfboard and arm. Fortunately, it struck me instantly this couldn't be a set-up with them all standing there, and I jumped on the first wave, paddling as quickly as I could. It was only then I discovered there was a shark circling behind me. It was 12 footer, so it could have done me some damage. I had not even been aware it was there.

When the boys were small, around eight and 10, I took them out on their little short foam surfboards. It was a nice day with a small swell and as we were paddling out, Dean on one side, Adam on the other, I looked up and saw a fin very close to us. Dean saw the look on my face and said, 'Don't worry, Dad, it's only a dolphin.' I thought it was a shark but he knew the difference.

On our property down south we have a plague of rabbits, plenty of tiger snakes, which are aggressive if cornered and quite lethal, and the infamous red-backed spiders, but I've only seen two or three of those in my entire life. They live in dark places and don't come looking for you. Ironically, as I write this book, one landed on Helen's neck as she climbed into our car in the garage in Perth. She thought it was just a harmless insect, grabbed it and tossed it out of the door. It was only when she saw it dead on the ground she realised the danger she had been in. They can be lethal. If you threaten them, they will bite.

Kangaroos can be a problem when you're driving, and if you hit one it would be like running into Jonah Lomu. My sister-in-law was driving no more than 40 kilometres an hour when a big one jumped out from the bush and landed on the car, destroying the front end. If they go through the windscreen, you can be in serious trouble because as they fight, they scratch and can rip you to pieces. They are tough creatures. If a dog approaches they will stand up and just rip with their front paws, disembowelling the dog. When Dad lived in the bush as a child, he had kangaroos as pets, but they are wild animals, not usually family pets.

CHAPTER TWENTY-FIVE

The best

The best batsmen I bowled against were, in order, Sir Vivian Richards, Sir Garfield Sobers, David Gower, Barry Richards, Graeme Pollock, Greg Chappell, Javed Miandad, Doug Walters, Allan Border and Ian Chappell.

For sheer ability to rip an attack apart, animal brutality and no fear in taking you on, I have to put Viv Richards at the top of the list. I just loved bowling against the man. I enjoyed it because it was such a challenge and I regarded him as one of the supreme players if not *the* supreme player. I think we finished about level – I got him as often as he got me.

When he first came in, he wanted to dominate you no matter what the pitch was like, how well you were bowling or whatever the situation of the match; he just wanted to attack you. I admired and respected him but at times it was also his downfall. Once he had scored his first 20 and settled down to batting properly, you were in trouble. If you didn't get him early, he was likely to score a big total. Viv was like a heavyweight fighter, whatever came his way, he would take it on, fighting fire with fire.

I have Sir Garfield Sobers in second place, even though his career was coming to a close as mine was starting. One experience was enough to convince me he was right up there with the very best, even at the end of his career, aged 36, playing on broken-down knees with more urgent things on his mind. I never saw Garry Sobers bat at four, making those huge scores, but I saw enough and I can imagine from that one cameo role how awesome the man was.

David Gower never looked like getting out while making runs look so easy and scoring them so quickly. In the end, he would play a lazy shot and lose his wicket because that was the way he played, although with him, even the good shots could look lazy because he played them with such ease. I would bowl just outside the off stump and bring in a short cover with cover a bit squarer because he would take on the outswinging ball. To some that's negative play, but it's horses for courses.

I played against both Barry Richards and Graeme Pollock just a couple of times. Barry Richards played one of the best innings I have ever seen but it was in a Shield game on a pitch where no one got wickets and every bowler had hundreds against his name. I have also seen him play county cricket and World Series where he scored hundreds making them look so easy it made me wonder just how good he could have been. He was difficult to bowl to because he could play every shot in the book and then some. He was a magician. Like Viv, he created shots that I had never seen before but he was elegant and brutal in effect.

It was clear Pollock was an exceptional cricketer. He played in 23 Tests and I don't know what the opposition was like but people who saw him and played against him said he was effective and played some terrific shots. If I'd played against him more often than I did, I think I would have concentrated on getting the ball up around the ribs, with a couple of short-leg fielders. He did pull the ball, but when I was bowling a bit quicker, I would have put it there for him to take me on. You would have to bowl bloody well.

Greg Chappell could not only tear an attack apart but he could also be so solid, so technically proficient. In form, he was a beautiful technician, as good as anyone. I have watched in wonder as he played against some of the best attacks I have ever seen. I have also seen him failing against them but then fighting his way back to compile really big scores. I'm convinced he was even better after his brief slump than before. My way to curb him was to bowl six to nine inches outside his off stump, just on a length, inviting him to drive, not just at the start of the innings but any time. I would also bounce him over his left shoulder down leg side, hoping he would be caught at fine leg or by an edge to the wicket-keeper. This could be effective because he would like to take you on.

I had my problems with Javed Miandad but that has nothing to do with my judgement. On all sorts of wickets and against all sorts of bowling, he has to be up there. He was a busy player, especially against the spinners, as he would be down the track taking them on, but prepared to wait if they were on top. He would take on the fast bowler outside the off stump, as if to say, 'Well, what are you going to try next?' He was busy with his feet, busy with his bat and busy with his mouth. I have nothing but respect for his ability to play. He was also a massive in-your-face competitor. I realise now I was too attacking against him when I bowled; if I had the chance again, I would be less so, which shows how he wound me up and won the battle of the minds, too often for my liking.

My old mate Doug Walters would have been higher up the list except he never succeeded in England. His Test average was around 48 over 74 matches, but if England are taken out of the equation, his average is huge. I have seen him change the course of a match regularly in an hour or an hour and a half. He was a wonderful player of spin and fast bowling and his only failing was against the little niggly medium pacers in England. He wanted to get on with the game and didn't have patience. I think the ball didn't come on to him and it moved through the air and off the pitch a little more than elsewhere. He had a unique technique with a high backlift, which increased the chances of him being beaten by a moving ball. I tried everything against him. We had plans and failed with them, standby plans and they failed, too. He always scored runs against us, which is a major reason why I have him in this list.

What a problem the last two were! I could have chosen Clive Lloyd, Zaheer Abbas, Gundappa Viswanath, Martin Crowe, Sunil Gavaskar or Geoff Boycott but, after careful consideration, I went for Allan Border and Ian Chappell.

It was a toss-up between Allan Border and Clive Lloyd. Lloyd had two careers in my opinion. The first was before he was made captain of the West Indies, when he was as flamboyant as Gower and scored lots of runs with plenty of ups and downs. When he became captain, he batted lower down the order and took on the role of father of the team, protecting the lower order. He took his time and became a more methodical and more correct batsman with a much better defence. It was like watching two different people. Border was similar in that he had the guts, worked with the lower order, took on the best bowlers. He played beautiful shots but could also place it around. He was a great guy to have in the team and he made even the best bowlers work hard to get him out. He would not let them dictate to him or the team. I bowled to him just short of a length most of the time, around off stump, throwing in the occasional short ball, fast and straight. I would throw up the odd one at off stump going away to entice the drive and try to get him caught around the gully area.

If I had to pick any one of those guys to play for my life in any match situation against any bowling, on any wicket, in any conditions, and especially if we had our backs against the wall, I would have no hesitation in picking Ian Chappell. If a team ever needed runs in any situation, I would put my money on him to come through. He was so strong minded, strong willed, and would not be bogged down or dictated to by the bowlers in the way Boycott or Gavaskar were. He had a great defence and would turn defence into attack with short singles and boundaries.

Sometimes I bowled well to Ian Chappell and sometimes not so well. The best way was to bowl at the stumps, perhaps with the ball going away, because he did like to turn the ball on the on side as much as he could. When you got a bit wide, he took you on and if I bowled short to him, he would take me on. I guess over the years, we finished 50–50. He was a bat-for-your-life type of player and always exciting.

Apart from Lloyd, Zaheer Abbas and Crowe came close. I saw Zaheer bat beautifully but I also saw him struggle, particularly against the shorter ball, which he did not always cope with. Viswanath just missed out because, if anything, he was too flamboyant and, like Zaheer, could struggle and I didn't see Crowe play much. Gavaskar and Boycott are not included simply because they were not my type of player; and when I look at the new era of Test players, I understand they are a dying breed, not seen as up to the modern stroke players who score their runs quickly. You may have one in the side if you have half a dozen real stroke makers, but they are on their way out.

If I had to choose the best of the current crop, I'd go for, in order, Sachin Tendulkar, Brian Lara, Steve Waugh, Adam Gilchrist and Mark Waugh. This selection cannot be nearly so comprehensive as those I played against because I've only seen some of them on television.

However, I have no hesitation in nominating Sachin Tendulkar at the top of the list; you don't really need to say much more than he is the 'Little Master'. He plays on all wickets against all sorts of bowling and doesn't appear to have any weakness. He will be the first batsman in history to score a century of centuries in one-day and five-day Test cricket.

I first saw Tendulkar when he was 14 and he was outstanding then. I was doing an MRF coaching stint in India, setting up a one-day game, telling the captains and bowlers what I was looking for with their field placings, and where to bowl. The other players were standing around listening. A youngster ran in to bowl and the batsman hit the ball straight out of the ground. The bowler looked at me and I told him not to worry, it was a good length but it didn't have the zip in it. I told him to think about it.

The second ball was a bit short, the batsman swayed back and it was gone again. I explained to the bowler that the batsman had read him, and not to go from one extreme to the other, adding this is where the thinking process comes in.

The third ball was much better with a bit of swing but the batsman thumped it off the back foot to the boundary. I thought it wasn't a bad ball and not a bad shot. I looked at the little lad down the other end for the first time and saw he was a young teenager, and quite small.

Two overs later, I asked Sekar, my head coach at MRF, if we had prepared a flat wicket. They hadn't and I checked the balls. Sure enough, they were new. So I asked who the young lad was and was told I had rejected him a couple of years earlier. I shook my head and said I had definitely never seen him bat or I would have remembered him. Sekar laughed, saying no, I had rejected him as a fast bowler!

I decided to watch from behind, rather than with the bowlers and was so impressed I told the others he was not only going to be scoring runs but would be scoring lots of runs. I didn't need to be an expert. That was Sachin Tendulkar.

It is remarkable how players mature at different ages in different countries; the advent of the academies may bring through English and Australian kids younger than in the past. I remember being surprised at England picking Graham Gooch at 20 because it was so much against the trend. He proved it can and should be done with exceptional talent.

Brian Lara blows hot and cold, making big hundreds then a series of low scores. Maybe we have not seen the best of him and maybe we never will. That's the nature of the man. He can be absolutely brilliant but he can look pedestrian. His weaknesses have been exposed by very good bowling, but who knows what he can produce in the future.

Steve Waugh is one of the few guys in cricketing history to have markedly improved his batting average after his first 25 Tests. With almost all batsmen, after 25 Tests their averages tend to stay about the same. Steve took a good look at himself and came up with what was needed to reach the next level and become a great player, at the same time as shouldering the responsibilities of captaincy.

Some will be shocked by Adam Gilchrist's inclusion as he has been playing a short time only, and he bats at number seven. He is better than that and shows it when he opens the batting in one-day games. I've picked him on the Viv Richards premise – exciting to watch, ready to take them all on and, like Viv, if he decides to build an innings, the opposition had better look out. He is an amazingly talented bat.

I wonder how far Mark Waugh could have gone if he had had a killer instinct as well as looking brilliant. He did not always hammer home advantages and maybe he could have put his innings together more carefully and built them up like Bradman, Chappell, Lloyd or even his brother Steve used to do. Everyone is different but I put him in for the same reasons I included David Gower and Doug Walters in my previous list – he is such a beautiful bat who plays the game with ease. He is a natural.

Two others who nearly made the selection are Andy Flower and Richie Richardson. Andy has achieved his average in a Zimbabwe side which is always under pressure. Much like the guys in Sri Lanka, he goes from not particularly strong club cricket into Tests, a big ask worth extra points when assessing a player. Richie Richardson could have done a lot more but he was a typical West Indian player – casual but often truly brilliant.

Graham Gooch deserves a special mention as he is the only opener, apart from Barry Richards, who only played a handful of Tests, I have picked. He faced some of the greatest fast bowlers the world has seen in a career which spanned 20 odd years and came out of it averaging around 40. For sheer guts and determination, combined with a top technique, he came through with flying colours.

I must also mention Greenidge and Haynes, as they took on all and contributed in no small way to the West Indies' domination of cricket for over a decade. I have had many a laugh with Desi over the years off the field but there was a dead serious rivalry on it.

On to fast bowlers and I would say the best in my time were, again in order, Andy Roberts, John Snow, Jeff Thomson, Michael Holding, Richard Hadlee, Joel Garner, Malcolm Marshall, Imran Khan, Bob Willis, Kapil Dev, Curtly Ambrose and Graham McKenzie.

Of those, Andy Roberts was the most complete; he had almost perfect line and length with an economy of run-up and action, and he was really whippy at the end. It was X factor stuff. He was uncompromising, unsmiling, and just got on with the job. He had an outswinger, an off-cutter, a slower ball and two bouncers. Andy once asked Ian Chappell, after they had finished playing, why he did not take on his bouncers. Ian replied, 'Do you think I'm stupid? I knew what you were about and I knew you had two bouncers. It wasn't a percentage shot.' One of the bouncers was a slower ball, not that slow, but Andy used it to set up the unsuspecting batsman and then he would nail them with the faster ball.

I must admit that I tried it but not as successfully as he did. I would bowl as quickly as I could to a compulsive hooker but would try the slower one to tempt a batsman who did not usually hook. I would use it as an enticement, three-quarter pace, to suck him in. But I tried it more in Shield cricket and Andy did it at the highest level. Andy was unusual because there weren't many around in those days who had such a good change of pace. It wasn't just that, it was the control. He was always on the right spot. He almost crept in rather than indulge in the big arm-pumping run most of us used. His secret was stealth.

Playing against John Snow, I watched him lope in to bowl and he'd let go of leg-cutters, then an inswinger, occasionally an outswinger and a great bouncer. Just about the only ball I did not see him bowl was the slower one, certainly not in a Test match where he mainly bowled flat out. Illingworth used him well as a strike bowler, never toiling away just to save runs. This guy was pure strike and just exceptional. I was young and impressionable, of course, and maybe he looked exceptional to a youngster, but I believe he holds his own. If he had bowled in Australia instead of county cricket, who knows how good his record would have been. The excessive cricket played on the county scene must have blunted his edge. I put him above some big names because it is what I saw from the pavilion and from out in the middle. This man could run through a side. The Aussies held him in total respect.

Jeff Thomson was a man to put the fear of God into batsmen in any era through pure and simple pace. It was nothing to do with guile or where the ball was going. His was a short, explosive career. When he was on top of the world, he sustained an awful injury, breaking his collar bone. It meant changing from loping in, wound up like a spring, to, later, creating his pace from a long, fast run-up, like the rest of us. Because of losing his shoulder action, he lost the ball which came sharply off a length. That was his best weapon before he was injured. For outright natural ability, and a bloke who didn't seem to train a lot, lived life to the full and played cricket for fun, he was amazing.

Michael Holding, otherwise known as 'Whispering Death', was the man closest to poetry in motion. I believe he achieved perfection in his run-up and action, and it was done with such ease it was frighteningly deceptive. Initially, he just ran up and bowled fast, but when he learned to swing the ball both ways, even though he lost some pace, he was a better all-round bowler. When bowling flat out, he was beautiful to watch with that fluid, unhurried action – a great athlete.

Richard Hadlee was just a machine, made in New Zealand and polished in Nottingham. I reckon he was the first truly professional fast bowler I ever saw. I saw the raw item when he was a youngster and I saw the mature finished product. There was no stone left unturned in his bid to perfect his action and shorten his run. He was prepared to listen and learn. He had a very good but sparingly used bouncer which rocked them on to the back foot, and he used inswing and outswing so well. Without doubt, he was one of the greatest bowlers of all time.

I would have loved to see Joel Garner taking the new ball, in the early days with the West Indies, instead of coming on to bowl eight or nine overs straight on a good line and length. With that 6ft 8ins frame, he kept it tight, kept the batsmen honest, and was miserly with runs against him. He didn't do a lot with the ball, just ran his fingers a bit for the odd off-cutter; his fingers were twice as long as most people's. It was impossible to know whether to come forward or go back to him. At the end of his career, when he was in his 30s, they gave him the new ball and he really charged in. Opening with the new ball as a youngster, he would have been awesome. I have nothing but respect for the way he bowled. I am bracketing Malcolm Marshall and Joel together. Both are great bowlers, with Marshall going on to be acknowledged by a top judge as one of the best ever. I only played against him at about 18 or 19 years old, so perhaps he shouldn't qualify for this section.

Imran was a very fit, lionhearted fast bowler, capable not only of bowling extremely fast but also of bowling for long spells. His aggressive approach helped Pakistan become a top force in Test and one-day cricket. His success and Pakistan's emergence as a powerful cricket nation is no coincidence. He deserves a top ten place and he was one of the best all-rounders I saw.

Graham McKenzie is in there on merit. He was also a hero of mine. He was quick but he could fill the workhorse role for Australia. He didn't have a lot of support; he didn't have a colleague who was a strike bowler of top quality for most of his career. On his first tour, he was support to the great Alan Davidson but after that, a lot of his partners were into the wind, bowlers who could support but not strike like him. He carried the Australian attack on his shoulders for many years. For a guy who could bowl as quickly as he did, he probably found the hack work a bit tedious. I looked up to him then and still do.

Bob Willis was maybe not the fastest guy around but he bowled fast spells and was hard and uncompromising, prepared to work his socks off for his country day-in and day-out. A dour man, he did not have super skills with the ball but he was skilful enough to be a great servant for his country, coupled with sheer guts and determination. The game he played against Australia at Headingley in 1981 was the greatest spell of fast bowling I have ever seen.

Kapil Dev was not up there in terms of pace by any means, but he's on my list simply because of the skill factor. A wily bowler with inswing and outswing and the slower ball, he was prepared to bowl 35 to 40 overs an innings to get his four or five wickets. He was not far short of Hadlee as a true professional.

Of the modern fast bowlers, these would be my choice: Ambrose/ Marshall, Wasim Akram, Glenn McGrath, Bruce Reid, Courtney Walsh, Craig McDermott, Allan Donald, Shaun Pollock, Brett Lee, Darren Gough and Jason Gillespie.

Marshall and Ambrose share the number one position for the following reasons. Curtly Ambrose could hold his own with anyone on his day. Anyone who bowls from nearly 7ft tall has an advantage, but you still have to have the ability. He had very good pace and he was hard to handle. He developed an outswinger, a yorker and a change of pace. In any conditions, on any sort of track, he could take wickets. Malcolm Marshall was a magician, a more complete bowler than Ambrose, but Curtly, because of his trajectory, even on the deadest wicket against the best batsmen, was dangerous. I can't split them.

Wasim Akram is at number two for his economy of action, his swing and his ability in all conditions, in one-day cricket as well as in Test matches. He is just an incredible player. He sometimes allows batsmen to get on top of him mid innings, but reverse swing made him as dangerous late on as he was with the new ball.

Glenn McGrath is like a metronome, the ultimate bowling machine, who can bowl all day if asked. Bruce Reid was as close to unplayable as anyone I saw in the short time he was around. If his body had held together, he would have gone right to the top. At around 6ft 7ins, he could bowl inswing, outswing and a beautiful line and length, which for a left-arm bowler was quite rare, like Wasim and Alan Davidson. He had a bouncer, too, and never gave you any reprieve. Courtney Walsh was a workhorse, another Willis type, with a remarkable body which never broke down.

The choice gets tougher after that. Craig McDermott started his Test career very young, bowling a good line and length with a good outswinger and off-cutter at pace. He was also a fine competitor, fierce and uncompromising. There was a period of five or six years when he was a real tough-nut bowler.

South African Allan Donald lived up to his nickname of 'White Lightning'. He did not come into international cricket until the age of 27 or 28, which is the peak for a fast bowler. He missed six or seven years before that, and I suspect he could have been even better had he played earlier.

Shaun Pollock is another who bowls inswingers and outswingers, and has a bouncer which hurries on from nowhere. He's very accurate, gets on with the job, and is a tough competitor with a good cricketing brain. An excellent all-rounder, as a bowler he has the ability to think batsmen out, finding and probing their weaknesses.

If Australian Brett Lee keeps fit, he can be up there with those other guys. He has a great outswinger, terrific pace, a yorker, reverse swing, an off-cutter, a slower ball, a good work ethic, and is a great competitor – that's an entire armoury of weapons. Who knows what he could do if injury does not gobble him up.

Darren Gough is too inconsistent for me to call him one of the all-time great bowlers. He has great matches rather than great series. You never know when he's going to do amazing things, such as take a hat-trick, but he's just as likely to be ordinary in the next game. The county cricket circuit's workload could be too much for him to stay fresh for Tests and, indeed, he has missed a lot of cricket with injury. I'm sure it affects some players more than others. Fred Trueman, for example, thrived on lots of work while Gough maybe needs to peak and then wind down his workload. That system suited me, and a few others.

Gough can look good and he can look exceptional. If he could put the package together, he would be one of the greats. He bowls great yorkers and good slower balls, and they are top weapons. Perhaps he tries to do too much and should bowl line and length with good variety instead of two outswingers, an inswinger, a slower ball and a yorker followed by a bouncer. I would like to see him develop a good stock ball.

I have chosen Jason Gillespie as the future because of his ability to bowl bloody well on dead tracks when the chips are down, a breakthrough is needed and no one else is putting up his hand. He is becoming more refined but he can still produce that really quick ball or quick spell. I have heard Justin Langer say the quickest spell he ever faced was from Gillespie for an hour or so. Probably he always has plenty up his sleeve, and knows how to bowl within himself. He is a solid, all-round fast bowler who could end up having a great career if his body holds together.

It was very difficult to leave out Merv Hughes, Waqar Younis, Shoaib Akhtar, Javagal Srinath and Chaminda Vaas. Leaving out Waqar is almost sacrilege but he has struggled over the last few years. Merv Hughes was a great competitor, great team man, good in the dressing room and a great mate, but just couldn't quite make the cut although you would have him in the trenches. He was more a competitor than a gifted fast bowler and I take my hat off to him.

There has been much discussion on the validity of Shoaib's bowling. Medically, he has a lever in his arm that goes back about 15 degrees the wrong way, which can make the action look worse. We have videoed him, put his action through computers, analysed him, and I don't have an argument with him generally. There are times when he bowls a bouncer that the front arm pulls away towards gully and not the batsman, putting the extra bit of shoulder in. I worry then because it looks bad. My advice to him is not to try to do all the bowling with the right arm. If he uses the left arm and trunk to bowl fast, he will not have a problem. His weapon is his pace. I have not seen him bowl regular outswing and not any new ball inswing. There is some reverse swing but his outright pace is his great asset and I don't think it is good enough to have just that to do well in top-class cricket in the long term.

He is only young and most of us go through that period, but it is the smarter ones who survive by enlarging their repertoire with something different. That makes you a more complete bowler rather than one-dimensional. All Shoaib is bothered about at the moment is being the fastest in the world. That is what he loves, but that single objective can cloud the real issue, which is to be a fast bowler for your country, not a sideshow trying to bowl the 100 miles per hour ball at every outing. We will see if he has the character to back it up and, knowing the man and having worked with him, I would say he has.

Often you bowl your quickest when you are not trying. The quickest I bowled was when I didn't steam in but when I was running in more relaxed, using a smoother action than usual. In England, it surprised me at times that I felt more coordinated when I was not charging in trying to let fly. It's like a sprinter who tightens up instead of being relaxed and forceful.

Vaas swings the ball both ways at a brisk pace without being express. He is almost the perfect one-day fast bowler, an Alan Davidson type with a lovely run-up and perfect rhythm – an athlete with a smooth action combined with a good command of length. He is not a big exponent of the bouncer or yorker, or even of the odd slower ball, but there is more to come from him.

Srinath has suffered from being a fast bowler bowling on dead wickets designed to take spin. He has had to adapt more than most of the others because that's his own turf. Had he played in another country, perhaps England, he would have had better figures and taken more wickets. He has battled injuries and I have a lot of respect for him, consistently bowling well in difficult conditions.

The guys I would have liked to see behind the stumps when I was bowling are Rod Marsh, Alan Knott, Bob Taylor, Jack Russell and Ian Healy.

Rod Marsh is my yardstick. I felt totally comfortable with him. He rarely dropped the ball, even creating catches by taking half chances. He has been known to dive past first slip an inch above the ground when the ball wouldn't have carried to the fielder, and he anticipated batsmen's flicks down the leg side. He's the man.

Of the rest, Alan Knott stood out with Bob Taylor not far behind. Taylor would have played more Tests if he had been a better batsman. There are those in England who say he was as good a wicket-keeper as Knott, and some think he was even better.

Jack Russell, next on the list, was undoubtedly a better glove man than Alex Stewart, but Alex was often preferred because he was a superior batsman, worth his place in the side for that alone. He finished up by becoming a very good wicket-keeper through sheer hard work. Ian Healy, of course, is a consistently good keeper and a great asset behind the stumps.

It is difficult to leave out some other fine wicket-keepers – Adam Gilchrist, Deryck Murray, Moin Khan, Ian Smith, Syed Kirmani, Wasim Bari, Jeff Dujon and Mark Boucher, for instance. A case can be argued for the inclusion of each of them in the top five, and every argument would be valid.

It seems there is often rivalry between two wicket-keepers for the international place, and the one who can combine the role with being an outstanding batsman gets the nod, even if he's not quite as good behind the stumps. Apart from Knott and Taylor, and Russell and Stewart,

mentioned above, there was Deryck Murray and Jeff Dujon. Murray was
a fine glove man but Jeff Dujon replaced him because he was younger
and a good batsman. Dujon would have got a game in the very fine
West Indian side on the strength of that alone, and had he been allowed
to concentrate on batting, he could have been world class. He was very
difficult to bowl to. The South African, Boucher, is another fine
batsman–wicket-keeper, with more to come.

If Western Australia keeper Tim Zoehrer had been given an extended
run and convinced the selectors he was the man for the job, I think he
could have gone down as one of the greats because he was also a very
good batsman. I think he was as good a glove man as Healy.

Often wicket-keepers and bowlers form a good combination. Dujon
took 71 from Marshall in 68 matches; I had 95 in 69 with Rod; Botham
had 60 in 51 with Taylor; Boucher keeping to Donald had a remarkable
52 in only 31. Boucher and Donald having the best average with 1.67.
This shows how great a bowler Donald was and what he could have
done, had he been given the opportunity.

Any list of top spinners is exciting to contemplate. I've taken the licence
to select seven, with the last three equal: Shane Warne, Muttiah
Muralitharan, Saqlain Mushtaq, Bishen Bedi, Danny Vettori, Abdul
Qadir and Lance Gibbs.

I have no hesitation whatsoever in picking Shane Warne as my
number one spin bowler. This may surprise some people but I have
picked him out because when he was at his absolute best, I did not see
anyone play him with any certainty. He took a couple of hammerings
from the Indians in recent times but I believe that was because he came
back from major surgery far too soon. At his best, he is the best I have
seen at first hand, the only spinner who has made the hairs on the back
of my neck stand up. If I'm watching him on the television, I can't leave
the room. No other spinner has ever done that to me. Before his injuries,
he could do everything with the ball. His main asset, compared with any
other wrist-spinner apart from Qadir, is that he can turn the ball with
unbelievable accuracy. There have been those who could turn the ball

miles without the accuracy, and those who were on the spot every ball but did not turn it that much. He's a hard nut, relishes a challenge, and there's nothing he likes better than knocking the Poms over.

After him, it becomes difficult because there are so many ifs and buts – on what sort of pitches do they usually play? Are they mainly suited to certain conditions, or can they take wickets when the conditions do not suit them? Using those criteria, I've chosen Murali as my number two because he seems to get wickets everywhere. Even if he is given just 10 overs, he will always be a change to take a couple of wickets. He is one of the biggest turners of the ball I have seen as an off-spinner, getting bite and bounce. He doesn't need the variety but he has it; he can turn the ball on a sheet of glass. My one concern is that there has been a cloud over his action for years but it has been officially cleared and we have to accept his arm is bent naturally. He is the victim of an abnormality in his physical make-up; we have to be careful not to brand players because they are different. The authorities must continue to monitor him, as they should anyone who has been called, but we should celebrate him for his talent.

Murali is closely followed by Saqlain, who could conceivably overtake both him and Warne as the greatest spinner of all time. In fact, I would be surprised if he doesn't. He has the capacity. He is the first spinner to develop a new ball which is not an arm ball or an outswinger but seams away after it pitches. He can turn the ball, maybe not as much as Murali, but it is the seamer that is his great weapon. You don't know when it's coming or what it will do. Batsmen are, rightly, very wary and therefore vulnerable.

Bishen Bedi was not a big turner, but he used the angles and the crease; if they let him, he would bowl over the umpire's head just to get a different angle. Batsmen rarely got on top of Bish and he loved batsmen as much as I did! He treated Australian batsmen like a game, bamboozling us and almost playing cat and mouse – a bit like a fast bowler who keeps batsmen at the crease for a little while to hit them on the thigh and the inside of the thigh, to soften them up for future meetings.

The young Kiwi Vettori is another who could move up the pecking

Rod Marsh once said that he didn't trust fast bowlers who didn't drink – here I am getting into the habit.

PATRICK EAGAR

With Jeff Thomson during the 1975 World Cup. It may not have been our finest hour, but we struck up a wonderful partnership.

Lots of excitement. Alan Knott succumbs to the most prolific partnership in Test history: c Marsh b Lillee. We got him twice in this Old Trafford Test in 1972.

The remarkable Centenary Test at Melbourne in March 1977. Derek Randall, cheeky as ever. What an innings!

umbling action in
one-dayer. Great
alance but perhaps
hy I have such a
d neck now!

he ball flies away
uring an Australia v
West Indies World
eries match – these
mes were played at
high level of
tensity and helped
volutionise cricket.

Bouncing Ian Botham in 1981. I
was sure this was the right metho
to get him, but at Headingley it
resulted in the most remarkable
turnaround.

Geoff Boycott is LBW at The
Oval in 1981 at the end of one c
the most remarkable series of all
time. I still don't understand hov
we didn't win it.

We couldn't afford overseas telephone calls so I wrote long letters. Well I tried, but couldn't match Helen's seven- to ten-page letters.

Rod Marsh, Greg Chappell and I draw a close on a great era at Sydney in January 1984. At the time we held the Test records for most dismissals by a keeper, most catches by a fielder and most wickets by a bowler respectively.

Helped off by the team physiotherapist and Rob Bailey after tearing every ligament and breaking an ankle bone playing for Northamptonshire in 1988.

Still with a Pom in my sights all these years on. Bowling to Mark Butcher at Lilac Hill in October 1998 while Mike Atherton watches on.

Ashley Mallett enjoys my attempt to 'fill' Rod Marsh. Futile really.

My 50th birthday. Rod Marsh, Thommo and Greg. If you believe what Thommo is trying to put over then you believe pigs fly. I reckon Thommo just made it through the photo before collapsing.

Ian Chappell and myself coaching at the MRF Pace Foundation in India. He may not have been the greatest fast bowler, but if I needed a man to bat for my life, he's the one I'd choose.

Australia's Team of the Century ceremony. My hero Keith Miller and Australian Prime Minister and cricket tragic, John Howard.

order in time. He was the youngest spinner to reach 100 Test wickets, and in a country that does not play a lot of Test cricket. I believe he is in there with a chance of eventually making 300 or 400 in a few years' time if he steers clear of injury. Like Bedi, he does not turn the ball a lot but he does not yet have quite the variety of Bedi. In the years to come he may surpass him.

Abdul Qadir, the Pakistani bowler who played from the seventies to the nineties, was a lot like Warne, a bit faster but without the variety. He was a big spinner of the ball from his quick run-up. Even now, at over 45 years of age, he still turns his arm over with some success in club cricket in Melbourne. Recently he took 70 wickets in a Melbourne season, shattering the previous record in a very high standard of cricket. This is one of the reasons he is in my top five.

Lance Gibbs was similar to Bedi, a finger spinner and master of flight, but unlike Bedi, Gibbs was right-handed, and enjoyed an extensive variety. He was not averse to throwing the ball up high to bring the batsman down the wicket. The ball dropped sharply, the batsman didn't quite know where he was and was stumped. Gibbs was a real quality act.

It was hard to leave out Mushtaq Ahmed and Harbhajan Singh. Other bowlers shone in their own conditions; Derek Underwood and Anil Kumble, for instance, were both successful on their home pitches but not in Australia, which is where I mainly saw them. They did great jobs and won matches for their teams but neither of them can be classed as outstanding in all conditions.

If you go back in history, it is not often you find great records of combined runs, wickets and catches – Keith Miller and Alan Davidson, W.G. Grace and Warwick Armstrong perhaps. Yet I have no doubt that the era in which I played was the most abundant for all-rounders. It's difficult to choose five, let alone put them in any order, except for the top slot. To make it easier, I'm going to knock out the three South Africans, Mike Procter, Clive Rice and Vince Van Der Bijl, because I didn't see them at their best, nor did I play against them. Given these reservations, my top five are Sir Garfield Sobers, Ian Botham, Imran

Khan, Malcolm Marshall and Kapil Dev.

I have no hesitation at all in putting Sobers first. If there was a guy more all-round in any sport, he must have been a joy to watch. To come into top-class cricket as a spinner at 16 years of age is incredible. In a very good West Indian side, he progressed from number nine or ten to number four in the batting order, and moved from wrist-spin to chinamen, swing and fast bowling – not medium fast because he hit the bat hard. He was also a wonderful fielder in close, in the slips or in the covers. If there was a superman of cricket it was Garry Sobers. There is no chance there has been, or will be, anyone who will be a better or more complete all-rounder.

Ian Botham doesn't figure in my lists as a bowler or a batsman because he was a genuine all-rounder, with his batting and bowling on an equal standing. He was also a fine fielder, and certainly a better slip fielder than all the others except Sobers. Marshall, Imran and Kapil Dev were better bowlers, but Botham could make things happen with bat and ball equally.

Imran Khan would be included in most sides of his era as a batsman if he had concentrated on that skill. He was not flamboyant but he had the ability. However, for me, it was as a bowler that he had the edge, dangerous on any wicket and in almost any conditions.

Malcolm Marshall was an outstanding bowler, as good as Kapil Dev, but his batting potential was rarely realised because the West Indies had such a powerful line-up. He did not often get to bat in a role where he could build an innings and make a big score. Both Marshall and Kapil Dev, given the opportunity to bat more than they did, could have been even greater all-rounders than they were. Kapil Dev could be brilliant, but at others times, you hardly noticed him come and go.

My first reserve in this glittering array of supermen would be Richard Hadlee. It may look like I'm living in the past, but when you compare this group with the players around now, we are not brimful of real quality all-rounders. There's Pollock, Gilchrist, Kallis, Stewart and Cairns – and two of those are wicket-keepers. None of them is quite there although one or two are on their way. Jacques Kallis, for example, bats at number three against top bowlers; he opens the bowling and is a very fine into-the-wind swing bowler with good pace; and he is also an excellent fieldsman. South Africa are remarkably lucky to have Shaun Pollock as well as Kallis. Pollock could still go down as one of the great all-rounders, but his stint as captain was an added burden.

Darren Gough looked like he could be a genuine all-rounder early in his career but I understand the reasons why he hasn't, not least because of the daily grind of county cricket. He throws the bat instead of playing conventional cricket shots, and has become a recognised tailender.

I can see Brett Lee in the current Australian side developing into an all-rounder because he has shown such potential with the bat. Shane Warne, too, has potential with the bat and is close to being an all-rounder especially as he is such a good fielder – but time is running out for him to be classed as one of the real greats.

As a kid, Sobers was one of my heroes and I would have loved to emulate him and become an all-rounder. I loved batting and averaged over 40 when I came back from stress fractures to play for Perth, and I scored 73 at Lord's. I was told not to waste a lot of energy batting. I could be bowling within half an hour and it was a directive from some captains not to hang around. It meant I went out and threw the bat. At times, when I concentrated and hung around with some of the better guys, I started to gain confidence and rhythm. Although they weren't classic shots, I felt I had the ability to score runs and had I put the work in, could have contributed a lot more. In the modern era, I would have been encouraged to bat and practise more, which can only help your game.

Fielding is not often regarded in a category on its own but some class performers turned it into an art form. I'd nominate Jonty Rhodes as the maestro, with the rest on an equal footing because I cannot for the life of me separate them: Jonty Rhodes, Sir Garfield Sobers, Clive Lloyd, Viv Richards, Ricky Ponting, Derek Randall, Roger Harper and Greg Chappell.

Neil Harvey, I was told, was outstanding as was Colin Bland, but I've seen these two just briefly on television, so I cannot count them among my contenders. Ross Edwards was without the natural ability but he took on the workload. He was an innovator, the first to run and dive, and he made himself into a top fielder. He never gave up and would chase right to the boundary if the dive failed.

Maybe Jonty Rhodes stands out because he overlapped two eras. Nowadays every team has a host of brilliant fielders, although not in this superstar category. More interesting is the fact that most top sides do not have a bad fielder. Fielding is like any other aspect of cricket these days with better practice and specialisation, just as with batting and bowling.

You would pay good money to watch Lloyd in his early years, Richards with those three run-outs in a World Cup final, and Garry Sobers with his versatility. I include Randall because he was so different, especially compared with other English fielders.

Ricky Ponting typifies for me the run and dive of the modern fielder – he can catch, pick up and throw from his knees, flick the ball in and is Australia's answer to Jonty Rhodes, perhaps following in the footsteps of the great South African. Ponting is a product of the academy, taught to pick up on either side, throw off either foot, off his knees or off his belly.

Maybe future cricketers will show the benefits of everyone being able to field, bowl to first-class or even Test standard for five to ten overs, and bat well even at number eleven, defensively or aggressively. One-day cricket is the catalyst and is helping to push the all-round skill of the next generation in Test cricket. In other words, every cricketer will become more competent in every discipline.

Rating umpires is a very personal thing. In my judgement, they must not only be a very good umpire but also a personable human being. You can forgive them for not being right on all occasions, but the best conduct themselves well, are not officious, and try to fit in without becoming one of the boys. Then there are the special umpires who are prepared to see there is a grey area and will give and take. With those criteria in mind, it comes down to just a few. My selection is Dickie Bird, Douglas Sang Hue, Charlie Elliott, Dusty Rhodes and Tommy Spencer.

Separating them was difficult but Dickie Bird has to be at the top of the list. He and I got on very well. He fulfilled all the criteria – he was a decent human being, enjoyed the *craic*, liked the lads but kept his distance. He had the balance correct. He treated the players with great respect. Towards the end he wavered a little, but overall his career was long and excellent. The only criticism I had of him was that he erred on the safety side of lbw decisions by using the rule if in doubt, give it not out. But it applied to everyone so it was an even playing field.

Douglas Sang Hue was not much of a communicator but the respect was there because he made great decisions with no fear in front of crowds who might – and did – riot. He made honest decisions against the West Indies, knowing he could be going home to a pile of ashes instead of a house. That requires commitment and guts.

Behind those two, in no specific order, are Charlie Elliot, Dusty Rhodes and Tommy Spencer, all super competent umpires who, by no coincidence, were also very good cricketers in their own right.

I would also single out Australia's Col Egar, Peter O'Connell, Mel Johnson, Tony Crafter, and someone a lot of cricket fans will not have heard of, Garry Duperouzel. Others from Australia were Tony Crafter and Rob O'Connell. There were a lot of good umpires in England, apart from the four mentioned, and I particularly admired the Australian Bill Alley who took up umpiring after a playing career with Somerset.

Mel Johnson was a top bloke. He got on with the guys and openly admitted he made mistakes, something you didn't hear from many others. Here was a guy who did his best – which is all you can ask. Peter O'Connell was a long servant to Western Australia and a Test umpire. He was very similar to Mel Johnson; they even looked alike and performed just the same.

Garry Duperouzel was a good cricketer whose brother played for Western Australia as a batsman and was also a great Australian Rules player for St Kilda. Garry, sadly, never stood in a Test match. He was an umpire in World Series Cricket with Douglas Sang Hue. He shone like a beacon and was accepted by all the players as a very fine umpire. He was fair, made good decisions and was prepared to make the hard decisions, whereas many lived by the motto 'If not sure, say not out'. He was a good all-round guy, composed, natural and not impressed by names or status. I have no idea why he vanished from the face of the earth after World Series Cricket; perhaps it was because he had thrown in his lot with us. I just wish that he had stayed around. He was a loss to the game.

Of today's umpires, Buckner, Shepherd, Venkat and Willey stand out. With regard to the system of the International Umpiring Panel currently in use, the authorities must be careful to select on merit and not just try to have a representative from most countries for the sake of impartiality.

My final say on umpires is that in any sport it has got to be the most difficult job to do well and please everyone. I admire top umpires because of that, but find it hard to stomach incompetence and over-officiousness.

CHAPTER TWENTY-SIX

The modern game

One of the most important developments in recent years at the top level of the game has been the use of technology. If it is overused, it may undermine the umpire's decisions and I'm not in favour of that. With too many new concepts and innovations, the umpires will end up as ball counters. An example is replays. I understand they are good for television viewers, but I don't like it when they show an incident over and over again to reveal a mistake. Umpires have to make an instant decision without any help. More often than not, commentators use the technology to prove the umpire's decision is wrong. The fairest method is to show the incident just a couple of times and leave viewers to make up their own minds, which seemed fairer.

You have to take the good with the bad, though, because television also replays the good decisions. I would like to see more of them and less of the bad ones because it would be good for the game and a confidence builder for the umpires.

Cricketers should be honest to help the umpires; catches off bump balls are a classic example. The fielder knows 99 times out of 100 if the ball is caught but there are some who cheat. Fortunately, the umpires quickly get to know them and appeals from these players are viewed differently. Modern technology still does not always conclusively give the correct answer, particularly for catches in the outfield and some slip catches. An umpire is there to make the decisions and if you take that away from him, what is he there for? You might as well have a robot.

I still believe an umpire is in the best position and should be the sole judge of an lbw decision. The technology appears to be so accurate, but as a ball wears, conditions change, and that's not picked up. It's a gimmick and clever, but that's what it is – a gimmick. I'm not convinced someone's out because the machine says so, but the pundit in front of his television is sure the umpire has made another mistake.

Snickometers were introduced to enhance television viewing, but it's fallible even with a computer chip in the bat. If they are not careful, they are going to change the game from the sport kids play at grass roots level to one which can't be duplicated in back yards, streets and clubs.

I'm not saying get rid of the technology – just don't overdo it. Used sensibly, the technology could help to raise umpiring standards because umpires know they have to remain sharp and alert throughout a televised match, and not make errors. They have to make decisions rather than say not out as the safe option.

I would not be averse to an umpire checking for an edge on to the pad or a caught behind if he loses sight of the ball in the flurry of bat, gloves and body, as long as these things do not take too much time. Bat-pad may well be another area where he can use the third eye to make a judgement because this causes more angst than anything, especially on the sub-continent. It may also stop batsmen making fools of themselves by showing dissent after their dismissal.

One area of the game I'm very hot on is no balls, and I'm sure some sort of Cyclops could be used to check a bowler's feet placement. This would relieve the umpire of the onerous task of watching the feet, followed immediately by watching the ball in flight and what it does at the other end. That fraction of a second can be the difference between making a good decision and bad one.

No balling is a particular bugbear of mine when I'm coaching and I see bowlers go well over the crease in the nets and practice. Some are six inches over but others are two to three feet over the line, and they don't seem to care.

If a light ray, similar to Cyclops in tennis, with a beeper to tell everyone when a bowler bowls a no ball, could be used in the nets, three things will happen. The first is the bowler will know and be embarrassed if he continues to do it. Secondly, the batsman will not be happy and may well harangue the bowler about it. The third thing is the coach will be straight on to it.

The front-foot rule is the fairest way to make sure everyone is bowling from the same spot. It's not perfect, but it's the best option we have. In the past we had draggers – the bowler dragged his back foot to gain maximum advantage and the back foot was the focus point of a no ball. Guys of over 6ft dragged and slid in on the back foot and gained a huge advantage. With the advent of the front-foot rule, virtually no one drags because they have a barrier where they have to stop. It's a fairer rule except it puts more pressure on the umpire, who has to follow the front foot before following the ball's flight.

Since the introduction of technology for run-outs, more batsmen are given out than in the past. Almost every time a batsman was within six or nine inches he had to be given not out because there was no way an umpire could note the moment the bail fell off and where the bat was at that precise millisecond. That to me is a great use of technology, along with the stumpings, but it's only available at the very top level. The umpire goes back to his everyday cricket after Test matches, sees a close run-out and turns to ask for the third umpire when there isn't one. How embarrassing is that? Again, it's unfair on the umpire.

I like to see umpires make decisions and we should not interfere too much even if mistakes are made because they will even out unless you are the unluckiest person in the world.

If we continue to witch-hunt umpires, we will not find anyone who wants to do the job. The pay is better than it used to be, encouraging former players to take it on, but will they want to do it if we are putting so much pressure on them?

I have not got enough confidence in the technology to be convinced it's right all the time, and therefore that must colour my view. Maybe in the future the technology will be perfect; only then should we embrace it wholeheartedly.

The game itself goes through peaks and troughs in terms of behaviour and it's largely up to the governing bodies and the umpires to control it. Players are no longer in it just for fun and glory; they are playing for big stakes. Successful teams and successful players are always going to be more in demand and earn more money than the less successful ones. I saw that coming with the county championship when winning for financial gain became so important. Players quizzed umpires more and more and over-zealous appealing became the norm. There is so much money and prestige involved, a win-at-all-costs attitude takes over and players try anything on. I would like to see umpires sit down with coaches, administrators and players to talk it right through because it has got to the stage where it could spoil the game. People will always try to bend the rules, but there must be boundaries for cricketers just as there are for young children. There are rules and they must be adhered to. A commitment from everyone involved could help halt the trend and bring back fairness.

Maybe the introduction of a yellow-card system could help although it's not as easy as that. What misdemeanours are worth yellow cards? How far do you go? Perhaps a set of regulations could be drawn up, enforced by a warning followed by a yellow card. Then if someone oversteps the mark again, he is sent from the field of play for a session. If it's a batsman, maybe he should have a proportion of his runs deducted.

Fines don't work any more. I laugh when I see a tennis player fined $5,000. It's pin money for most top players. They have to be hit where it hurts, something to make them think twice the next time they are considering committing the same offence.

In cricket you can hurt the cheats by hurting the team. The other players would quickly come down on the villain if he was affecting the team's chances. In that way, it would be self-correcting within the team.

Another thing I despise is orchestrated appealing. The bowler sees the wicket-keeper go up, then the slips and he follows, or the bowler goes up followed a few heartbeats later by the fielders. When someone at mid-off, or anyone other than the wicket-keeper and the bowler, appeals for lbw he cannot be serious because he is in no position to judge.

A nasty habit creeping into our sport is that of appealing bowlers and/or fielders running at umpires. Claiming catches which come off the ground would also be an offence. Send these people off and they will soon think again. Sin-bin a player if he's bad and he will soon have his coach and officials in his ears. I guess it would stop it pretty quickly.

Bad language is becoming another problem now there are microphones everywhere and what people say can be heard a long way from the pitch, even in people's front rooms. I would start by banning the mikes because the pitch is the inner sanctum and there will be a few heat-of-the-moment things going on – I remember them only too well. The viewer will still see the close-up of the faces; why have the noises to go with it, especially if they can cause offence? I cannot see any advantage of stump microphones.

If a situation can be contained out in the middle, it can be sorted out on the square and not blown up out of all proportion. We have to be careful not to take the passion out of the game, sanitise it. When people are passionate and competitive, the odd incident will occur. Being abusive to someone is one thing, but when it's directed at the world in general, maybe it's different. Players need consistency. What I found suited me was an umpire who, as I walked back or at the end of the over, had a quiet word with me to cool it, or to warn me to watch it with my front foot. I respected that and took notice.

The only rule change I would like to see is the one governing throwing. The problem we have is technical. In the past it was all done by naked eye with the umpire looking from side-on and making a judgement. It's very difficult to judge with a naked eye unless someone cocks the arm like a pitcher. I have seen some obvious throwers but I have also seen some who look different and I cannot say whether they throw. Now that we have digital computer technology, it's possible to view any section of the action. With such precise equipment, we may be jumping at shadows and I would emphasise to any throwing panel the videotape must be perfectly clear and not in any way blurred. It has to be viewed side-on to the bowler and not from square-leg, and from directly in front of or behind the arm on the same delivery. It's no use filming different balls from the two angles because your action changes from bowling a slower ball to an inswinger to an outswinger or a leg-break or even a straight ball. Even wrist movements can make an arm action look different. This all has to be taken into account.

Many years ago when Andy Roberts first went to England he must have taken around 140 wickets in a county season; he was breaking arms, hitting people on the head and bowling express. The cry started to come out that he must throw because no one could bowl so quickly. Why didn't they say that when Thommo bowled? You cannot accuse someone because he is bowling really quickly. Now they can find out with technology – but it has to be done in the manner I have suggested. We are no longer talking about telling someone to take a spell and work it out. Having a player sit out while people pore over his action could cost him a small fortune with the risk of being branded for the rest of his career. We cannot play God with players' careers. Committee members must have specialised knowledge about the mechanics of bowling, and not just be great former players or umpires.

Throwers are rare; with a true thrower you can see the elbow leading. Others can produce some minor flicks or push the ball in from wide of the crease, which can look like a throw. Even the occasional thrower is a rarity, and the action may look worse because the bowler is trying harder. The odd bowler with a suspect action may throw when trying to bowl a quicker ball.

What I would like to do is find film of all those who were branded throwers, along with others who were suspect, and sit down in a forum or for a television programme to inform the public more fully.

I don't like tampering with the great game. It has survived its ups and downs and controversies for over a hundred years. If you change the rules too much, you are tampering with history and casting doubt over results and players' averages. Things do change, and I'm always prepared for little changes to make the game better, but I don't want it to change totally.

Another major development has been the growth of limited-overs cricket. This year's World Cup comprised 54 matches, as opposed to 15 in 1975. In fact, we did not play one-day cricket at all in Australia until about 1971. It was first introduced in England, because the county championship was struggling, with three competitions. Talk about overkill. For a time it was great and the public supported all of them. Then people got tired of it and it became a slogathon instead of a scientific game. It also took spectators away from the county game, which is the nursery for Test cricket. For a while there was confusion between the three, one-day, county and Test cricket. England now has two major one-day competitions; maybe one would be sufficient.

Kerry Packer saw the benefit of one-day cricket, but as a totally separate game, not a shortened version of the four or five-day game with an instant result. He brought in coloured clothing, more cameras and different rules to make it a more exciting spectacle than the hit and giggle game it had been.

One of the biggest bonuses was that fielding improved dramatically because everyone had to field well, and this flowed over to the longer game. On the downside, batsmen took risks not seen before and bowlers bowled too defensively. The public and the sponsors embraced it and now youngsters are saying they want to play one-day, not just Test cricket.

When I first started playing one-day cricket, it was something I had to do, and after a few years I became bored with it. Initially, we had regulation fields with several slips, similar to the longer game; then, through necessity, we started to have defensive fields and, to me, it was boring. We were not forced to go off short runs or to restrict bouncers, but it was too negative.

There are lots of things I don't agree with such as the rules on wides and limited bouncers, although restricting wides down the leg side is fine, because formerly that was a very professional trick, particularly with the little medium pacers who could slot it in the hole every time. But I don't understand why there are such strict limits on short-pitched deliveries, which are often a perfect ball to bowl. Are they going to stop the yorker next? If they are not careful, they might as well use a bowling machine. Let's experiment but let's not change the game too much. Take out the hook and you take away one of the greatest parts of the game. All we are seeing at the moment are shots in the 'V' and square shots.

The introduction of floodlights was a marvellous innovation. When the weather is closing in, you can play right up until the rain starts. In England, when it goes dark at the back end of the summer, you are off as much for bad light as you are for rain. Melbourne and Tasmania have similar problems.

We have gained so much from World Series Cricket, with the lights and coloured gear, the razzmatazz, the marketing and innovative television coverage introducing a whole new audience to cricket. I don't mind coloured clothing, white balls or night cricket, as long as the fans are comfortable watching it. Initially, there was a problem with white balls but they have improved, although a lot more research and money needs to be invested to bring their standard up to that of the red one.

Who knows what will happen with the development of indoor stadiums after the efforts in Japan for football's World Cup when conditions were even and play was certain. Long-term, I envisage a lot of dome-type enclosed arenas. One of the problems with that is it changes the atmosphere, allowing the ball to swing more. The roof would be closed when the umpire decided. On the positive side, rain would no longer stop play.

Cricket's World Cup has developed into an important competition. It was an interesting event when it was launched in 1975, and we thought it would be nice to win. Now it's a meticulously planned and very professional campaign. When I was playing, it was just a nice extra; we did not see the future of the Prudential Cup.

For the second World Cup in 1979, India introduced a team of mostly all-rounders. We were surprised they did not have many specialists. As it turned out, however, they were the smart ones and we were not so smart. That's the way one-day cricket will probably go in the future, with more multi-skilled players rather than specialists.

For years I have been pushing to have two separate teams, one for one-day cricket and one for traditional cricket. The idea is gaining popularity but is still years away from fruition. I'm sure it will come and when the transition is complete, you could play a one-day tournament in another country, totally separate from the Test team, and therefore play more cricket around the world. Players will specialise more and more. We have already reached a stage where five or six Australian Test players have been replaced by one-day specialists. This will escalate until all nations can produce two specialised sides, together with support staff, including selectors.

With two sets of selectors, there is sure to be a period when the two teams want some of the same players but this will gradually fade out and there will be two separate squads with players concentrating on one game or the other.

This is all still some way off. In Australia, for example, there is still not a huge amount of one-day cricket, but gradually the sponsors will embrace it because the public will want to see more instant cricket. We may end up with an extended one-day competition.

One thing which has changed out of all recognition has been the preparation and coaching of young players on the verge of making a breakthrough. The success of the Australian Cricket Academy has been due in large part, in my eyes at least, to Rodney Marsh. As head of the Academy, Rod was very keen on everyone playing attacking cricket, with the batsmen being aggressive from the start. At first I felt it could backfire on Rod, but saw that, following the success of one-day cricket, Test cricket had to measure up and be a lot more entertaining to attract both spectators and sponsors.

He took the view that we were in the business of entertainment and not self-indulgence. I went to see Eric Burdon and the Animals in concert, and at one stage they left the drummer alone on stage for five minutes to play jazz style. He was fantastic but, to me, it seemed a negative indulgence. I likened it to Geoff Boycott who often seemed to be batting for himself. I had gone to see Eric Burdon and the Animals, and while the crowd enjoyed a very good drummer, it was not what they had gone along to see. It might suit some to listen to a long drum solo, and I suppose there are the odd one or two who will happily watch a century scored over a day and a half, but these things are an indulgence.

Rod was trying to take that out of the young players' thinking and in so doing he affected the way world cricket was heading. It was starting to happen to a degree in Sri Lanka, especially in one-day cricket, but Rod wanted to make sure we went along at four an over instead of 1.27 in five-day Test matches.

There are few draws in Tests now unless it's because of the weather. Nevertheless, some of the great games I played in were draws – not contrived results but with four innings going down to the wire, games either team could have won over five days. That's the ultimate and I guess it's why Test cricket was played in the way it was. But if the game is over in three and a half or four days and is an exciting match, well and good, except the television coverage is compromised as they rely on income from the advertising time.

I did not like the format of the original Australian Academy, and refused to be involved. All the players had to play Grade cricket in Adelaide, which strengthened their sides and seemed unfair. South Australia had first pick of any Academy player for the Sheffield Shield, thus further strengthening South Australian cricket.

Also, I didn't think the people in charge of the Academy at the time would be able to enhance the future of our Test cricket. Rod Marsh changed the format so the players came to the Academy for the first part of the season until Christmas, playing games against second XIs and other Academy sides. Then they went back to their own States. I liked that concept and so I became involved.

It has had a good success rate although most of those guys would have made it anyway because they were the best youngsters around. But it shortens the learning curve and gives a better understanding of first-class cricket. Attending the Academy teaches the kids discipline, how to handle the press, look for jobs and gain an overall understanding of what to expect of a cricket career. It's a kind of finishing school. The boys leave the Academy as confident, experienced and almost complete first-class cricketers. It makes the step up to Shield and Test cricket so much easier. It has given us a head start on other Test-playing nations and we have become the best cricket-playing country in the world. It is quite incredible it has taken so long for the others to cotton on.

The only word of warning is that the players produced can only be as good as the coaching staff involved. The players must respect the staff, otherwise the whole thing breaks down. If you have an Academy run by second-rate personnel and coaches, you will produce second-rate players. You also need the right people for fitness, conditioning and diet; you need to have the right doctors, physios, psychologists and media specialists – it's a full service.

Over the last 30 years there has been a huge push in society to take the competitiveness out of sport. Winning isn't important, is the underlying message, just as long as everyone has a go. That concept contradicts history. Survival of the fittest relates not only to life but, in my opinion, to sport. You must have something to aim for, such as winning, improving yourself and lifting the overall standard.

The Academy has certainly done that and no one could have done it better than Rod. He earned everyone's respect by being a bloody good bloke as well as a tough disciplinarian and a great administrator. Not least, he picked the right players and had the best people to look after them. England has done the right thing in turning to him. I think the Australian administrators were foolhardy to let him go, of course, although I realise he needed a change and maybe a challenge. While Rod was still director of the Academy, he set up a deal with the ECB whereby they send out their people during the off-season to work at the Academy when our boys are out playing games. Having done the deal, they persuaded him to switch sides. England were looking for someone to organise some infrastructure and provide some direction for the young blokes, and they've got a great person to do it. It will not only help England but it's fabulous for the good of world cricket, and from that point of view I'm behind the move.

Both Rod and I believe Australian cricket has a problem, even though it is ranked number one in the world. We let people play too long – myself included. It's hard to know when to quit a game you love as a player. You want to extend it for as long as possible, particularly now with so much money involved. In my day, it was because you loved playing at the highest level; there were no big financial rewards to be made. Now it's a global business.

But if you go on for 14 or 15 years, you can impede the next generation of players. Australia has to be careful, otherwise a few years down the line, we may face a thin period, particularly with the batting, as I don't see a lot of players coming through. For a long time now, Australia has had a proliferation of top players who would have played for any other country in the world but who have hardly had a sniff at playing for Australia. Most of them seem to top the county averages in England, which further reinforces my argument.

We have had a great run, just as the West Indies did and England before them, with shorter periods of world supremacy for India and Pakistan. We are trying to even out the cycle so you do not have the big troughs because it's hard to claw your way back, as the West Indies are discovering and as Australia discovered in 1984 when a group of us packed it in at the same time. It was five or six years before the wheel turned again in our direction.

We have had a very good captain in Steve Waugh, demanding his players set goals for themselves, very much like Ian Chappell's leadership style. Mark Taylor and Allan Border put in the hard yards with a side Waugh was able to take to the next level. In our current side there is some great talent, especially among the fast bowlers, and they have been prepared to work on it. It has been a very good era but we have to face the fact that it may be coming to a conclusion.

England is experiencing the total opposite. English cricket had been on a slide but at the turn of the century there were many good signs. However, with Australia so dominant, it slowed them up and hit them so hard they were forced to regroup. They are still going in the right direction and becoming competitive; they are not the easy beats they were for a decade. That's a good thing because when English cricket is strong, world cricket is strong. History tells you the hardest side to beat were England, the great foe, and the game needs to see them strong again. When England are playing well, they are hard nuts and difficult to beat.

I believe several factors contributed to the slide of English cricket. Three-day county cricket was contrived; pitches were doctored. In addition, the one-day game eroded Test cricket because its format was carried over into county and Test matches without good planning. The one-day game discouraged real fast bowlers and spinners, and encouraged the medium pacers to drop the ball on the spot and wait for the doctored pitch to do the work for them. Bowlers relied on the help of the pitch instead of using line, length and movement. It carried over into the three- and five-day games.

The Academy will help enormously and I see England getting better and better. I don't know what the answer is with county cricket; it needs to be a more natural contest where you have to work hard for the wickets and the runs. Fewer matches will help the mental attitude, and the experiment of having two divisions, along with bringing in overseas coaches with new ideas, are all positives. England led the way for so long it was hard for them to see they were targeted as a benchmark and eventually overhauled. Now they have realised and have started to claw back.

The game worldwide is getting bigger and bigger and the introduction of new countries brings a breath of fresh air. However, I thought Sri Lanka came into Test cricket too early, before they were ready, and the same could be said of Zimbabwe but they have quickly learned to become more competitive. I reserve my judgement on Kenya and Bangladesh – I don't know enough about their cricket.

Ideally, all countries should have a first-class competition because it is a big step up from club cricket to the Test arena, as Sri Lanka and

Zimbabwe discovered. New Zealand had a long apprenticeship, but that may not be the answer now. Maybe the ICC should step in to help countries develop to Test level.

It has been an advantage to the world game that South Africa has recovered their status so quickly. You can never underestimate them. They emerged very strongly after the ban, with similar style and passion to Australian cricket. Twenty years is a long time out but they have proved they were more than ready to resume.

The West Indies have to do what England has done and look at their structure. They were lucky in the past because they had so much natural talent to call upon, but competition from basketball and other American sports has taken its toll, and not every top young sportsman there automatically takes up cricket.

Their new Academy should help so long as they can overcome their internal problems. It's like trying to make a team out of Australia, New Zealand, Hong Kong and Indonesia. Who would like the job? I like a challenge but I don't like hitting my head against a brick wall. A lot of people don't understand that the West Indies is not one country, but several. Every island is different from the others, with different cultures and different people. They could be in for a long lean spell if they are not careful.

Pakistan are the enigmas of the world game. They are hot, they are cold, brilliant then ordinary, exciting then dull, smooth and then controversial. At times, I cannot believe how well they play and at others, not long afterwards, how badly.

India expects to win at home and is surprised if they win away. To me, they haven't kept up with the times and have done themselves and their players a disservice by continuing with this attitude of 'as long as we beat them at home we will be fine'. The wickets are so different from anywhere else, and the sooner they produce wickets for a fairer contest, the sooner they will compete outside their country. When that happens, I fear for the rest of the world because they are amazing cricketers when it all comes together. I have seen at first hand the passion, the religion of the sport, and the quality of the players.

When I first started going to India more than 15 years ago, you couldn't stop people talking about the game wherever you went; it drove me mad at times. You quickly realised their passion for the sport; they live and breathe it. There are a billion Indians who love the game.

I was there when the bribery scandal was exposed and it was as if someone had suddenly told them that religion did not exist, that there was no good in the world any more. They would not even talk about it and were in a state of complete denial. Cricket was deleted from the topics of conversation because they were embarrassed and upset. They could not believe what was going on. It was incredible.

Gradually, it is getting back to normal, but slowly. That's how seriously they take it. It has hit the game hard and there have been a lot of empty seats at some recent Test matches, although the one-day games seem to be as well supported as ever.

The world order has changed. England was the power base but now the Asian countries have the numbers and that is where the money is with television rights. Financially, before television rights, cricket in India was poor; before the middle class emerged, there weren't many who could afford to go to watch a match or buy a television. Now, apparently, there are 250 million middle-class people in India. That involves a lot of money and is the reason why the balance of power has shifted. It's where the money is and where the sponsorship lies. It's going to be interesting to see how it develops.

The first public sign of them flexing their muscles was over the series with South Africa. Mike Denness made some decisions as match referee which the Indians felt were biased against them, and almost caused a chasm in the cricket world.

The Asian countries have been told what to do for so long by the former powerful cricket nations, and they are now saying they must have equal standing, or be in charge, and a big share of the purse strings. I hope sense prevails but I believe there is going to be a huge cricket revolution of a magnitude we have never seen before. World Series Cricket will pale into insignificance. It could split the game into two distinct centres. What a shame if that happened. We would all get on with it but cricket would be a weaker game.

It may be India and Pakistan find they cannot form even an uneasy alliance and it may be the one thing that will keep the world game. The smaller countries such as Bangladesh, Sri Lanka and Kenya will wait to see where the balance of power lies, and you cannot blame them for that.

CHAPTER TWENTY-SEVEN

The art of fast bowling

Things change in all walks of life and I'm sure there have been major changes in most sports, especially as sports science has developed. It has taken a while in cricket, however. For years, we all went by Don Bradman's *The Art of Cricket*, or the *MCC Coaching Manual*. By and large, the same principles applied for all roles, from batting to wicket-keeping.

Fast bowling had been coached in the same way for 100 years and was in desperate need of repair. The coach would stand there and say things like, 'Well bowled', 'You're not following through enough', 'Don't let your shoulder fall away'. It dawned on me one day that everyone was telling the bowlers about their problems but not how to fix them because no one knew the solutions.

I've lost count of the number of times I've heard a coach say, 'You're falling away – stand up straight.' It just makes me laugh because nobody deliberately tries to fall over when attempting to bowl. The reason they are falling away is because, mechanically, something is wrong. If you cannot explain to the player why it's happening and show him how he can fix the problem, it will not go away. He might be able to stand straight for a couple of balls, but inevitably he will start to fall away again. It was band-aid coaching, not corrective teaching.

Even now, we need more people to become more involved in the mechanics of bowling, to find the reasons why an action clicks or why some bowlers bowl continually down leg side when they are trying not to. You cannot just tell the player; you have to show him and explain so he can understand the mechanics, and then work it out for himself by watching a video of his action. Thus the coach coaches himself out of that particular job and moves on to the next one. Some coaches don't want to work that way, but I do. Get in, do the job and get out.

In the old days, we had Outside Broadcast Units in huge vans. They beamed pictures of the cricket from the ground back to the local television station, which then relayed them to the rest of Australia. When I was having problems with my bowling, John Inverarity and I, sometimes with Rod Marsh and maybe one of the other bowlers, would ask the television technicians to replay the tapes slowly so we could pick out the faults and see why I was making them. We focused on all the basic, little things – nothing as specific as today because we knew nothing about biomechanics.

In later years, when I started coaching, we advanced to video and filmed the players. The quality was blurry and sketchy, but it was still useful. Real progress was made when jog wheels were introduced. This meant we could slow the film down frame by frame, which was fabulous; now we have digital equipment, which is absolutely amazing. The film can be slowed down to whatever speed you want, superimposing one action on top of another, taking exact measurements to show the player the difference between what he is actually doing and what we want him to achieve. I wonder how much better it can get.

We can now break the action down, right from the run-up to the follow-through. If the run-up is not correct, the subsequent delivery action is not likely to be satisfactory. We can assess the run-up for all sorts of things – what's happening with arms, what's happening with the head, is he too far forward or too upright, too fast or too slow?

Fast bowling requires special preparation and these days fitness is tailored to the individual, with strength, flexibility and weights programmes. This attention to detail helps prevent injuries, which is better than treating them after the event.

The trunk is the main part of the body used by fast bowlers; if you have a strong and flexible trunk, it enables you to pull your shoulders and arms through quicker than you otherwise would, and therefore to bowl faster and safer. It's not necessary to have six-pack stomach muscles, the beach look, but to strengthen the internal muscles, the deeper trunk muscle. Strength but not bulk is the aim and it can be achieved with specific weight and strength training. Research and development on this subject is ongoing.

Diet is another issue to be considered specifically for fast bowlers. Recently I came across a situation where the guys were losing weight and strength during the season, and were feeling a bit flat. The dieticians were using high carbohydrate diets for performance. Suddenly the penny dropped – all these carbs are fine for the match or training days, but in between you need protein to rebuild the muscles you are using to perform. Otherwise, you lose strength. We are learning all the time.

From a technical point of view, we have moved radically from the theory that every fast bowler has to be side-on, to accepting there are three different actions. One is the old side-on, then there's front-on and also the semi, which is halfway between the two and not to be confused with a mixed action, which causes such a lot of back problems. What we have to do now is to discover whether having the different actions reduces back problems, and the initial indications are that it does. The crucial factor is to make sure the hips and shoulders are aligned at the set-up. Alignment means if you dissect your body through the top, your shoulders and hips are pretty close to being in one line. Set-up refers to when you land on the back foot with your front arm up high in front of your body and about ready to pull down. If your hips and shoulders are in alignment then, you can't go very far wrong. Where possible, particularly at indoor centres, we have cameras to check the alignment from above. Mark Portus, who is with the A.C.B., the Academy and the

Institute of Sport, is working on this, along with other fast-bowling research, and I enjoy working with him.

The modern observation is that bowlers don't swing the ball as much as they used to, and this is something to do with the front-on action. That's rubbish! It doesn't matter whether you are front or side-on; it's where your arm is positioned for delivery which counts, and how you use your wrist. Check whether the wrist is in the right position behind the ball for an outswinger and follows through the same line, or whether it is behind the ball and high up for an inswinger and behind that line with no movement across the seam with finger or wrist. I emphasise, following through correctly is paramount.

Understanding is, of course, evolving all of the time. Naturally, there are problems and we are tackling them in the modern way, with sports doctors, orthopaedic surgeons, physiotherapists, biomechanics and experts in human movement. The coach has to take on board the results of all the latest research that are being thrown at him from every quarter. This has been part of my work over the last decade with the Australian Board of Control and MRF in India, allowing me to help coaches understand more about fast bowling.

One problem I have, especially with youth scouts and coaches, is that the kids who run in and bowl a good line and length at medium pace and get their five wickets regularly at school, are the ones who are sent to me as future state and Test bowlers. Most of them are not going to get much further, and certainly not a lot quicker. They look good at that age because they can bowl accurately and are quick in school cricket, but when they come to see me, I can often tell instantly they are not going to be fast bowlers.

It is an acquired skill to know what to look for among the youngsters to find a potential fast bowler. The first thing I look for is to see whether the person has reasonable coordination in their run-up and action. After that, the most important observation is how the bowler contracts through their trunk. In other words, it's really about how the trunk pulls through, rather than how fast the bowler appears to be. If they can contract through the trunk region, which pulls the shoulders and the arms through, that creates speed. What we want is a fast-twitch fibre muscle. You cannot take an autopsy, so you have to judge it by the ability to react fast, turn quickly and sprint, the way they pick up a ball and they throw it, and how fast and how far they throw it, among other things. When they bowl, you look for how quickly the front arm comes down and through.

A lot of these bowlers may be written off when they are very young because they may be bowling short, wide or not swinging the ball. We are looking for other things in the youngsters. In fact, I don't care how badly they bowl, or if they take only one or two wickets in a game. What I'm watching for is whether they are athletes with the right overall make-up.

I'm not even interested in build because you can go from someone of relatively small stature, such as Larwood or Gough, to someone who is nearly 7ft tall. In the old days, we looked for fast bowlers in the range of 5ft 7ins to 6ft 3ins because they seemed to be more of the athletic type. Nowadays, taller boys are proving to be just as athletic. We can train them to be fast-twitch, even if they are a bit on the ploddy side, as we have done in India with the son of a big-boned, 7ft plus basketball player. With his son, and others like him, we tailor the individual programmes to include more short, sharp workouts to help improve fast-twitch muscle make-up.

With the élite players, we are looking for a lot of other assets on top of those already mentioned. What we want at this level is attitude and determination, someone who can go through the pain barrier, someone who will work harder than most physically and someone who has something a bit different. It may be a glint in the eye, or the fact that he can unleash one now and again, or swing the ball naturally, or maybe mental toughness. A combination of all those assets and you are looking at superstar potential.

As sports become professional and good money is involved, some people may be tempted to use drugs in a bid to gain an advantage, and there may, of course, be fast bowlers among them. I don't believe any players are involved in that scene in Australia, but who knows, drugs from steroids right across the spectrum to EPO could become a problem. I hope the testing is very thorough and the authorities keep a careful and close eye on the situation.

A lot of players take supplements, but a warning has been sounded about them because apparently they can produce nandrolene, which is a banned performance-enhancing substance. This has resulted in sportsmen at very high levels being banned in soccer and in athletics; they denied taking steroids and subsequently discovered supplements were the problem. That's the sort of thing which could happen to a young fast bowler, keen to make it. They could find themselves banned without even knowing they have taken steroids. The sensible thing is to make sure all the favoured supplements are clean and cleared; otherwise there could be serious embarrassment. The academies should push this point and check everything the players take.

I am totally against all drugs, performance enhancing or recreational. To take performance-enhancing drugs is cheating – nothing more, nothing less.

There is one problem I'm not quite sure how to address, and it's come about partly due to the strategy of containment in the one-day game. What is the point of bowling a beautiful outswinger when, with no slips, batsmen can have a go at you with an outside edge predominant and intentional use of an open face? After conceding a couple of fours, the bowler gives it away and just bowls line and length. With inswing, the batsman plays it off the pads, or often a no ball results down the leg side. Bowlers have been forced to bowl a lot straighter. They also run the fingers over the ball to make it drift in a little. It's almost like cutting the ball, a mini swing, but definitely not as effective as normal swing in five-day cricket. In school cricket, we encourage the young bowlers to swing the ball and show them how to do it, but once they leave, they are encouraged to jam the ball into the pitch in areas designed to contain.

Another thing about swing bowling is you have to pitch the ball a bit fuller. With one-day cricket and today's more aggressive approach to Test cricket, you are not necessarily encouraged by captains and coaches to pitch the ball up and bowl swing. Also, you cannot bowl dangerous swing if you are bowling just short of a length, which so many quick bowlers tend to do. Indeed, there are so many factors stacked up against it that swing bowling is in danger of becoming a lost art. I would love Bob Massie, Terry Alderman and Mick Malone to demonstrate it to the young players.

An inswinging yorker was always a wicket-taking ball, but now we have the devastating late reverse swinging yorker, which is a menace to any batsman, even one with his eye in. Almost everyone has to be able to bowl a slower ball. When I played, if you saw a few guys bowl a slower ball in a season you were surprised. The first slower ball I saw was from Graham Taylor, who opened the bowling at the Perth Cricket Club. He bowled a fast leg-spinner which actually turned, and if he left me a legacy, it was that he encouraged me to try it. He called it his 'zorf ball' and it was called that thereafter. I tried to bowl the leg-break but it just blooped out and slowed up, nowhere near today's well-concealed weapon. Steve Waugh had a very good slower ball out of the back of his hand.

I have talked to several retired players about it, and they say the slower ball has always been around but it wasn't perfected until recently. Now you have bowlers playing around with leg-spin, off-spin, back of the hand, knuckle balls, palm of the hand and three fingers or one finger behind the seam, the way Max Walker bowled it, running the fingers down the side. There are all sorts of different ways, but the ones that give the most control and are the easiest to hide are where the wrist comes from behind, or the ball is in the back of the palm.

If I was just starting out, I would work on the one where there appears to be no wrist differential. It's so important not to show it as you run in because the top batsmen watch the ball from the hand. Greg Chappell used to say it was like a television set in front of him and he would concentrate on head, shoulder and arm until finally his vision would shift to the wrist. From there he could judge what the bowler was attempting to do. I guess that's one of the reasons why the great batsmen are great.

I'm often asked in India how I would bowl to Tendulkar. My answer is, 'With a helmet on,' but I'm not sure they see the joke. Some bowlers who have come up against Tendulkar in full flight might agree. In his autobiography, Viv Richards claimed he used to deliberately smash the ball straight back at the slow bowlers to frighten them. When bowling my slower ball, or a leg-cutter, I used to run in as usual, and then as I took the ball up, I fiddled with it to get it into the finger position I wanted. It takes a while to perfect but you can deceive the batsman because your delivery stride looks no different from usual.

The first thing any kid who wants to be a fast bowler does is mark out a long run-up to look fearsome. That's the wrong way round. A run-up should be just long enough to coordinate with your delivery. A reasonably long run-up takes the pressure off the back whereas a huge run-up is tiring and counter-productive. You can bowl quickly off a short run, but if you are trying to bowl at 90 miles per hour off a short run, you are going to have problems sooner rather than later because of extra stresses.

One thing which used to be constantly overlooked was the necessity to rehydrate. We were allowed water only at drinks intervals, but the damage has already been done once you feel thirsty. Because I sweated so much, I was thirsty after two or three overs, but I was not allowed to have a bottle of water on the boundary, and it was also wrong to keep a bag of ice in the underground box used to house helmets. I was told I was wasting time. I would regularly lose as much as half a stone in fluid every day I bowled, whether it was a hot or cool day. Thank goodness it's different now.

Nowadays, fast bowling is coached as a specific skill, as are all other aspects of the game. Players used to be treated the same and coached generally, but that has all changed, not only in our sport but also in most of the others. It's called evolution.

APPENDIX

Dennis Lillee

A STATISTICAL SURVEY OF HIS CAREER

Compiled by BILL FRINDALL

FIRST-CLASS CAREER

BOWLING AND FIELDING SUMMARY

Season	Venue	Matches	Overs	Mdns	Runs	Wkts	Avge	Best	5wI	10wM	Ct
1969-70‡	A	8	197.2	17	705	32	22.03	7- 36	1	–	6
1969-70‡	NZ	5	92.4	16	296	18	16.44	6- 40	1	–	4
1970-71‡	A	11	312.5	44	1096	31	35.35	5- 65	2	–	4
1971-72‡	A	9	232.2	32	932	48	19.41	8- 29	4	2	5
1972	E	14	456.5	119	1197	53	22.58	6- 66	3	1	3
1972-73‡	A	9	302.3	56	1131	56	20.19	6- 30	3	–	2
1972-73	WI	5	54	9	238	5	47.60	4- 21	–	–	–
1974-75‡	A	13	444.4	68	1559	62	25.14	4- 43	–	–	3
1975	E	9	345	107	886	41	21.60	7- 67	2	1	1
1975-76‡	A	13	312.3	29	1490	62	24.03	7- 41	4	1	2
1975-76	SA	2	70.4	22	180	15	12.00	7- 27	1	–	–
1976-77‡	A	11	354	59	1368	70	19.54	6- 26	8	4	4
1976-77‡	NZ	4	122.4	25	392	23	17.04	6- 72	2	1	3
1979-80	A	8	368.5	83	1062	48	22.12	6- 60	4	1	3
1979-80	P	3	102	19	303	3	101.00	3-114	–	–	1
1980	E	4	116.2	25	391	20	19.55	6-133	1	–	–
1980-81	A	13	545	138	1462	69	21.18	6- 53	4	–	3
1981	E	8	377.4	102	1028	47	21.87	7- 89	3	1	3
1981-82	A	8	301	66	819	37	22.13	7- 83	3	1	4
1981-82	NZ	4	79	23	183	7	26.14	3- 13	–	–	2
1982-83	A	8	343	103	907	32	28.34	4- 29	–	–	3
1982-83	SL	2	52.2	12	179	7	25.57	3- 26	–	–	1
1983-84	A	13	610.5	143	1513	59	25.64	6- 62	3	–	5
1987-88	A	6	223.2	45	600	16	37.50	4- 99	–	–	2
1988	E	8	245	45	778	21	37.04	6- 68	1	–	3
TOTALS		**198**	**4290.5** ‡2370.3	**1061** 346	**20695**	**882**	**23.46**	**8- 29**	**50**	**13**	**67**

Venue	Matches	Overs	Mdns	Runs	Wkts	Avge	Best	5wI	10wM	Ct
Australia	130	2392 ‡2155.3	578 305	14644	622	23.54	8- 29	36	9	46
England	43	1540.5	398	4280	182	23.51	7- 67	10	3	10
New Zealand	13	79 ‡215	23 41	871	48	18.14	6- 40	3	1	9
Pakistan	3	102	19	303	3	101.00	3-114	–	–	1
South Africa	2	70.4	22	180	15	12.00	7- 27	1	–	–
Sri Lanka	2	52.2	12	179	7	25.57	3- 26	–	–	1
West Indies	5	54	9	238	5	47.60	4- 21	–	–	–

Venue	Matches	Overs	Mdns	Runs	Wkts	Avge	Best	5wI	10wM	Ct
HOME	130	2392	578	14644	622	23.54	8- 29	36	9	46
		‡2155.3	305							
AWAY	68	1898.5	483	6051	260	23.27	7- 27	14	4	21
		‡215	41							
TOTALS	**198**	**4290.5**	**1061**	**20695**	**882**	**23.46**	**8- 29**	**50**	**13**	**67**
		‡2370.3	**346**							

‡ Eight-ball overs

ALL FIRST-CLASS MATCHES

TEAM SUMMARY
BOWLING

Team	Matches	Overs	Mdns	Runs	Wkts	Avge	Best	5wI	10wM
AUSTRALIA (Tests)	70	2102.5	547	8493	355	23.92	7-83	23	7
		‡731.2	105						
Australia v World XI	4	‡117.4	17	482	24	20.08	8-29	2	1
Australia B	5	‡92.4	16	296	18	16.44	6-40	1	–
Australians (Tours)	27	537.4	118	1786	82	21.78	7-67	3	1
		‡40	12						
International Wanderers	2	70.4	22	180	15	12.00	7-27	1	–
Northamptonshire	8	245	45	778	21	37.04	6-68	1	–
Tasmania	6	223.2	45	600	16	37.50	4-99	–	–
Western Australia (Shield)	70	1022.2	262	7544	323	23.35	7-36	18	4
		‡1309.5	178						
Western Australia (v Tourists)	6	89	22	536	28	19.14	6-30	1	–
		‡79.4	18						
TOTALS	**198**	**4290.5**	**1061**	**20695**	**882**	**23.46**	**8-29**	**50**	**13**
		‡2370.3	**346**						

‡ Eight-ball overs

FIRST-CLASS FIVE-WICKET INNINGS ANALYSES

		Analysis			For	Against	Venue	Season
1	16.2	4	36	7	Western Australia	South Australia	Perth	1969-70
2	11.4	–	40	6	Australia B	New Zealand U-23 XI	Napier	1969-70
3	**28.3**	**–**	**84**	**5**	**AUSTRALIA**	**ENGLAND 6**	**Adelaide**	**1970-71**
4	18.6	3	65	5	Western Australia	New South Wales	Perth	1970-71
5	24	3	75	5	Western Australia	Victoria	Perth	1971-72
6	7.1	3	29	8	Australia	Rest of the World	Perth	1971-72

	Analysis				For	Against	Venue	Season
7	11	4	24	6	Western Australia	Queensland	Brisbane	1971-72
8	16.3	1	48	5	Australia	Rest of the World	Melbourne	1971-72
9	**30**	**8**	**66**	**6**	**AUSTRALIA**	**ENGLAND 1**	**Manchester**	**1972**
10	**24.2**	**7**	**58**	**5**	**AUSTRALIA**	**ENGLAND 5**	**The Oval**	**1972**
11	**32.2**	**8**	**123**	**5**	**AUSTRALIA**	**ENGLAND 5**	**The Oval**	**1972**
12	7.7	2	30	6	Western Australia	Pakistanis	Perth	1972-73
13	12.2	4	43	6	Western Australia	New South Wales	Sydney	1972-73
14	24	4	87	5	Western Australia	South Australia	Adelaide	1972-73
15	27	10	67	7	Australians	MCC	Lord's	1975
16	**15**	**8**	**15**	**5**	**AUSTRALIA**	**ENGLAND 1**	**Birmingham**	**1975**
17	11	1	58	5	Western Australia	Victoria	Perth	1975-76
18	**11.3**	**–**	**63**	**5**	**AUSTRALIA**	**WEST INDIES 6**	**Melbourne**	**1975-76**
19	9.3	–	41	7	Western Australia	South Australia	Adelaide	1975-76
20	24	4	72	5	Western Australia	South Australia	Adelaide	1975-76
21	14	5	27	7	International Wanderers	SA Invitation XI	Johannesburg	1975-76
22	12	1	68	5	Western Australia	South Australia	Adelaide	1976-77
23	20	3	78	6	Western Australia	Victoria	Perth	1976-77
24	**47.7**	**10**	**163**	**5**	**AUSTRALIA**	**PAKISTAN 1**	**Adelaide**	**1976-77**
25	**23**	**4**	**82**	**6**	**AUSTRALIA**	**PAKISTAN 2**	**Melbourne**	**1976-77**
26	13	2	44	5	Western Australia	South Australia	Perth	1976-77
27	13.6	4	37	5	Western Australia	South Australia	Perth	1976-77
28	**17.3**	**4**	**51**	**5**	**AUSTRALIA**	**NEW ZEALAND 2**	**Auckland**	**1976-77**
29	**15.7**	**2**	**72**	**6**	**AUSTRALIA**	**NEW ZEALAND 2**	**Auckland**	**1976-77**
30	**13.3**	**2**	**26**	**6**	**AUSTRALIA**	**ENGLAND CT**	**Melbourne**	**1976-77**
31	**34.4**	**7**	**139**	**5**	**AUSTRALIA**	**ENGLAND CT**	**Melbourne**	**1976-77**
32	22.3	4	94	6	Western Australia	Queensland	Brisbane	1979-80
33	**24**	**3**	**78**	**5**	**AUSTRALIA**	**WEST INDIES 3**	**Adelaide**	**1979-80**
34	**33.1**	**9**	**60**	**6**	**AUSTRALIA**	**ENGLAND 3**	**Melbourne**	**1979-80**
35	**33**	**6**	**78**	**5**	**AUSTRALIA**	**ENGLAND 3**	**Melbourne**	**1979-80**
36	29.4	4	133	6	Australians	Nottinghamshire	Nottingham	1980
37	25.5	8	57	5	Western Australia	Victoria	Perth	1980-81
38	46	13	97	6	Western Australia	Queensland	Brisbane	1980-81
39	**15**	**1**	**53**	**6**	**AUSTRALIA**	**NEW ZEALAND 1**	**Brisbane**	**1980-81**
40	**23.5**	**5**	**63**	**5**	**AUSTRALIA**	**NEW ZEALAND 2**	**Perth**	**1980-81**
41	11	1	41	5	Australians	Middlesex	Lord's	1981
42	**16.4**	**2**	**46**	**5**	**AUSTRALIA**	**ENGLAND 1**	**Nottingham**	**1981**
43	**31.4**	**4**	**89**	**7**	**AUSTRALIA**	**ENGLAND 6**	**The Oval**	**1981**
44	**9**	**3**	**18**	**5**	**AUSTRALIA**	**PAKISTAN 1**	**Perth**	**1981-82**
45	**20**	**3**	**81**	**5**	**AUSTRALIA**	**PAKISTAN 2**	**Brisbane**	**1981-82**
46	**26.3**	**3**	**83**	**7**	**AUSTRALIA**	**WEST INDIES 1**	**Melbourne**	**1981-82**
47	30.5	12	62	6	Western Australia	New South Wales	Perth	1983-84
48	**50.2**	**8**	**171**	**6**	**AUSTRALIA**	**PAKISTAN 3**	**Adelaide**	**1983-84**
49	28.4	7	63	5	Western Australia	Victoria	Perth	1983-84
50	29	8	68	6	Northamptonshire	Gloucestershire	Northampton	1988

FIRST-CLASS TEN-WICKET MATCH ANALYSES

	Analysis			For	Against	Venue	Season
1	7.1	3	29	8	Australia	Rest of the World XI	Perth	1971-72
	14	2	63	4				
2	11	4	24	6	Western Australia	Queensland	Brisbane	1971-72
	10	–	46	4				
3	**24.2**	**7**	**58**	**5**	**AUSTRALIA**	**ENGLAND 5**	**The Oval**	**1972**
	32.2	**8**	**123**	**5**				
4	19	4	65	3	Australians	MCC	Lord's	1975
	27	10	67	7				
5	9.3	–	41	7	Western Australia	South Australia	Adelaide	1975-76
	24	4	72	5				
6	20	3	78	6	Western Australia	Victoria	Perth	1976-77
	21.4	5	68	4				
7	**23**	**4**	**82**	**6**	**AUSTRALIA**	**PAKISTAN 2**	**Melbourne**	**1976-77**
	14	**1**	**53**	**4**				
8	13	2	44	5	Western Australia	South Australia	Perth	1976-77
	13.6	4	37	5				
9	**17.3**	**4**	**51**	**5**	**AUSTRALIA**	**NEW ZEALAND 2**	**Auckland**	**1976-77**
	15.7	**2**	**72**	**6**				
10	**13.3**	**2**	**26**	**6**	**AUSTRALIA**	**ENGLAND CT**	**Melbourne**	**1976-77**
	34.4	**7**	**139**	**5**				
11	**33.1**	**9**	**60**	**6**	**AUSTRALIA**	**ENGLAND 3**	**Melbourne**	**1979-80**
	33	**6**	**78**	**5**				
12	**31.4**	**4**	**89**	**7**	**AUSTRALIA**	**ENGLAND 6**	**The Oval**	**1981**
	30	**10**	**70**	**4**				
13	**26.3**	**3**	**83**	**7**	**AUSTRALIA**	**WEST INDIES 1**	**Melbourne**	**1981-82**
	27.1	**8**	**44**	**3**				

ALL FIRST-CLASS MATCHES

BATTING SUMMARY

Season	Venue	Matches	Inns	NO	HS	Runs	Avge	100	50
1969-70	A	8	9	3	26	64	10.66	–	–
1969-70	NZ	5	4	3	26*	66	66.00	–	–
1970-71	A	11	16	5	32	159	14.45	–	–
1971-72	A	9	8	2	11	26	4.33	–	–
1972	E	14	13	7	11*	30	5.00	–	–
1972-73	A	9	11	2	14*	51	5.66	–	–
1972-73	WI	5	6	1	36	59	11.80	–	–
1974-75‡	A	13	20	5	46	247	16.46	–	–

Season	Venue	Matches	Inns	NO	HS	Runs	Avge	100	50
1975	E	9	9	4	73*	154	30.80	–	1
1975-76‡	A	13	16	4	36	211	17.58	–	–
1975-76	SA	2	4	1	22*	22	7.33	–	–
1976-77‡	A	11	13	4	27	162	18.00	–	–
1976-77‡	NZ	4	5	1	23*	54	13.50	–	–
1979-80	A	8	12	–	19	79	6.58	–	–
1979-80	P	3	4	2	12*	18	9.00	–	–
1980	E	4	4	1	33	81	27.00	–	–
1980-81	A	13	20	5	31*	251	16.73	–	–
1981	E	8	11	4	40*	158	22.57	–	–
1981-82	A	8	12	3	54*	125	13.88	–	1
1981-82	NZ	4	3	–	9	21	7.00	–	–
1982-83	A	8	9	3	26	84	14.00	–	–
1982-83	SL	2	1	1	12*	12	–	–	–
1983-84	A	13	13	4	25	86	9.55	–	–
1987-88	A	6	7	3	18	37	9.25	–	–
1988	E	8	11	2	22	120	13.33	–	–
TOTALS		**198**	**241**	**70**	**73***	**2377**	**13.90**	**–**	**2**

TEST MATCHES

MATCH RECORD

Season	Match	Venue	No	Runs	HO	O	M	R	W	Ct
1970-71	1 ENGLAND 6	Adelaide	10	10	c	28.3	–	84	5	1
			–			7	–	40	–	–
	2 ENGLAND 7	Sydney	10	6	c	13	5	32	1	–
			10	0	c	14	–	43	2	1
1972	3 ENGLAND 1	Manchester	11	1	*	29	14	40	2	–
			11	0	*	30	8	66	6	–
	4 ENGLAND 2	Lord's	11	2	*	28	3	90	2	–
			–			21	6	50	2	–
	5 ENGLAND 3	Nottingham	11	0	c	29	15	35	4	–
			–			25	10	40	2	–
	6 ENGLAND 4	Leeds	11	0	c	26.1	10	39	2	–
			10	7	b	5	2	7	1	–
	7 ENGLAND 5	The Oval	11	0	*	24.2	7	58	5	–
			–			32.2	8	123	5	–
1972-73	8 PAKISTAN 1	Adelaide	10	14	c	20.3	7	49	4	–
			–			15	3	53	1	–
	9 PAKISTAN 2	Melbourne	–			16.6	1	90	1	1
			11	2	c	11	1	59	1	–

Season	Match	Venue	No	Runs	HO	O	M	R	W	Ct
	10 PAKISTAN 3	Sydney	10	2	b	10	2	34	1	–
			11	0	*	23	5	68	3	–
1972-73	11 WEST INDIES 1	Kingston	–			26	4	112	–	–
			–			6	1	20	–	–
1974-75	12 ENGLAND 1	Brisbane	9	15	c	23	6	73	2	–
			–			12	2	25	2	–
	13 ENGLAND 2	Perth	9	11	b	16	4	48	2	–
			–			22	5	59	2	–
	14 ENGLAND 3	Melbourne	9	2	*	20	2	70	2	–
			9	14	c	17	3	55	2	–
	15 ENGLAND 4	Sydney	9	8	b	19.1	2	66	2	–
			–			21	5	65	2	–
	16 ENGLAND 5	Adelaide	9	26	b	12.5	2	49	4	2
			–			14	3	69	4	–
	17 ENGLAND 6	Melbourne	9	12	c	6	2	17	1	–
			11	0	*	–				–
1975	18 ENGLAND 1	Birmingham	10	3	c	15	8	15	5	–
			–			20	8	45	2	–
	19 ENGLAND 2	Lord's	10	73	*	20	4	84	4	–
			–			33	10	80	1	–
	20 ENGLAND 3	Leeds	10	11	b	28	12	53	1	–
			–			20	5	48	2	–
	21 ENGLAND 4	The Oval	10	28	*	19	7	44	2	–
						52	18	91	4	–
1975-76	22 WEST INDIES 1	Brisbane	9	1	b	11	–	84	3	–
			–			16	3	72	3	–
	23 WEST INDIES 2	Perth	9	12	*	20	–	123	2	–
			9	4	c	–				–
	24 WEST INDIES 3	Melbourne	9	25	c	14	2	56	4	–
			–			15	1	70	3	1
	25 WEST INDIES 5	Adelaide	11	16	*	10	–	68	2	–
			–			14	–	64	2	–
	26 WEST INDIES 6	Melbourne	11	19	*	11.3	–	63	5	–
			–			18	1	112	3	–
1976-77	27 PAKISTAN 1	Adelaide	10	0	c	19	1	104	1	–
			–			47.7	10	163	5	1
	28 PAKISTAN 2	Melbourne	–			23	4	82	6	–
			9	6	b	14	1	53	4	–
	29 PAKISTAN 3	Sydney	10	14	lbw	22.3	–	114	3	–
			10	27	c	4	–	24	2	–
1976-77	30 NEW ZEALAND 1	Christchurch	10	19	c	31.2	6	119	2	–
			–			18	1	70	2	–
	31 NEW ZEALAND 2	Auckland	10	23	*	17.3	4	51	5	1
			–			15.7	2	72	6	1

Season	Match	Venue	No	Runs	HO	O	M	R	W	Ct
1976-77	32 ENGLAND	Melbourne	10	10	*	13.3	2	26	6	–
	Centenary Test		9	25	c	34.4	7	139	5	–
1979-80	33 WEST INDIES 1	Brisbane	9	0	lbw	29.1	8	104	4	–
			–			2	–	3	–	–
	34 ENGLAND 1	Perth	9	18	c	28	11	73	4	–
			9	19	c	23	5	74	2	–
	35 WEST INDIES 2	Melbourne	8	12	c	36	7	96	3	–
			8	0	c	3	–	9	–	–
	36 ENGLAND 2	Sydney	8	5	c	13.3	4	40	4	–
			–			24.3	6	63	2	–
	37 WEST INDIES 3	Adelaide	8	16	c	24	3	78	5	2
			8	0	c	26	6	75	–	–
	38 ENGLAND 3	Melbourne	8	8	c	33.1	9	60	6	–
			–			33	6	78	5	–
1979-80	39 PAKISTAN 1	Karachi	10	12	*	28	4	76	–	1
			10	5	lbw	11	2	22	–	–
	40 PAKISTAN 2	Faisalabad	10	0	lbw	21	4	91	–	–
			–			–			–	–
	41 PAKISTAN 3	Lahore	–			42	9	114	3	–
			10	1	*	–			–	–
1980	42 ENGLAND	Lord's	–			15	4	43	4	–
	Centenary Test		–			19	5	53	1	–
1980-81	43 NEW ZEALAND 1	Brisbane	8	24	c	18	7	36	2	–
			–			15	1	53	6	–
	44 NEW ZEALAND 2	Perth	8	8	c	23.5	5	63	5	–
			–			15.1	7	14	2	–
	45 NEW ZEALAND 3	Melbourne	8	27	b	21	4	49	–	–
			8	8	c	13	3	30	1	–
1980-81	46 INDIA 1	Sydney	8	5	c	20.2	3	86	4	–
			–			18	2	79	3	1
	47 INDIA 2	Adelaide	9	2	c	34	10	80	4	–
			9	10	*	19	7	38	2	–
	48 INDIA 3	Melbourne	9	19	c	25	6	65	4	–
			9	4	b	32.1	5	104	4	–
1981	49 ENGLAND 1	Nottingham	9	12	c	13	3	34	3	–
			–			16.4	2	46	5	–
	50 ENGLAND 2	Lord's	10	40	*	35.4	7	102	–	–
			–			26.4	8	82	3	–
	51 ENGLAND 3	Leeds	10	3	*	18.5	7	49	4	1
			10	17	c	25	6	94	3	–
	52 ENGLAND 4	Birmingham	9	18	b	18	4	61	2	–
			9	3	c	26	9	51	2	–
	53 ENGLAND 5	Manchester	9	13	c	24.1	8	55	4	–
			9	28	c	46	13	137	2	–

DENNIS LILLEE

Season	Match	Venue	No	Runs	HO	O	M	R	W	Ct
	54 ENGLAND 6	The Oval	9	11	b	31.4	4	89	7	–
			9	8	*	30	10	70	4	–
1981-82	55 PAKISTAN 1	Perth	9	16	c	9	3	18	5	–
			9	4	*	20	3	78	1	–
	56 PAKISTAN 2	Brisbane	9	14	b	20	3	81	5	–
			–			19	4	51	4	–
	57 PAKISTAN 3	Melbourne	9	1	lbw	36.3	9	104	–	1
			9	4	c	–				
1981-82	58 WEST INDIES 1	Melbourne	9	1	c	26.3	3	83	7	–
			9	0	c	27.1	8	44	3	1
	59 WEST INDIES 2	Sydney	10	4	c	39	6	119	4	–
			–			20	6	50	2	–
	60 WEST INDIES 3	Adelaide	9	2	b	4.5	3	4	–	–
			9	1	c	4	–	17	–	1
1981-82	61 NEW ZEALAND 1	Wellington	–			15	5	32	–	–
			–			–				–
	62 NEW ZEALAND 2	Auckland	10	9	c	39	7	106	3	1
			10	5	c	13	5	32	1	1
	63 NEW ZEALAND 3	Christchurch	10	7	c	12	6	13	3	–
			–			–				–
1982-83	64 ENGLAND 1	Perth	10	2	*	38	13	96	3	1
			–			33	12	89	1	–
1982-83	65 SRI LANKA	Kandy	–			19	3	67	2	1
			–			11	3	40	1	–
1983-84	66 PAKISTAN 1	Perth	9	0	c	13	3	26	1	–
			–			29	6	56	–	–
	67 PAKISTAN 2	Brisbane	–			8	1	33	–	–
			–			2	–	10	–	–
	68 PAKISTAN 3	Adelaide	10	25	c	50.2	8	171	6	–
			10	4	*	–				
	69 PAKISTAN 4	Melbourne	11	2	*	38	11	113	2	–
			–			29	7	71	3	–
	70 PAKISTAN 5	Sydney	–			31.2	10	65	4	2
			–			29.5	5	88	4	–

* not out

TEST MATCHES

BOWLING AND FIELDING SUMMARY BY SERIES

Series		Tests	Overs	Mdns	Runs	Wkts	Avge	Best	5wI	10wM	Ct
1970-71‡	E	2	62.3	5	199	8	24.87	5- 84	1	–	2
1972†	E	5	249.5	83	548	31	17.67	6- 66	3	1	–

Series		Tests	Overs	Mdns	Runs	Wkts	Avge	Best	5wI	10wM	Ct
1972-73‡	P	3	96.1	19	353	12	29.41	4- 49	–	–	1
1972-73†	WI	1	32	5	132	–	–	–	–	–	–
1974-75‡	E	6	182.6	36	596	25	23.84	4- 49	–	–	2
1975†	E	4	207	72	460	21	21.90	5- 15	1	–	–
1975-76‡	WI	5	129.3	7	712	27	26.37	5- 63	1	–	1
1976-77‡	P	3	130.2	16	540	21	25.71	6- 82	2	1	1
1976-77†‡	NZ	2	82.4	13	312	15	20.80	6- 72	2	1	2
1976-77‡	E	1	47.7	9	165	11	15.00	6- 26	2	1	–
1979-80	WI	3	120.1	24	365	12	30.41	5- 78	1	–	2
1979-80	E	3	155.1	41	388	23	16.86	6- 60	2	1	–
1979-80†	P	3	102	19	303	3	101.00	3-114	–	–	1
1980†	E	1	34	9	96	5	19.20	4- 43	–	–	–
1980-81	NZ	3	106	27	245	16	15.31	6- 53	2	–	–
1980-81	I	3	148.3	33	452	21	21.52	4- 65	–	–	1
1981†	E	6	311.4	81	870	39	22.30	7- 89	2	1	1
1981-82	P	3	104.3	22	332	15	22.13	5- 18	2	–	1
1981-82	WI	3	121.3	26	317	16	19.81	7- 83	1	1	2
1981-82†	NZ	3	79	23	183	7	26.14	3- 13	–	–	2
1982-83	E	1	71	25	185	4	46.25	3- 96	–	–	1
1982-83†	SL	1	30	6	107	3	35.66	2- 67	–	–	1
1983-84	P	5	230.3	51	633	20	31.65	6-171	1	–	2
TOTALS		70	2102.5	547	8493	355	23.92	7- 83	23	7	23
			‡731.2	105							

BOWLING AND FIELDING SUMMARY BY OPPONENTS

Opponents	Tests	Overs	Mdns	Runs	Wkts	Avge	Best	5wI	10wM	Ct
England	29	1028.4	311	3507	167	21.00	7- 89	11	4	6
England‡		293	50							
India	3	148.3	33	452	21	21.52	4- 65	–	–	1
New Zealand	8	185	50	740	38	19.47	6- 53	4	1	4
New Zealand‡		82.4	13							
Pakistan	17	437	92	2161	71	30.43	6- 82	5	1	6
Pakistan‡		226.3	35							
Sri Lanka	1	30	6	107	3	35.66	2- 67	–	–	1
West Indies	12	273.4	55	1526	55	27.74	7- 83	3	1	5
West Indies‡		129.3	7							
TOTALS	70	2102.5	547	8493	355	23.92	7- 83	23	7	23
		‡731.2	105							

† Away series ‡ Eight-ball overs

TEST MATCHES
BOWLING AND FIELDING SUMMARY BY VENUE

Venue	Tests	Overs	Mdns	Runs	Wkts	Avge	Best	5wI	10wM	Ct
Adelaide	9	162.1 ‡188.2	37 26	1206	45	26.80	6-171	4	–	7
Brisbane	6	113.1 ‡62	24 11	625	31	20.16	6-53	2	–	–
Melbourne	14	353.3 ‡214	78 27	1798	82	21.92	7-83	7	4	4
Perth	7	232 ‡58	68 9	817	30	27.23	5-18	2	–	1
Sydney	8	196.3 ‡126.4	42 19	1036	43	24.09	4-40	–	–	4
In Australia	**44**	**1057.2 ‡648.6**	**249 92**	**5482**	**231**	**23.73**	**7-83**	**15**	**4**	**16**
Birmingham	2	79	29	172	11	15.63	5-15	1	–	–
Leeds	3	123	42	290	13	22.30	4-49	–	–	1
Lord's	4	198.2	47	584	17	34.35	4-43	–	–	–
Manchester	2	129.1	43	298	14	21.28	6-66	1	–	–
Nottingham	2	83.4	30	155	14	11.07	5-46	1	–	–
The Oval	3	189.2	54	475	27	17.59	7-89	3	2	–
In England	**16**	**802.3**	**245**	**1974**	**96**	**20.56**	**7-89**	**6**	**2**	**1**
Auckland	2	52 ‡33.2	12 6	261	15	17.40	6-72	2	1	4
Christchurch	2	12 ‡49.2	6 7	202	7	28.85	3-13	–	–	–
Wellington	1	15	5	32	–	–	–	–	–	–
In New Zealand	**5**	**79 ‡82.4**	**23 13**	**495**	**22**	**22.50**	**6-72**	**2**	**1**	**4**
Faisalabad	1	21	4	91	–	–	–	–	–	–
Karachi	1	39	6	98	–	–	–	–	–	1
Lahore	1	42	9	114	3	38.00	3-114	–	–	–
In Pakistan	**3**	**102**	**19**	**303**	**3**	**101.00**	**3-114**	**–**	**–**	**1**
Kandy	1	30	6	107	3	35.66	2-67	–	–	1
In Sri Lanka	**1**	**30**	**6**	**107**	**3**	**35.66**	**2-67**	**–**	**–**	**1**
Kingston	1	32	5	132	–	–	–	–	–	–
In West Indies	**1**	**32**	**5**	**132**	**–**	**–**	**–**	**–**	**–**	**–**
HOME	**44**	**1057.2 ‡648.6**	**249 92**	**5482**	**231**	**23.73**	**7-83**	**15**	**4**	**16**
AWAY	**26**	**1045.3 ‡82.4**	**298 13**	**3011**	**124**	**24.28**	**7-89**	**8**	**3**	**7**
TOTALS	**70**	**2102.5 ‡731.2**	**547 105**	**8493**	**355**	**23.92**	**7-83**	**23**	**7**	**23**

‡Eight-ball overs

TEST MATCHES

BOWLING ANALYSIS
MODE OF DISMISSAL

Bowled		54
Caught fielder	141	
Caught Wicket-keeper	97	
Caught and bowled	1	239
Leg before wicket		62
TOTAL		355

Note: 95 of Lillee's dismissals were caught by R.W.Marsh. The next highest combination of dismissals in Test cricket is 71 – ct P.J.L.Dujon b M.D.Marshall.

BATTING ORDER OF BATSMEN DISMISSED

Position	1/2	3	4	5	6	7	8	9	10	11	Total
	87	41	38	28	31	33	36	24	25	12	355

BATSMEN DISMISSED MOST TIMES

12 A.P.E.Knott (E).

9 D.I.Gower (E), I.V.A.Richards (WI).

8 D.L.Amiss (E), J.H.Edrich (E), G.A.Gooch (E).

7 I.T.Botham (E), G.Boycott (E), J.M.Brearley (E), K.W.R.Fletcher (E), R.W.Taylor (E).

6 A.W.Greig (E), R.Illingworth (E), Majid Khan (P), Mudassar Nazar (P), D.L.Murray (WI), Mushtaq Mohammed (P), A.M.E.Roberts (WI), Wasim Bari (P), R.G.D.Willis (E), Zaheer Abbas (P).

5 J.Garner (WI), M.W.Gatting (E), C.G.Greenidge (WI), B.W.Luckhurst (E), J.A.Snow (E), D.L.Underwood (E).

TEST MATCHES

BATTING SUMMARY BY OPPONENTS

Opponents	Tests	Inns	NO	HS	Runs	Avge	100	50	0
England	29	39	13	73*	469	18.03	–	1	3
India	3	5	1	19	40	10.00	–	–	–
New Zealand	8	9	1	27	130	16.25	–	–	–
Pakistan	17	21	6	27	153	10.20	–	–	3
Sri Lanka	1	–	–	–	–	–	–	–	–
West Indies	12	16	3	25	113	8.69	–	–	4
TOTALS	**70**	**90**	**24**	**73***	**905**	**13.71**	**–**	**1**	**10**

BATTING SUMMARY BY VENUE

Venue	Tests	Inns	NO	HS	Runs	Avge	100	50	0
In Australia	44	60	12	27	546	11.37	–	–	7
In England	16	21	9	73*	278	23.16	–	1	2
In New Zealand	5	5	1	23*	63	15.75	–	–	–
In Pakistan	3	4	2	12*	18	9.00	–	–	1
In Sri Lanka	1	–	–	–	–	–	–	–	–
In West Indies	1	–	–	–	–	–	–	–	–
HOME	44	60	12	27	546	11.37	–	–	7
AWAY	26	30	12	73*	359	19.94	–	1	3
TOTALS	**70**	**90**	**24**	**73***	**905**	**13.71**	**–**	**1**	**10**

TEST MATCH CAREER HIGHLIGHTS

#1: Adelaide Oval, 29 Jan-3 Feb 1971 – v England (6th)

Made his debut at the age of 21 years 195 days and recorded the first of his 355 wickets when he dismissed J.H.Edrich on the first day. Added the wickets of A.P.E.Knott, R.Illingworth, J.A.Snow and R.G.D.Willis to return figures of 28.3-0-84-5 in his first innings.

#3: Old Trafford, Manchester, 8-13 June 1972 – v England (1st)

Dismissed R.Illingworth, J.A.Snow and N.Gifford in four balls to return his first six-wicket analysis.

#4: Lord's, London, 22-26 June 1972 – v England (2nd)

Shared all 20 wickets with R.A.L.Massie (16 for 137 on debut) to end Australia's longest sequence without a victory against England – 11 matches since Manchester 1968 had produced four defeats and seven draws.

#7: The Oval, London, 10-16 August 1972 – v England (5th)

Dismissed P.H.Parfitt, R.Illingworth and J.A.Snow to take three wickets in four balls for the second time in the rubber. His first ten-wicket haul (10 for 181) gave him an aggregate of 31 wickets in the rubber and remained Australia's record in England until 1981.

#10: SCG, Sydney, 6-11 January 1973 – v Pakistan (3rd)

Although restricted by a vertebral injury he bowled unchanged throughout the 138 minutes of play on the final day to notch up his 50th wicket and help dismiss Pakistan for 106, their lowest total in this series until 1981-82, and gain Australia victory by 52 runs.

#18: Edgbaston, Birmingham, 10-14 July 1975 – v England (1st)

Returned the remarkable figures of 15-8-15-5 in the first innings as Australia became the first visiting team to win a Test at Edgbaston.

#19: Lord's, London, 31 July-5 August 1975 – v England (2nd)
Scored an undefeated 73 off 103 balls, hitting three sixes and eight fours in recording what remained his highest score in all first-class cricket.

#22: Woolloongabba, Brisbane, 28 November-2 December 1975 – v West Indies (1st)
Took his 100th wicket when he achieved the first of his nine dismissals of I.V.A.Richards at this level.

#28: MCG, Melbourne, 1-6 January 1977 – v Pakistan (2nd)
His match figures of 10 for 135 remained the best for Australia against Pakistan until 1979-80.

#31: Eden Park, Auckland 25 February-1 March 1977 – v New Zealand (2nd)
His match figures of 11 for 123, then the record for this series, remain the best in all Tests at Auckland and took his tally beyond 150.

#32: MCG, Melbourne 12-17 March 1977 – v England (Centenary Test)
His second 11-wicket haul in successive Tests included his best analysis to date – six for 26.

#34: WACA, Perth 14-19 December 1979 – v England (1st)
Became the eighth Australian to take 100 wickets against England and only the second after R.R.Lindwall to achieve this feat in post-war Tests.

#38: MCG, Melbourne 1-6 February 1979 – v England (3rd)
Returned match figures of 11 for 138 and became the fifth bowler to take 200 wickets for Australia.

#43: Woolloongabba, Brisbane, 28-30 November 1980 – v New Zealand (1st)
His analysis of 6 for 53 was the record for Australia against New Zealand until 1993-94.

#48: MCG, Melbourne 7-11 February 1981 – v India (3rd)
Overtook R.Benaud's Australian record of 248 wickets in 63 Tests and became the sixth bowler to take 250.

#51: Headingley, Leeds 16-21 July 1981 – v England (3rd)
Became the leading wicket-taker in Anglo-Australian Tests, a record he still holds, when he exceeded H.Trumble's tally of 141.

#53: Old Trafford, Manchester 13-17 August 1981 – v England (5th)
Became the first and, to date, only bowler to take 150 wickets in Tests between England and Australia.

#54: The Oval, London 27 August-1 September 1981 – v England (6th)
His sixth ten-wicket haul (11 for 159) included his then best innings analysis of 7 for 89 and took him to his best aggregate in any rubber – 39 wickets at a cost of 22.30 runs apiece.

#55: WACA, Perth 13-17 November 1981 – v Pakistan (1st)

Became the third bowler after S.F.Barnes (24) and C.V.Grimmett (21) to achieve 20 instances of five or more wickets in an innings.

#56: Woolloongabba, Brisbane, 27 November-1 December 1981 – v Pakistan (2nd)

Became the third bowler after F.S.Trueman and L.R.Gibbs to take 300 wickets. It was then the fastest in terms of fewest Tests (56) and innings (108) although Trueman (65 Tests) had reached the milestone in 340 fewer balls.

#58: MCG, Melbourne 26-30 December 1981 – v West Indies (1st)

At 2.55pm on 27 December he induced an edged stroke from H.A.Gomes to surpass the world Test record of 309 wickets held by L.R.Gibbs for almost six years. He gained the record on the ground where Gibbs had claimed it from F.S.Trueman and just four days after G.Boycott had broken its batting counterpart. His first innings figures of 7 for 83 remained his best in Test cricket. His three second innings wickets enabled him to equal the world record of seven ten-wicket hauls shared by S.F.Barnes and C.V.Grimmett. They also took his aggregate of Test wickets in 1981 to 85, a tally that remains the record for any calendar year.

#64: WACA, Perth 12-17 November 1982 – v England (1st)

In the last of his 29 appearances against England he took his record tally of wickets in this series to 167 at 21.00 runs apiece with 11 five-wicket and four ten-wicket analyses.

#68: Adelaide Oval 9-13 December 1983 – v Pakistan (3rd)

Took five wickets in an innings for the 23rd and final time to finish a single instance short of the world record held by S.F.Barnes.

#70: SCG, Sydney 2-6 January 1984 – v Pakistan (5th)

Extended his world Test record to 355 wickets, 95 of them caught by R.W.Marsh to establish an unbeaten record for any bowler/fielder combination in Test cricket. Retired from international cricket at the age of 34 years 172 days.

LILLEE'S PLACE IN TEST MATCH RECORDS
(Updated to 16 December 2003)

BOWLING RECORDS
300 WICKETS

	For	Tests	Wkts	Avge	A	E	I	NZ	P	SA	SL	WI	Z	B
C.A.Walsh	WI	132	519	24.44	135	145	65	43	63	51	8	–	9	–
S.K.Warne	A	107	491	25.71	–	132	29	75	76	101	23	49	6	–
M.Muralitharan	SL	78	437	23.52	22	43	51	39	68	77	–	44	73	20
Kapil Dev	I	131	434	29.64	79	85	–	25	99	8	45	89	4	–

Opponents (spanning A, E, I, NZ, P, SA, SL, WI, Z, B)

	For	Tests	Wkts	Avge	A	E	I	NZ	P	SA	SL	WI	Z	B
									Opponents					
R.J.Hadlee	NZ	86	431	22.29	130	97	65	–	51	–	37	51	–	–
G.D.McGrath	A	90	420	21.35	–	115	37	30	62	49	27	94	6	–
Wasim Akram	P	104	414	23.62	50	57	45	60	–	13	63	79	47	–
C.E.L.Ambrose	WI	98	405	20.99	128	164	15	13	42	21	14	–	8	–
I.T.Botham	E	102	383	28.40	148	–	59	64	40	–	11	61	–	–
M.D.Marshall	WI	81	376	20.94	87	127	76	36	50	–	–	–	–	–
Waqar Younis	P	85	369	23.24	30	50	8	70	–	20	56	55	62	18
Imran Khan	P	88	362	22.81	64	47	94	31	–	–	46	80	–	–
D.K.Lillee	**A**	**70**	**355**	**23.92**	**–**	**167**	**21**	**38**	**71**	**–**	**3**	**55**	**–**	**–**
A.Kumble	I	76	349	27.98	37	62	–	41	22	56	46	51	34	–
A.A.Donald	SA	72	330	22.25	53	86	57	21	27	–	29	43	14	–
R.G.D.Willis	E	90	325	25.20	128	–	62	60	34	–	3	38	–	–
L.R.Gibbs	WI	79	309	29.09	103	100	63	11	32	–	–	–	–	–
F.S.Trueman	E	67	307	21.57	79	–	53	40	22	27	–	86	–	–

100 WICKETS FOR AUSTRALIA

	Tests	Wkts	Avge	E	I	NZ	P	SA	SL	WI	Z	B
							Opponents					
S.K.Warne	107	491	25.71	132	29	75	76	101	23	49	6	–
G.D.McGrath	90	420	21.36	115	37	30	62	49	27	94	6	–
D.K.Lillee	**70**	**355**	**23.92**	**167**	**21**	**38**	**71**	**–**	**3**	**55**	**–**	**–**
C.J.McDermott	71	291	28.63	84	34	48	18	21	27	59	–	–
R.Benaud	63	248	27.03	83	52	–	19	52	–	42	–	–
G.D.McKenzie	60	246	29.78	96	47	–	15	41	–	47	–	–
R.R.Lindwall	61	228	23.03	114	36	2	4	31	–	41	–	–
C.V.Grimmett	37	216	24.21	106	–	–	–	77	–	33	–	–
M.G.Hughes	53	212	28.38	75	23	25	16	4	16	53	–	–
J.R.Thomson	51	200	28.00	100	22	6	10	–	–	62	–	–
A.K.Davidson	44	186	20.53	84	30	–	14	25	–	33	–	–
G.F.Lawson	46	180	30.56	97	–	10	33	–	1	39	–	–
T.M.Alderman	41	170	27.15	100	–	16	23	–	5	26	–	–
K.R.Miller	55	170	22.97	87	9	2	2	30	–	40	–	–
W.A.Johnston	40	160	23.91	75	16	–	–	44	–	25	–	–
W.J.O'Reilly	27	144	22.59	102	–	8	–	34	–	–	–	–
H.Trumble	32	141	21.78	141	–	–	–	–	–	–	–	–
M.H.N.Walker	34	138	27.47	56	–	28	17	–	–	37	–	–
J.N.Gillespie	37	137	26.17	53	13	11	3	24	–	33	–	–
A.A.Mallett	38	132	29.84	50	28	19	13	6	–	16	–	–
B.Yardley	33	126	31.63	29	21	13	21	–	7	35	–	–
R.M.Hogg	38	123	28.47	56	15	10	19	–	1	22	–	–
M.A.Noble	42	121	25.00	115	–	–	–	6	–	–	–	–
B.A.Reid	27	113	24.63	47	24	16	14	–	–	12	–	–
I.W.Johnson	45	109	29.19	42	19	–	4	22	–	22	–	–

	Tests	Wkts	Avge	E	I	NZ	P	SA	SL	WI	Z	B
								Opponents				
P.R.Reiffel	35	104	26.96	30	7	15	8	8	9	27	–	–
G.Giffen	31	103	27.09	103	–	–	–	–	–	–	–	–
A.N.Connolly	29	102	29.22	25	31	–	–	26	–	20	–	–
C.T.B.Turner	17	101	16.53	101	–	–	–	–	–	–	–	–

70 WICKETS IN A CALENDAR YEAR

	For	Year	Tests	Runs	Wkts	Avge	5wI	10wM
D.K.Lillee	**Australia**	**1981**	**13**	**1781**	**85**	20.95	5	2
A.A.Donald	South Africa	1998	14	1571	80	19.63	7	–
M.Muralitharan	Sri Lanka	2001	12	1699	80	21.23	7	4
J.Garner	West Indies	1984	15	1604	77	20.83	4	–
Kapil Dev	India	1983	18	1739	75	23.18	5	1
M.Muralitharan	Sri Lanka	2000	10	1463	75	19.50	7	3
Kapil Dev	India	1979	18	1720	74	23.24	5	–
M.D.Marshall	West Indies	1984	13	1471	73	20.15	9	1
S.K.Warne	Australia	1993	16	1697	72	23.56	2	–
G.D.McKenzie	Australia	1964	14	1737	71	24.46	4	1
S.K.Warne	Australia	1994	10	1274	70	18.20	6	2

35 WICKETS IN A SERIES

	Wkts	Avge	Tests	5wI	10wM		Venue	Series
S.F.Barnes	49	10.93	4	7	3	England v South Africa	SA	1913-14
J.C.Laker	46	9.60	5	4	2	England v Australia	E	1956
C.V.Grimmett	44	14.59	5	5	3	Australia v South Africa	SA	1935-36
T.M.Alderman	42	21.26	6	4	–	Australia v England	E	1981
R.M.Hogg	41	12.85	6	5	2	Australia v England	A	1978-79
T.M.Alderman	41	17.36	6	6	1	Australia v England	E	1989
Imran Khan	40	13.95	6	4	2	Pakistan v India	P	1982-83
D.K.Lillee	**39**	**22.30**	**6**	**2**	**1**	**Australia v England**	**E**	**1981**
A.V.Bedser	39	17.48	5	5	1	England v Australia	E	1953
M.W.Tate	38	23.18	5	5	1	England v Australia	A	1924-25
W.J.Whitty	37	17.08	5	2	–	Australia v South Africa	A	1910-11
H.J.Tayfield	37	17.18	5	4	1	South Africa v England	SA	1956-57
A.A.Mailey	36	26.27	5	4	2	Australia v England	A	1920-21
G.D.McGrath	36	19.47	6	2	–	Australia v England	E	1997
A.E.E.Vogler	36	21.75	5	4	1	South Africa v England	SA	1909-10
G.A.Lohmann	35	5.80	3	4	2	England v South Africa	SA	1895-96
B.S.Chandrasekhar	35	18.91	5	4	–	India v England	I	1972-73
M.D.Marshall	35	12.65	5	3	1	West Indies v England	E	1988

25 WICKETS IN A SERIES FOR AUSTRALIA

	Series	Venue	Tests	E	I	NZ	P	SA	WI
						Opponents			
C.V.Grimmett	1935-36	SA	5	–	–	–	–	44	–
T.M.Alderman	1981	E	6	42	–	–	–	–	–
R.M.Hogg	1978-79	A	6	41	–	–	–	–	–
T.M.Alderman	1989	E	6	41	–	–	–	–	–
D.K.Lillee	**1981**	**E**	**6**	**39**	**–**	**–**	**–**	**–**	**–**
W.J.Whitty	1910-11	A	5	–	–	–	–	37	–
A.A.Mailey	1920-21	A	5	36	–	–	–	–	–
G.D.McGrath	1997	E	6	36	–	–	–	–	–
G.Giffen	1894-95	A	5	34	–	–	–	–	–
G.F.Lawson	1982-83	A	5	34	–	–	–	–	–
S.K.Warne	1993	E	6	34	–	–	–	–	–
C.V.Grimmett	1930-31	A	5	–	–	–	–	–	33
C.V.Grimmett	1931-32	A	5	–	–	–	–	33	–
A.K.Davidson	1960-61	A	4	–	–	–	–	–	33
J.R.Thomson	1974-75	A	5	33	–	–	–	–	–
M.A.Noble	1901-02	A	5	32	–	–	–	–	–
H.V.Hordern	1911-12	A	5	32	–	–	–	–	–
C.J.McDermott	1994-95	A	5	32	–	–	–	–	–
G.D.McGrath	2001	E	5	32	–	–	–	–	–
J.V.Saunders	1907-08	A	5	31	–	–	–	–	–
H.Ironmonger	1931-32	A	4	–	–	–	–	31	–
R.Benaud	1958-59	A	5	31	–	–	–	–	–
D.K.Lillee	**1972**	**E**	**5**	**31**	**–**	**–**	**–**	**–**	**–**
C.J.McDermott	1991-92	A	5	–	31	–	–	–	–
M.G.Hughes	1993	E	6	31	–	–	–	–	–
S.K.Warne	2001	E	5	31	–	–	–	–	–
R.Benaud	1957-58	SA	5	–	–	–	–	30	–
G.D.McKenzie	1968-69	A	5	–	–	–	–	–	30
C.J.McDermott	1985	E	6	30	–	–	–	–	–
G.D.McGrath	1998-99	WI	4	–	–	–	–	–	30
C.V.Grimmett	1930	E	5	29	–	–	–	–	–
A.K.Davidson	1959-60	I	5	–	29	–	–	–	–
R.Benaud	1959-60	I	5	–	29	–	–	–	–
G.D.McKenzie	1964	E	5	29	–	–	–	–	–
J.R.Thomson	1975-76	A	6	–	–	–	–	–	29
G.F.Lawson	1989	E	6	29	–	–	–	–	–
H.Trumble	1901-02	A	5	28	–	–	–	–	–
W.J.O'Reilly	1934	E	5	28	–	–	–	–	–
A.A.Mallett	1969-70	I	5	–	28	–	–	–	–
W.M.Clark	1977-78	A	5	–	28	–	–	–	–
E.A.McDonald	1921	E	5	27	–	–	–	–	–
W.J.O'Reilly	1932-33	A	5	27	–	–	–	–	–

	Series	Venue	Tests	E	I	NZ	P	SA	WI
						Opponents			
W.J.O'Reilly	1935-36	SA	5	–	–	–	–	27	–
R.R.Lindwall	1948	E	5	27	–	–	–	–	–
W.A.Johnston	1948	E	5	27	–	–	–	–	–
D.K.Lillee	**1975-76**	**A**	**5**	–	–	–	–	–	**27**
B.A.Reid	1990-91	A	4	27	–	–	–	–	–
S.K.Warne	1994-95	A	5	27	–	–	–	–	–
S.C.G.MacGill	1998-99	A	4	27	–	–	–	–	–
S.K.Warne	2002-03	P	3	–	–	–	27	–	–
E.Jones	1899	E	5	26	–	–	–	–	–
H.Trumble	1902	E	3	26	–	–	–	–	–
R.R.Lindwall	1953	E	5	26	–	–	–	–	–
J.W.Gleeson	1968-69	A	5	–	–	–	–	–	26
M.H.N.Walker	1972-73	WI	5	–	–	–	–	–	26
G.D.McGrath	1996-97	A	5	–	–	–	–	–	26
C.V.Grimmett	1934	E	5	25	–	–	–	–	–
W.J.O'Reilly	1936-37	A	5	25	–	–	–	–	–
A.K.Davidson	1957-58	SA	5	–	–	–	–	25	–
D.K.Lillee	**1974-75**	**A**	**6**	**25**	–	–	–	–	–
A.G.Hurst	1978-79	A	6	25	–	–	–	–	–

LEADING CAREER AVERAGES
(Qualifications: 200 wickets; avge 25.00)

	For	Tests	Balls	Runs	Wkts	Avge	5wI	10wM
S.M.Pollock	SA	66	14709	5630	270	20.85	14	1
M.D.Marshall	WI	81	17584	7876	376	20.94	22	4
J.Garner	WI	58	13175	5433	259	20.97	7	–
C.E.L.Ambrose	WI	98	22103	8501	405	20.99	22	3
G.D.McGrath	A	90	21365	8971	420	21.35	23	3
F.S.Trueman	E	67	15178	6625	307	21.57	17	3
A.A.Donald	SA	72	15519	7344	330	22.25	20	3
R.J.Hadlee	NZ	86	21918	9612	431	22.30	36	9
Imran Khan	P	88	19458	8258	362	22.81	23	6
R.R.Lindwall	A	61	13650	5251	228	23.03	12	–
Waqar Younis	P	85	15906	8576	369	23.24	22	5
M.Muralitharan	SL	78	26147	10281	437	23.52	36	11
Wasim Akram	P	104	22627	9779	414	23.62	25	5
M.A.Holding	WI	60	12680	5898	249	23.68	13	2
D.K.Lillee	**A**	**70**	**18467**	**8493**	**355**	**23.92**	**23**	**7**
C.V.Grimmett	A	37	14513	5231	216	24.21	21	7
C.A.Walsh	WI	132	30019	12688	519	24.44	22	3
J.B.Statham	E	70	16056	6261	252	24.84	9	1
A.V.Bedser	E	51	15918	5876	236	24.89	15	5

LIMITED-OVERS INTERNATIONALS

BOWLING AND FIELDING SUMMARY BY OPPONENTS

Opponents	LOI	Balls	Mdns	Runs	Wkts	Avge	Best	4wI	R/Over	Ct
England	16	953	22	615	31	19.83	4-12	3	3.87	5
India	5	252	6	115	10	11.50	4-32	1	2.73	–
New Zealand	15	810	23	433	28	15.46	3-14	–	3.20	2
Pakistan	5	285	5	155	8	19.37	5-34	1	3.26	1
Sri Lanka	3	168	–	97	–	–	–	–	3.46	–
West Indies	17	999	22	660	24	27.50	4-28	1	3.96	2
Zimbabwe	2	126	2	70	2	35.00	2-47	–	3.33	–
TOTALS	**63**	**3593**	**80**	**2145**	**103**	**20.82**	**5-34**	**6**	**3.58**	**10**

FOUR-WICKET ANALYSES

	Analysis				Against	Venue	Season
1	12	2	34	5	Pakistan	Leeds	1975
2	10	–	56	4	England	Sydney	1979-80
3	8.5	–	28	4	West Indies	Sydney	1979-80
4	10	6	12	4	England	Sydney	1979-80
5	11	1	35	4	England	The Oval	1980
6	10	1	32	4	India	Sydney	1980-81

BATTING SUMMARY BY OPPONENTS

Opponents	LOI	Inns	NO	HS	Runs	Avge	0	Balls	R/100b
England	16	10	3	21	74	10.57	2	87	85.05
India	5	2	1	5	9	9.00	–	7	128.57
New Zealand	15	5	1	7	11	2.75	1	21	52.38
Pakistan	5	2	–	8	15	7.50	–	24	62.50
Sri Lanka	3	1	–	5	5	5.00	–	5	100.00
West Indies	17	14	3	42*	126	11.45	3	176	71.59
Zimbabwe	2	–	–	–	–	–	–	–	–
TOTALS	**63**	**34**	**8**	**42***	**240**	**9.23**	**6**	**320**	**75.00**

WORLD SERIES SUPERTESTS

Season	Match	Venue	No	Runs	HO	O	M	R	W	Ct
1977-78	1 WEST INDIANS	Melbourne	9	37	c	16	4	77	2	1
		(VFL Park)	9	5	c	20	1	100	2	1
	2 WEST INDIANS	Sydney	9	1	b	17	1	75	1	–
		(Showground)	9	27	c	5	–	32	–	–
	3 WEST INDIANS	Adelaide	9	1	lbw	11	–	48	2	–
		(Football Park)	9	9	*	14.3	–	61	3	–
	5 WORLD XI	Perth	10	1	lbw	27	1	149	4	–
		(Gloucester Pk)	10	8	b	–		–		
	6 WORLD XI	Melbourne	–	27.1	2	141	2	–		
		(VFL Park)	10	8	*	15	2	82	5	–
1978-79		WORLD XI	Auckland	11	0	*	18	4	59	7	–
		(Mt Smart Stad)	11	0	*	14	7	30	5	–
1978-79	1 WORLD XI	Melbourne	11	2	c	32.4	13	51	4	–
		(VFL Park)	11	0	c	38	16	63	1	–
	3 WEST INDIANS	Melbourne	11	10	*	42	16	91	3	–
		(VFL Park)	11	20	*	12	6	13	–	–
	4 WEST INDIANS	Sydney	10	2	c	15	4	33	2	–
		(SCG)	–	14	3	23	7	–		
	5 WORLD XI	Sydney	10	8	c	18.5	6	51	5	–
		(SCG)	10	9	*	17	4	57	1	–
1978-79	1 WEST INDIANS	Kingston	10	1	c	18.2	3	68	4	–
		(Sabina Park)	10	12	c	25	4	100	4	1
	2 WEST INDIANS	Bridgetown	9	6	c	13	2	56	3	–
		(Kensington)	9	8	*	14	3	53	1	–
	3 WEST INDIANS	Port-of-Spain	9	30	c	22	4	76	1	1
		(Queen's Park)	9	12	c	31	5	77	3	–
	4 WEST INDIANS	Georgetown	9	3	c	24	4	98	1	2
		(Bourda)	–	–		–				
	6 WEST INDIANS	St John's	9	6	lbw	31.2	2	125	6	–
		(Recreation Gd)	–	–		–				

Note that the above matches, played under the banner of 'World Series Cricket', were administered by private companies and were not sanctioned by the International Cricket Conference or by any of the national cricket authorities in the countries in which they were staged. In 1979 the ICC ruled that no WSC match would be classified as first-class.

WORLD SERIES SUPERTESTS

BOWLING AND FIELDING SUMMARY

Season	Venue	Matches	Overs	Mdns	Runs	Wkts	Avge	Best	5wI	10wM	Ct
1977-78	A	5	152.4	11	765	21	36.42	5-82	1	–	2
1978-79	NZ	1	32	11	89	12	7.41	7-59	2	1	–
1978-79	A	4	189.3	68	382	23	16.60	7-23	2	–	–
1978-79	WI	5	178.4	27	653	23	28.39	6-125	1	–	4
TOTALS		**15**	**552.5**	**117**	**1889**	**79**	**23.91**	**7-23**	**6**	**1**	**6**

BATTING SUMMARY

Season	Venue	Matches	Inns	NO	HS	Runs	Avge	100	50
1977-78	A	5	9	2	37	97	13.85	–	–
1978-79	NZ	1	2	2	0*	0	–	–	–
1978-79	A	4	7	3	20*	51	12.75	–	–
1978-79	WI	5	8	1	30	78	11.14	–	–
TOTALS		**15**	**26**	**8**	**37**	**226**	**12.55**	**–**	**–**

* not out

Index

["

THE INFERNAL GROVE

DEFILER'S GATE

THE SPECTRAL FIELDS

THE DEFILED RIFT

THE DESOLATE SEA

THE WHITE GROVE

THE EMERALD COVE

THE CINDER GROVE

HELLFAST

THE DREADFUL STEPPES

The World of Eventide

THE EMERALD REACH

THE FERAL EXPANSE

THE LOWLAND GROVE

WATCHER'S LOOKOUT

DUUNHEIM

THE MIST MOUNTAINS

PEDDLER'S POINT

THE BILLOWING BOG

THE

THE CELESTIAL SEA

WILLOBROOK

FAELYNDELLE

THE AGELESS ISLES

SPRINGMOUTH HIGHLANDS

WOLFBERRY HINTERLANDS

THE ELDER GROVE

THELYNAR GROVE

Druid's Oath: The Raven Spell Copyright © 2023 by Ryan Carriere All rights reserved.

This is a work of fiction. Names, characters, places, and incidents either are the product of the author's imagination or are used fictitiously. Any resemblance to actual persons, living or dead, events, or locales is entirely coincidental.

Cover and Interior design by Ryan Carriere Printed in Canada

First Edition:

ISBN: 9798870595726